BORN TO
DRUM

BORN TO

DRUM

THE TRUTH ABOUT THE WORLD'S GREATEST DRUMMERS—FROM JOHN BONHAM AND KEITH MOON TO SHEILA E. AND DAVE GROHL

TONY
BARRELL

DEY ST.
AN IMPRINT OF
WILLIAM MORROW PUBLISHERS

DEY ST.

HarperCollins books may be purchased for educational, business, or sales promotional use. For information please e-mail the Special Markets Department at SPsales@harpercollins.com.

A hardcover edition of this book was published in 2015 by Dey Street Books, an imprint of William Morrow Publishers.

FIRST DEY STREET BOOKS PAPERBACK EDITION PUBLISHED 2016.

Designed by Renato Stanisic

Library of Congress Cataloging-in-Publication Data has been applied for.

ISBN 978-0-06-230786-6

24 25 26 27 28 LBC 12 11 10 9 8

FOR THE FIRST MUSICIAN I EVER MET:
MY MOTHER, JOAN BARRELL

INTRODUCTION

I think drummers are amazing. I've been listening to them and watching them now for a long time, having been a fan of pop and rock music since I was a boy. Drummers play the most wonderful, exciting, and complex rhythms. A band without a drummer is like a rocking chair that somebody has cruelly bolted to the floor: while it may appear to rock, it actually doesn't. And yet drums don't simply add rhythm to the music we listen to: these apparently primitive acoustic instruments bring drama, warmth, texture, and humanity to it as well.

"Are you a drummer?" the brilliant British drummer Bill Bruford asked me outright when I requested an interview for this book. Other percussionists seemed equally anxious to know whether I played the kit, whether I was one of them or not, as though a non-drummer would not be sufficiently qualified to understand them properly. I can immediately see why they would be so cautious, if not paranoid. A heck of a lot of writing about drummers seems to recycle the same old clichés about these people being crazy, stupid, or somehow so different from their fellow humans that they might as well be six-legged aliens from the planet Zildjian.

No, Bill, I'm not a drummer. But I am a musician as well as a writer, I do know a great deal about music, and I had no intention of writing a book about the insanity or dumbness or weirdness of drummers. Instead I wanted to go deeper and examine what it really takes to be one of them. What kind of person becomes a professional drummer? What qualities do they need? What makes drummers different from ordinary people who don't use wooden sticks for a living? What sort of kicks do people get out of drumming? I wanted to take the clichés apart, separate the tired old mythology from the truth, and see if I could reach some profound or thought-provoking conclusions about the role of the drummer in a band and in the wider world, as well as the culture, history, and psychology of drumming.

I ended up talking to around forty brilliant professional drummers, plus other important musicians who have worked closely with drummers, and I came away with some great stories and some ideas and opinions that surprised and amazed me. I also found that most drummers are great company: they're sane, intelligent people with interesting things to say. Whether I was shooting the breeze backstage with Clem Burke of Blondie, having a long chat with Phil Collins, or on the receiving end of a stream of jokes from Nick Mason of Pink Floyd, I had enormous fun. I learned a heap of stuff, too: every single drummer I spoke to had different insights to offer me, which only goes to prove that drumming is a more complex and sophisticated subject than some people would have you believe.

This book is dedicated to drummers everywhere. But it certainly isn't just a book for drummers: it's for everybody who loves music, and wants to know much more about these incredible musicians. Take it from this non-drummer—drummers really do rock.

BORN TO
DRUM

INTO THE ASYLUM

magine this. One day, you're given the opportunity to be a musician in a band. It's a really cool band, playing powerful and addictive rock music for an army of appreciative fans worldwide. You're going to travel the globe and bring pleasure to hundreds of thousands of people, with fans screaming your name and queuing round the block to say hello and touch the hem of your garment. How awesome is that?

Except that there's a catch. Every night you will be relegated to the back of the stage, all but concealed behind an assortment of hefty, round objects that you are required to whack continually using a pair of wooden sticks. You have to hit a snare drum, a big drum that stands on the floor (appropriately known as a floor tom), a series of other toms, and God knows what else. Oh, yes, and there is a whole array of cymbals that you need to ding and bash and caress as you go. And maybe you should think about striking that cowbell or that other oojamaflip on the offbeat during the second part of the middle eight in the fifth song of the second half.

Meanwhile, your feet are operating pedals to hit the big bass drum in front of you, the one emblazoned with the name of the manufacturer or the name of the band (also known as the kick drum), and to activate the hi-hat, which is a special pair of cymbals on a stand that crash together. You can't do all this stuff randomly and haphazardly, either: it all has to fit with the music the band's playing. In fact, it's your job to keep all the other musicians in time and playing to the correct rhythms. And in case all that isn't daunting enough for you, let's say you're a prog-rock band and several of your numbers are epic twenty-two-minute suites with about fourteen tempo changes in each one, along with several bars of seriously tricky time signatures—like 13/8 (thirteen quavers to the bar) instead of the 4/4 of standard, no-nonsense rock music (four crotchets to the bar).

Your arms and legs are beginning to ache. The sweat pouring down your face, your chest, your arms, and your legs is partly the result of the physical exertion that is required to play your instrument, and partly the result of a profound terror that you're going to screw up, momentarily forget how one of the songs goes, play one half beat out of place that confuses the bass player, the guitarist, the singer, the backing singers, and the entire horn section and turns a great number into a chaotic cacophony.

On top of all that, while you're playing, you're mostly hidden from view; while hundreds of adoring fans are ogling the lead singer and the guitarist, regarding them as the ultimate sex gods, you're being seriously ignored. What's more, you have the most enormous collection of equipment to transport from gig to gig, to laboriously set up and take down again. So do you really want that gig? Do you really fancy being a drummer?

Well, somebody has to do it. "What is the most important instrument in a band?" asked a recent online poll on musicban ter.com, an American website where tens of thousands of music lovers chew the fat over their favorite subject. When the dust had settled, the clear winner was the drum kit, with nearly 36 percent of the vote, ahead of guitar (nearly 29 percent), bass (just over 18 percent), and vocals (just over 14 percent). The result confirms that drummers are absolutely vital to modern music.

So it's just as well, isn't it, that plenty of people want to be drummers. Thousands of willing volunteers step forward and accept the challenge of playing this monstrously cumbersome instrument, and most of them not only do it well but absolutely love doing it. In many cases, they can't imagine anything that would give them greater pleasure.

The big question that has bothered me, for more years than I care to remember, is: Why? Why would anybody choose to be a drummer? It was a question that ultimately took me on a long journey, into a long series of concert venues, hotel rooms, and recording studios, as I met dozens of top drummers and tried to get to the bottom of their peculiar, percussive passion.

For some people, there is one quick and easy answer to the big why. This is an idea about drummers that is so powerful, and so deeply ingrained in our culture, that it will not go away. Exactly how this idea arrived in the world is unknown. It may have been conceived in the early twentieth century by a jealous boyfriend who discovered that his girlfriend was sexually attracted to a man who played the drums in a band. It might go back much, much earlier, to a time when a bunch of prehistoric humans noticed, to their intense irritation, that one rogue member of their tribe enjoyed beating stretched animal skins instead of doing something more useful, such as making flint tools or hunting saber-toothed tigers. The idea is this: people who play the drums are crazy. Insane. Nuts. Cracked. Several hit records short of a jukebox.

Plenty of people have occupations that can be regarded as crazy. They risk their lives as stuntmen for the sake of a movie. They rob banks, sell illegal hard drugs, run prostitution rackets, organize vicious dog fights, or produce nasty, exploitative "reality" television shows. But drummers are musicians; they display considerable skill and artistry, drive the rhythms of some amazing pieces of music, and bring pleasure to millions of people. What's crazy about that?

Well, professional drummers are people who hit things for a living. That does make them bonkers, in one sense at least. And some drummers themselves are willing to accept the diagnosis, though the late British sticksman Cozy Powell may have had his tongue in his cheek in 1989 when he reflected: "I think drummers have an unfair reputation because, let's face it, first of all you have to be MAD to play the drums! I mean, nobody sane is going to spend their life hitting various objects with two pieces of wood."

Superficially, Dennis Wilson was a healthy, all-American boy—a tanned Adonis who was the only real surfer and heartthrob in the Beach Boys. But underneath that sun-bleached mop of hair, and the bushy beard that arrived later, the drummer seemed a little too ardent in his enthusiasms, a touch too restless in his quest for adventure and pleasure. Fast cars were raced to the limit and beautiful women were adored and divorced, with the result that hundreds of thousands of dollars disappeared in alimony payments. Ultimately he threw himself into booze and drugs with the same impetuosity he had once reserved for music and sports. An association with the notorious lunatic Charles Manson, who moved in with Wilson in 1968, didn't help. Fleetwood Mac's Christine McVie, who had a relationship with Wilson between 1979 and 1981, is said to have concluded that he was "half little boy and half insane."

Another famous drummer with a reputation as a madman was John Bonham of Led Zeppelin. The case for the prosecution rests mainly on the thunderous sound of his playing, his enormous capacity for booze, and a pattern of irreverent behavior in hotels—the sort of antics performed by a select number of debauched rock stars on tour in the 1970s. The band's singer, Robert Plant, didn't help Bonham's reputation when he introduced him onstage in Los Angeles as "the man who broke every window in room 1019 last night, the man who set fire to his own bed . . ."

Inside the Led Zep entourage, it was well-known that Bonham could become extremely homesick on tour, and that he had a Jekyll and Hyde personality. In Robert Louis Stevenson's famous story, Dr. Henry Jekyll is transformed into a hideous embodiment of evil by a boiling, smoking mixture of chemicals—and in the drummer's case, the fun guy people knew as Bonzo would metamorphose into a violent and unpredictable character known as "the Beast" after his yearning for home combined with a large quantity of alcohol. In 1975, he reportedly ordered twenty Black Russians in an LA bar, and after gulping about half of them down he saw a woman he knew from the music industry looking at him and smiling. He went straight over to the woman, punched her to the floor, and told her never to glance at him with that particular facial expression again.

Bonham was also prone to less violent impulses. He once looked outside his hotel in Dallas, Texas, to see a stunning customized 1959 Chevrolet Corvette, and decided he had to have it. He asked a security worker to find the owner and shelled out an extremely generous $18,000 to buy the car on the spot.

He could also be a maniac when he actually got inside one of his many cars. Tony Iommi, Black Sabbath's guitarist, would often socialize with him, enjoying his company at clubs and parties. "He was a wild character," Iommi recalled recently, "and he was good fun—unless we went out and he was driving. Then that was bad fun, because he used to get really pissed—drunk—and then drive back." On one occasion, says Iommi, Bonham had just bought a flash new car—"something like a Maserati. And we were driving the wrong way up this road, and I said, 'We're going the wrong way!'" Bonham decided to solve the problem by turning the steering wheel and driving right over a traffic island, so that they would move into the correct lane. "And we got stuck on this island. [He'd] ripped all the bottom of this new car . . . So we had to get out and get a cab and get home. He left it there!"

Peter "Ginger" Baker, too, has been portrayed as lacking the full set of marbles. In 2013, *Esquire* magazine gave the former Cream and Blind Faith percussionist the title of "the world's craziest drummer." Ginger Baker's crimes are a perfect catalog of vintage rock behavior; they include destroying hotel furniture in the course of practicing his skills, taking heroin to improve his drumming, violently assaulting his bass-playing colleague Jack Bruce, and leaving his first wife to run off with his daughter's boyfriend's teenage sister.

The award-winning 2012 film *Beware of Mr. Baker* revealed that even in his early seventies, Baker was still a redoubtable and fearsome character, a nightmare for interviewers, and still capable of violence. When the maker of the film, Jay Bulger, informed him that he was going to conduct interviews with an assortment of people from Baker's past, the drummer exploded. "I'm going to put you in fuckin' 'ospital!" he growled, lashing out at Bulger with a metal walking stick, bloodying his nose—seemingly unconcerned that the whole incident was captured on film.

Sometimes the "crazy" things that drummers do are hilarious. In the summer of 2012, Mick Brown, the drummer with Ted Nugent's band, made an unusual getaway after playing a gig in the town of Bangor, Maine. Having found a golf cart in the building, Brown gleefully drove off in it, picked up some girls he knew from the audience, and resisted attempts by local law enforcers to apprehend him. The official police report tells the rest of the story: "As [police officers] attempted to stop Brown, he accelerated past them, past a third officer and when a security officer got close enough to stop him, Brown allegedly shoved the officer. At that point two other security officers physically removed Brown from the cart and placed him on the ground. He was arrested. No damage was reported to the cart although two traffic cones were damaged, one still under the cart, significantly so." The drummer, who had apparently enjoyed some refreshment before his joyride, was charged with operating a vehicle under the influence of alcohol, driving to endanger, theft, and assault, but was released after $4,000 was paid in bail.

A year later, Brown opened up about the incident, saying he loved riding around on golf carts. "The bass player and I do it a lot: we get drunk and we drive around. It's a lot of fun. Whenever I see a key in one, we hop in and go. It was nothing out of the ordinary."

That golf-cart episode is reminiscent of the rib-tickling adventures of the late Keith Moon, who had fun with various vehicles, including his own personal hovercraft and milk float. If anyone deserves an award for the Craziest Drummer Who Ever Lived, it is surely Moon, who not only drummed like a man possessed but was the human equivalent of an unstoppable runaway train, with a passion for shocking and destructive pranks. When the Who appeared on *The Smothers Brothers Comedy Hour* on US television in 1967, their performance of the song "My Generation" climaxed with the detonation of super-loud explosives in Moon's bass drum, to the surprise of everybody else in the studio, including the drummer's bandmates. Moon's arm was cut by shrapnel from his cymbals, and the explosion caused the actress Bette Davis, another guest on the show, to faint.

Moon was a hyperactive drummer who seemed to be just as hyperactive away from the kit. His passion for destruction extended to blowing up lavatories, and he proudly confessed to bringing mayhem to a hotel in Copenhagen during a Who tour. While he may have embroidered and exaggerated the story, there does seem to have been an incident with a waterbed that he found in his suite. According to his version of events, he decided to have the water-filled bed shoved into an elevator—so it would pop out as a surprise for people on another floor. But the bed burst before it could be taken to the lift, and the gushing water started a disastrous domino effect: after it wrecked the floor of Moon's room, it poured down and created more damage below. "I ruined three rooms in one fell swoop— one swell flood!" Moonie boasted later.

Theories about the specific mental conditions that Moon the Loon suffered have come thick and fast in the years since his death. He may have had ADD (attention deficit disorder) or, worse, ADHD (attention deficit hyperactivity disorder) or BPD (borderline personality disorder). Non-medical types called him "barking mad" or, if they were being kind, "eccentric." "When you've got money and you do the kind of things I get up to, people laugh and say that you're eccentric . . . which is a polite way of saying you're fucking mad," he said. "Well, maybe I am. But I live my life, and I live out all my fantasies, thereby getting them all out of my system. Fortunately, I'm in a position where financially I'm able to do it."

After a while, the naughtiness became driven by his public image; he felt compelled to act up because he was Keith Moon, and people expected it of him. Who guitarist Pete Townshend once recalled that he was in a car with Moon, on the way to catch a plane to take them to the next gig, when the drummer insisted on returning to the hotel where he had stayed the night before. As Townshend explained, "We were late for the plane, and Keith was like, 'Oh my God, I've got to go back to my hotel room.' We thought he'd left drugs in his room or something. We turned around; we know we're going to miss the plane and we might be late for the gig. We rush back to the hotel and he rushes in, comes out with the TV set and throws it into the swimming pool, gets back in the car, and goes, 'Phew, I nearly forgot!'"

The drummer did spend short periods in psychiatric institutions, and Townshend has been searingly frank about his bandmate's mental health. In a recent documentary about the making of the 1973 Who album *Quadrophenia*, the guitarist stated: "It was quite clear that Keith Moon was certifiably insane, and if he hadn't had a drum kit to play with, he probably would have ended up in jail." Hopefully, that jail would have offered some form of remedial psychiatric treatment. For the real tragedy of Keith Moon is that he was never diagnosed as insane during his lifetime; indeed, it's likely that his fame, popularity, talent, and public image prevented such a diagnosis from even being contemplated. As the writer Tony Fletcher puts it in his biography, *Dear Boy: The Life of Keith Moon*, "Clearly, Keith needed psychiatric help. Perhaps if he had been treated and diagnosed . . . when his violent alter ego began emerging from the shadows with alarming frequency, his personal demons could have been confronted, his rage brought under control, his energy harnessed when he was away from his drum kit, not just when he was on it. But how do you convince someone to go to a shrink when he is being hailed as the greatest drummer in rock 'n' roll history, when he is being lauded as the funniest man of his generation, when he is being held in wide regard as kind-hearted, generous and hopelessly lovable? How do you suggest to such a person that he might not be completely sane?"

When Moon died in September 1978, there was a lot of wishful thinking from fans about him being replaced in the Who by Rat Scabies, the drummer of the Damned, the notorious British punk band. Scabies—whose real name is Christopher Millar—appears to be a perfectly sane individual. However, in the early days of the Damned, he not only displayed a hyperactive style of drumming similar to Moon's, but also had a Moonish line in destructive pranks. Earlier in 1978, a Damned gig at the Rainbow Theatre in London climaxed with Scabies pouring petrol over his drum kit and setting it alight. In 1979 the band played Wirrina Stadium in the English city of Peterborough, and Scabies repeated the trick. The flames spread across the stage, the fire brigade arrived and turned on their water hoses, and the audience rioted, fighting and smashing windows.

Flaming percussion is not a punk invention, as John Bonham would point out if he were still with us. A frequent sight at Led Zeppelin gigs was the ignition of Bonham's big symphonic gong, which would be set alight by a roadie using the magic of alcohol. And similar pyromaniac stunts have been performed by other drummers. In the early 1990s, about a decade before he started playing drums with the Flaming Lips, Kliph Scurlock was performing in a punk band at the Outhouse, a famously spartan cinder-block music club in Lawrence, Kansas, when he decided on a whim to enhance the show with some special effects. "My drum set was a 1963 Ludwig kit, or maybe it was 1964, and it was the same kind of silver sparkle set that Ringo Starr played," he recalled. "I bought it for two hundred dollars from somebody who had had it sitting in their basement forever. It was like, 'Yeah! Ringo drums! All right!' Anyway, I thought it would be neat if I set fire to the drums. I was thinking it would be really punk rock. I wasn't thinking through that these were really old drums, and the wood was probably very dry, and it went up in flames really quick. Some friends and I were able to get the fire put out, but not quickly enough to salvage the kit. It was a bummer, because I loved that drum set."

Tré Cool of Green Day used to have a habit of torching his drums onstage, when he wasn't smashing them up. Away from the kit, Cool has followed the punk-rock tradition of hellraising in other ways. After Green Day won a Moonman award for Best Alternative Video at the MTV Music Awards in 1998, he excited spectators with an impulsive act in Orlando, Florida. During a broadcast interview with the band, he suddenly left the stage and started climbing the metal framework of the big, rotating Universal Studios globe. He sat on the globe for a while, waved to cheering fans, then climbed back down and returned to the interview. Asked why he'd done it, he smiled and was speechless for a while, before explaining: "I hadn't broke anything for, like, six hours!"

"Crazy" antics like these are rarely evidence of real insanity, and may be attributed to individual drummers attempting to live up to (or live down to) the generalized reputation that drummers have somehow acquired. But sometimes the mental state of drummers is a much more serious business. In 1995, Joey Kramer was due to begin recording a new album in Miami with Aerosmith, the band he had been in since 1970 and whose name he had coined himself. The band was on top of the world, selling millions of records and playing to huge, adoring crowds, and Kramer had succeeded in staying away from drugs and alcohol for nine years. However, after withdrawing from the world and spending alarming stretches of time in bed at home in Boston, he finally flew to Florida to take up his position on the drum stool—and suffered a severe emotional breakdown. Kramer was taken to a mental-health facility called Steps, in Oxnard, California, where he underwent group therapy and gradually found a way through his paralyzing condition. He tells his story with great candor in the 2009 book *Hit Hard: A Story of Hitting Rock Bottom at the Top*.

The case of the drummer Jim Gordon is much more tragic. Gordon was a six-foot-three-inch giant from California who became an in-demand session player by the end of the 1960s. His CV includes work with many big names, including the Everly Brothers, the Byrds, Glen Campbell, the Carpenters, and the Beach Boys. After playing for the husband-and-wife duo Delaney & Bonnie, Gordon became the drummer for Derek and the Dominos, featuring Eric Clapton. Gordon was one of the drummers on George Harrison's epic album *All Things Must Pass*, and went on to work with John Lennon, Frank Zappa, Carly Simon, Joe Cocker, and Traffic. But at some point he began to hear voices in his head, giving him peculiar instructions: they would tell him to go to certain destinations, and they would restrict the food he ate. It was textbook schizophrenia. "The voices were chasing me around," he explained later, "making me drive to different places. Starving me—I was only allowed one bite of food a meal. And if I disobeyed, the voices would fill me with a rage, like the Hulk gets."

Gordon's career as a drummer began to fail as he repeatedly checked into hospitals for treatment, desperate to shake off the inner voices. In 1979 he had to refuse an offer to tour with Bob Dylan. On June 3, 1983, at the age of thirty-seven, Gordon drove to the apartment of his seventy-one-year-old mother, Osa Marie Gordon, in North Hollywood.

When she opened the door, he attacked her, bludgeoning her head with a hammer before finishing her off with a butcher's knife in the ribs. "I just snapped," he admitted later. Convicted of second-degree murder (use of the insanity defense had recently been restricted in California law), he received a prison sentence of between sixteen years and life.

In July 1994, ten years into his sentence, Gordon—prisoner C89262 in the California Men's Colony at San Luis Obispo—was quoted in the *Washington Post*: "When I remember the crime, it's kind of like a dream. I can remember going through what happened in that space and time, and it seems kind of detached, like I was going through it on some other plane. It didn't seem real." The newspaper said he had associated some of the inner voices with his mother. "My mother, she persecuted me a great deal, I felt," he said. "And it finally got so bad that I just gave up and got a condominium and just stayed indoors. I didn't ever go anyplace. That's when I started hearing voices, and having delusional thoughts and hallucinations, and all of a sudden the crime occurred." He no longer heard the voices, he said, and was taking the high-potency medication Navane (thiothixene) for acute paranoid schizophrenia. But at a hearing in April 2013, sixty-seven-year-old Jim Gordon was flatly denied parole, having been deemed "a danger to society if released from prison."

Sadly, Gordon's isn't the only case of a matricide in the world of drumming. William Marrufo was once the drummer in the LA Latin-rock band Ozomatli. On January 5, 2005, he suddenly attacked his fifty-eight-year-old mother, Teresa, outside the home where they both lived in Santa Ana, California. After beating her head against the ground, he went into the house, emerged with a knife and two meat cleavers, and slashed and stabbed her to death.

After the attack, Marrufo explained to detectives that he believed his mother had been possessed by Satan. He was later convicted of first-degree murder and appeared to be facing a life sentence, but that verdict was overturned and the thirty-five-year-old drummer was found "not guilty by reason of insanity" and confined in a state mental institution.

Another drummer who suffered from psychological problems was Paul Hester, who played in the Australasian band Crowded House. Although Hester was a life-and-soul-of-the-party type, adored by the band's fans for his cheekiness and wit, he was also prone to extreme mood swings. This was the boy who had written in an essay at school that he wanted to be "a leading drummer in the world and to have a successful pop group." But, rather than making him happy, the increasing success of the band in the early 1990s perversely became a cause of discontent. In April 1994, during a North American tour, Hester walked out of Crowded House, leaving the band to play a gig in Atlanta, Georgia, without him. Neil Finn, the Crowdies' main songwriter, was scathing about Hester in a subsequent interview. "He's always been a bad-tempered little bastard," he said. "As much as he's incredibly funny when he's up—totally funny and [with] an incredibly gifted sense of humor—the other side of that is very black. We'd wake up on any given day and not know whether we'd find him up or down. He was casting a shadow over the whole organization."

Hester was frank about his aversion to success, revealing in an Australian newspaper: "I was thinking if things pick up, then we are on a course for world domination. The idea of being the most popular band in the world didn't appeal at all."

One day in March 2005, Paul Hester left his home in Melbourne, Australia, to take his two dogs for a walk. He never returned. The next morning, police found his body hanging from a tree in nearby Elsternwick Park. It later emerged that he had undergone years of therapy for depression, he had frequently taken antidepressants, and his relationship with the mother of his two young daughters had just ended.

Is it possible that many drummers are insane or eccentric, to varying degrees, but that their very occupation—the cathartic, stress-relieving act of beating the drums—keeps their craziness or eccentricity in check? Or is it just a coincidence that in the twenty-first century, so many people are using drums for therapy? Most of them aren't serious musicians who play proper drum kits in real bands: they are ordinary people who spend their spare time playing African-style hand drums in drum circles, groups of like-minded people who find creating rhythms beneficial to their health. There are now thousands of drum circles around the world, with many astonishing claims being made for the therapeutic effects of regularly bashing a membrane stretched over a wooden shell. Drums are regarded as a balm for all sorts of psychological conditions, from ADHD to bipolar disorder and from Alzheimer's disease to full-on insanity. Drum therapists claim that drumming can improve your self-esteem, heighten your ability to focus on important tasks, increase your ability to listen and learn, and convert negative, destructive tendencies into positive, creative behavior.

Several of the professional drummers I interviewed said that playing drums was a therapeutic, stress-relieving activity. "Drumming, for me, has always been a form of therapy," said the drummer and producer Butch Vig. "It allows you to release all this energy in a positive way."

Steven Drozd, multi-instrumentalist in the Flaming Lips, went further. "Drums are my first love," said Drozd. "I find that if I go for really long periods of time without playing the drums, I get some kind of pent-up anxiety and anger, which I can let loose if I can play on the drum kit. Sometimes, at home, I'll pull the drums out of the closet, set them up, and beat on them for a while."

In a recent online confession, an anonymous drummer diagnosed with ADHD shared some insights into the therapeutic benefits of drumming, based on personal experience: "I suspect my ADHD helped draw me towards drumming—I found it suitably maniacal . . . So for years there were no lessons or books or any kind of studious approach—just going hell for leather. Since I was a social pariah it suited me to spend hours daily on the kit . . ."

That could almost be the late Keith Moon speaking. It seems that drums do provide a valuable outlet for some people, and that a certain number of those people are, indeed, mentally unbalanced. This is confirmed by the stories of Moon, Jim Gordon, and Paul Hester, and by those of other, lesser-known drummers whose stories have not been publicized. But we are still talking about a tiny number of people—a minuscule percentage of the millions of people in the world who play the drums. And in the context of global mental illness, this is a drop in the ocean. In 2011, a research project reached some startling conclusions about the mental health of Europe alone. The study—by the European College of Neuropsychopharmacology (ENCP)—found that 38 percent of the population of Europe suffers every year with some kind of mental or neurological disorder, including depression or schizophrenia. That works out at a total of around 165 million Europeans. A 2013 study of children in New York City between the ages of six and twelve found that around 20 percent of them—over 145,000 kids—struggle with conditions such as bipolar disorder, ADHD, or depression. Even the fact that New York children are apparently saner, overall, than the average European is no comfort: mental illness often strikes later in life, so that New York's 20 percent is likely to rise as the city's children exchange their diapers and toys for jobs and mortgages.

So if psychological problems are quite common among non-drummers, and not as common as we may suppose among drummers, why does the idea of the "mad drummer" persist? I put the question to Richard Jupp, the apparently sane and sensible drummer with the British rock band Elbow, who since their emergence from Greater Manchester in the 1990s have won a clutch of prestigious prizes, including a Brit Award for Best British Group and an NME Award for Outstanding Contribution to British Music. "I think it's because we *look* mad," he replied. "We look a bit funny, because when you're behind a drum kit there's a lot to think about, there's all this shit going on around you, you're concentrating and putting all your energy into it, and you start pulling all these faces. You have this intensity, and I think that's where the look of insanity comes from.

"But also, we're like kids. You're surrounded by shiny stuff that you hit to make a noise, and you get all giddy and giggly about it. You see a new cymbal and you're mesmerized—'Ohhhh . . . What does that sound like?'—and you immediately have to go over and tap it. You get excited about different woods, finishes, skins, drumsticks . . . We've all got that giddiness, and that same look in our eyes."

Of course, the mass media are to blame, too, for perpetuating the idea of insanity among drummers so entertainingly. When *The Muppet Show* aired on British TV in 1976, millions of viewers were introduced to Animal, a hairy, berserk drummer who played in a band called Dr. Teeth and the Electric Mayhem. Animal's intelligence appeared to be extremely limited: his growling communication was limited to simple English phrases or unintelligible shouting, and he took figures of speech (such as the theatrical phrase "Break a leg") literally. It has been claimed without foundation that Animal, who was designed by the late Muppetmeister Jim Henson, was based on Keith Moon of the Who. Both drummers had heavy, dark eyebrows; however, Animal's profusion of facial hair also resembled that of a young Ginger Baker or John Bonham. When Jay Bulger was asking famous drummers to appear as talking heads in *Beware of Mr. Baker*, he tried to get Animal to say a few words, but the Muppet was reportedly unavailable.

Another form of comedy seems to haunt the profession of drumming. For example, one day, a drummer announces that he has had enough of being ridiculed by people who don't consider him to be a proper musician: he decides he is going to learn to play some "proper" musical instruments. So he walks up to the counter in his local music shop and asks: "Could I have that big red trumpet over there, please . . . oh, and that accordion over there?" The man behind the counter thinks for a while, then says: "Okay, I suppose you can have the fire extinguisher . . . but the radiator's got to stay."

The many "drummer jokes" that circulate today highlight a curious mismatch in the public perception of drummers. These jokes have been coined and passed on by musicians for decades, and have since entered the mainstream via word of mouth and the Internet. Just as some Jewish and Irish comedians have often told deprecating jokes about their own kind, so drummers seem happy to tell their favorite drummer jokes, joining in with the laughter. I discussed the subject with one of Britain's finest rock timekeepers, Simon Kirke, who played with the bands Free and Bad Company. "How do you know when the stage is level?" asked Kirke, quickly providing the punch line: "When the drummer drools out of both sides of his mouth."

Nick Mason, drummer and cofounder of Pink Floyd, gave me another: "A drummer walks up to the counter and says, 'I'd like some fish and chips, please.' And the girl behind the counter just rolls her eyes. And he goes, 'For fuck's sake, what's the matter? Why can't I just have some fish and chips?' And she rolls her eyes again and looks up at something above her. He looks up and sees this sign that says PUBLIC LIBRARY: QUIET PLEASE. And so he goes [whispering], 'Could I have some fish and chips, please?' "

Many of these jokes have the same theme, and it certainly isn't that drummers are insane. In fact, there is a notable lack in these witticisms of padded cells, straitjackets, and electroshock therapy. What they push, over and over again, is the notion that drummers are stupid, dumb, dim-witted, slow, educationally subnormal. "'Mummy, when I grow up I want to be a drummer,'" recited Nick Mason in the voice of a little boy. "'Don't be ridiculous, darling—you can't do both.'"

In a 1989 music magazine, Cozy Powell railed against the widespread assumption that drummers were "a bit thick." "There are probably a lot of drummers out there who are," he wrote, "but then there are many who are highly intelligent too—the Simon Phillips of this world. I've just been flicking through a drum magazine and they seem to be getting more intelligent all the time. Of course, you've got the earthy members of the drumming fraternity as well, like the late Keith Moon and John Bonham, and myself of course; not Brains Of Britain perhaps, but we had and have something else to offer . . . Perhaps all the people I've listened to in the past haven't had such a great education because they've always been too busy playing drums. For instance, I got chucked out of school at an early age because I was always arriving late, being tired from gigs the night before . . . my ONLY interest was playing the drums. As far as I was concerned, school was a waste of time because I knew exactly what I wanted to do."

Even in the noughties, the idea that drummers are mentally inferior shows no signs of going away. As recently as May 2013, more supposed evidence of this "fact" was trotted out for the entertainment of British television viewers. On an edition of the BBC satirical quiz *Have I Got News for You*, one of the guest panelists, the Reverend Richard Coles—a Church of England priest and broadcaster who was once in a 1980s pop band called the Communards—recalled a memory from his days on the road. "I was on tour with the Style Council once," he said, "and Steve White, the drummer—lovely chap—was staying in this posh hotel in Scotland." The hotel had apparently once been a castle and retained some its historic treasures. "And he walked into the library, which was full of books, and Steve White said, 'Blimey, what a lot of videos!'"

Note that patronizing little phrase "lovely chap," which seems to be shorthand for "I'd like to make it clear that I'm not being unkind or disparaging about him at all, but he's a drummer and let's have a laugh about him nevertheless."

Aggrieved drummers pour their hearts out on Internet message boards, complaining that the guitarists and euphonium players they jam with harbor nasty prejudices about their musical skills and their mental abilities. "I'm personally appalled at the amount of people who think that no thought whatsoever goes into playing the drums," moans one. "I'm the drummer in my band, and my bandmates keep on making fun of me because I'm a drummer so I must be stupid," laments another. "Ask them to play without you for a day and hear how much they suck," advises a fellow drummer. John Densmore, the intelligent man who played drums in the Doors, was clearly similarly rattled when he spluttered in a 2007 interview that "The drum was the first fucking instrument!"—turning the primitive nature of skin bashing into a positive statement.

One message board recently asked the question "Why do drummers look dumb most of the time?" and attracted some enlightening remarks. One of the contributors echoed Richard Jupp's insight about "mad drummers," saying that drummers have so much to think about that they unconsciously make a variety of ridiculous facial expressions as they play. Just as some of these facial contortions can give the impression of madness, a good many of these expressions—such as the wide-open mouth or the protruding tongue—can make drummers look oafish, simple-minded, and comical. This is then compounded by the medium of still photography, which preserves those dumb looks for eternity. "Guitarists, bassists, singers can all be captured easily by the camera," said one of the commenters, "but drummers are hard. It's the movement that makes the drummer so beautiful and spectacular to watch, and it's hard to capture that in a single photo."

But drummers can consciously aim to look more intelligent, explained another contributor; they can intervene and change the expressions they make when they play: "After having managers and so forth tell me to change my expressions and such while I played, I put up mirrors to watch myself. I concentrated on how I looked while I played . . . It's become part of the playing . . . It simply becomes part of the nature of the beast when you work on it."

There is another stereotype about drummers that needs to be examined. Is there an unwritten rule, tucked away at the back of an invisible contract drawn up by an unseen hand, that obliges the drummer to be "the comedian of the band"? Even in a group as chock-full of humor and wit as the Beatles, Ringo Starr quickly acquired the role of clown—as opposed to the clever, acerbic Beatle (John Lennon), the cute, public-relations Beatle (Paul McCartney), and the quiet, deep-thinking Beatle (George Harrison). The image branding was parceled out in a similar way with the Monkees, America's Prefab Four of the 1960s, with Micky Dolenz ending up on the drums and managing to become the zaniest member of a pretty kooky band.

Of course, there was no contest in the Who: offstage, Keith Moon would dress up as a veritable parade of characters, from a Nazi officer to Queen Elizabeth II, with a silly voice for each one. Paul Hester's genial personality and sense of fun were frequently at the fore during Crowded House concerts. At the end of a 1987 tour of Canada, a series of pranks between the band and their support act, Chalk Circle, culminated in Hester shedding his clothes and running across the stage during Chalk Circle's encore. Hester was nicknamed, inevitably, Hester the Jester.

When I asked Nick Mason if he had been "the comedian in the band," he seemed reluctant to accept the accolade and name-checked his two former Floydmates Roger Waters and David Gilmour: "Well, actually, Roger can be incredibly funny. I really enjoy Roger's company from that point of view; we can make each other really laugh. And Dave can be amusing." However, Mason betrayed himself by littering the interview with witticisms. When I asked, "What's the strangest thing you've ever hit with a stick?" he deadpanned: "Erm . . . I can't remember her name now." To a question about the relative merits of human drummers and drum machines, he said: "You can't get a drum machine to be sick over the coats in the cloakroom, and throw a television out the window, can you?" Asked if he had ever been injured as a drummer, he joked: "Yes. By really angry guitar players—'Shut the fuck up!'"

Chad Smith of the Red Hot Chili Peppers indulged his mischievous sense of humor in 2014 when he challenged the actor and comedian Will Ferrell to a drum battle. It all began when Ferrell, interviewed online, highlighted the physical resemblance between himself and the drummer. The actor took it further by declaring in a video that he actually was Chad Smith, and the drummer responded by telling Ferrell to "stop impersonating me" and by throwing down the drum-off gauntlet. Ferrell accepted and suggested they use the event to raise $300,000 for the charity Cancer for College. Total pledges of nearly $312,000 confirmed that the event would go ahead.

When I spoke to Smith before the drum battle, he delivered

a deadpan monologue about Ferrell that was hard to take seriously. "There's obviously something wrong with him, because he's impersonating me," he said. "He says that he is me. But I don't know if he's off his medication or a little delusional. I'm concerned for his mental health and well-being, you know, because he is a very talented comedian and actor, and I think he's great. I look forward to seeing what he's got," he laughed. "He's very famous for that skit on *Saturday Night Live* where he played the cowbell to that Blue Öyster Cult song, and that's very funny, so I think that his cowbell skills are in some way going to be incorporated into our battle. But unless he's been secretly practicing, I don't think it's going to be in his favor to go drum set to drum set, him and myself. I'm sure some sort of musical hilarity will ensue, and I'm up for it. It's for a great cause. But I hope he doesn't bring any of his children—I don't want him to be publicly embarrassed or anything."

The Smith-Ferrell drum battle took place in May 2014 on *The Tonight Show Starring Jimmy Fallon*. The two men, wearing identical backwards baseball caps and Kiss T-shirts, traded jibes and beats behind two drum kits. Most of the beats came from Smith, and most of the jibes came from Ferrell. ("That was cute. Do you play for the Lukewarm Chili Peppers?") Finally Ferrell picked up a cowbell, the rest of the Chili Peppers ran out onstage to perform Blue Öyster Cult's "(Don't Fear) The Reaper," and Ferrell was arbitrarily awarded a big golden cowbell as a trophy.

Just as there are different styles of drumming, so comedy comes in a variety of shades. In 2011, Premier, "the world's leading manufacturer of drums and percussion," announced a series of fifteen special shows in Germany and the UK by Nicko McBrain, the drummer with the British band Iron Maiden. Each date would be An Evening with Nicko—"a night of drums, drumming and entertainment" with this "charismatic figure . . . renowned for his humor, showmanship and live performances." I met McBrain before he played the final date of the tour, which was at Bush Hall in Shepherds Bush, London. Though highly respected as a hard-rock drummer, he made it clear that the show would not be a "drum clinic," exactly—a serious session in which drummers demonstrate their skills and pass on technical tips and tricks to an audience consisting mostly of other drummers. "I don't do drum clinics, I do a drum show," explained the cheery long-haired Londoner. "I leave the drum clinics to the guys who can really impress people with their prowess on the drum set. The way I've always looked at it is, I see these guys and I don't know what the fuck they're doing."

He told me he would be playing a few Maiden songs during the performance and promoting some Premier drums, including the Spirit of Maiden kit, made in his honor. There will also be a good deal of comedy. "There are a few gags that I stole off my old mate Jimmy Jones," he said.

This was interesting. Jimmy Jones, a veteran British stand-up comic, is often politely described as "outspoken" and "uncompromising" and is known for telling old-fashioned, politically incorrect "adult" jokes about Irishmen, flatulence, and "colored fellas" with "big choppers."

McBrain had played seven dates in Germany, including Munich, Frankfurt, and Cologne. The German shows had gone well, he said, attracting a combination of Iron Maiden fans and drummers. "But I got into trouble, because I tell a few politically incorrect jokes. Some bloke walked out. He said [adopting a comedy German accent], 'I do not like zis man—he is homophobic and racist.' He marched out the venue." What sort of jokes was he telling? "I talk about this survey that says one in three men in England are gay," he said, "and I just tell gay jokes. That's all—there's nothing meant by it. If you happen to be that way inclined, fine! Leave my bottom out of it, though."

Back in 1988, McBrain appeared on *The Sooty Show*, the British TV institution featuring a lovable bear puppet who never speaks to the audience, and his puppet friends, including Sweep and Soo. On the show, McBrain had a drum-off with Sooty and Sweep on their miniature kits. Iron Maiden fans wouldn't let him forget about it afterward—flocks of Sooty puppets would come flying through the air onto the stage—but Sooty subsequently became a mascot on his kit. The bear also made an unscheduled appearance during the penultimate Evening with Nicko, in Reading, revealed McBrain. "We had a signing session last night, and this guy came up with a Sooty. And I said, 'Do you know why Sooty doesn't speak? Because he's got Tourette's!' I animated him and had him saying, 'You fuckin' shit-faced bastard!' Everyone was laughing their bollocks off." McBrain only realized after the bear's outburst that there were small children in the audience who perhaps shouldn't have been exposed to that kind of language, and might now be cruelly disillusioned about their favorite puppet.

During the show that night, McBrain drummed along to some Iron Maiden songs, with footage of the band on a big screen behind him. He talked about Maiden, about Premier drums, and about cymbals and foot pedals. And the jokes came thick and fast, populated by characters including "colored guys" and "queers." The audience was a mix of Maiden fans and drummers—mostly men in black T-shirts—and some of them roared with laughter. But there were some sharp intakes of breath as well, and expressions that appeared to say, "Did he really say that?"

Before the show, McBrain had told me he usually started a drum solo with a "Max Wall shuffle." Max Wall was a peculiar British comedian with a long career in the twentieth century, remembered for his lugubrious voice and his comedy walk, which were often accompanied during his stage shows by military-style drumming. "I got off the kit the other night and I was in hysterics," said McBrain, "because I was thinking of Max and his funny walk, and him saying, 'Good . . . evening . . .'"

And as McBrain was saying this, it occurred to me that drummers may unconsciously become comedians because their instrument has so many comical associations—which other instruments, such as an electric guitar, don't. In addition to the Max Wall business, there's that old tradition requiring the drummer in a house band to punctuate the punch line of a joke, especially a bad one, with a short percussive sequence known as a sting or rim shot. Usually employing two drums and a crash cymbal, this is also known as the "ba-dum-tish." Millions of people recognize that sound when they hear it, but not a single person, it seems, knows who started it and when. It may well have originated soon after the appearance of the one-man drum kit, in the early days of vaudeville. The ba-dum-tish is now available in a variety of smartphone apps so you can instantly and electronically show your lack of appreciation for a friend's wisecracks. The comedy rim shot even has its very own joke: "Two drums and a cymbal fall off a cliff . . ." "Ba-dum tish!"

The American comedian Fred Armisen, the *Saturday Night Live* performer who cocreated the sketch show *Portlandia*, has shown that drumming humor doesn't have to be clichéd or simple-minded: it can be dry and subtle as well. Around the time he reached his forties, in the mid-noughties, Armisen fused his talent for comedy with his ability on the drums (he had played in the Chicago-based "post-hardcore" band Trenchmouth in the 1990s). He began playing the comedy character Jens Hannemann, a supposed virtuoso who gives earnest and utterly ridiculous video drum tutorials that smartly parody the educational clips of drum teachers that proliferate on the Internet. Hannemann plays horrible-sounding, laughably intricate passages of drumming that no pupil would even want to play. He combines this with outrageous deadpan comments such as "It's going to sound disgusting, but, you know, music is always for me like when you're with your partner physically. Your body does the same things: lot of sweating, a lot of sweating." His advice to novices is equally suspect: "Spend all your money and buy the most expensive equipment you could ever find."

In Armisen's DVD *Jens Hannemann: Complicated Drumming Technique*, he plays two characters: Hannemann, and the drum tech Victor Benedetto, summed up by one reviewer as "a considerably less accomplished but well-meaning schlub who isn't fit to carry Hannemann's Rototoms or gong bass drum." The humor has shot over the heads of many nonmusicians who miss the esoteric muso jokes, and it has even eluded some drummers. After a clip from the DVD appeared online, one critic with twenty-three years' drumming experience complained that Hannemann "does not even play the same thing from a slow pattern compared to when it is sped up"—which was exactly the point of one of the gags. I feel sorry for the aspiring drummers who bought *Complicated Drumming Technique* in good faith, then spent weeks banging their heads against the nearest wall as they tried to master the nonexistent and impossible time signature of 29/3.

Since an unwritten law dictates that the drummers are co-medians, they are often involved in the practical jokes that are perpetrated within a band. This can work two ways: they can be the pranksters themselves, or they can be the victims of pranks—a fate that often befalls people who are known to have a terrific sense of humor. Inevitably, some drummers became the target of their fellow percussionist Keith Moon—as when Herman's Hermits toured America with the Who in 1967, and the Hermits' drummer, Barry Whitwam, was about to turn in when he discovered that *somebody* had placed the head of a suck-ling pig in his bed.

When the Doors played the Winterland Ballroom in San Francisco in 1967, their highly enigmatic and unpredictable lead singer, Jim Morrison, decided to put the flowers that fans were giving him to a mischievous purpose. Morrison kept plac-ing them between John Densmore's drumsticks and his drums, apparently knowing that the drummer wouldn't want to ruin the concert by ceasing to play. Densmore was forced to smash the flowers to pieces. "Maybe," the drummer rationalized later, "it was his way of fucking with my image as a flower child."

Bill Ward, the original drummer in Black Sabbath, was often singled out for cruel treatment by other members of the group. In 1973, Sabbath went to record an album in Beverly Hills. The guitarist, Tony Iommi, told an interviewer in 2006 that they found some gold spray paint in the garage of the house they were renting and decided it would be perfect for their drummer. "We waited until he'd had a few drinks and was out of it, took all his clothes off, then sprayed him gold from head to toe," recalled Iommi. "Then we found this tin of lacquer and lacquered him. He was violently ill when he came round. So we phoned an ambulance. You can imagine what they thought when they arrived—seeing this bloke lying there, naked and sprayed gold. They asked us if we realized what we'd done, and said we could have killed him by blocking up all his pores. They were really pissed off. They gave him a shot of something to sort him out, and told us to clean him up. So we went back in the garage and found some paint stripper. His skin went this horrible red, really sore. We laughed about it the next day, but God, it wasn't funny on the night."

Iommi added that he wasn't averse to incendiary pranks, as well. "Bill and I used to have this party piece where I'd set him on fire," he said. "I'd pour alcohol on him—the studio alcohol we used to clean marks off the machines. I'd pour it on his hands, light it, flames would appear, and it would burn off. The effect was completely superficial—no damage done. One day I wanted to do this trick for our producer. I said to Bill, 'Can I set fire to you?' 'Not just yet,' he said, 'I'm busy.' A couple of hours later he said, 'I'm going home now, Tone. Do you want to set fire to me or what?' I got the alcohol, poured it over him, and as I lit him he went 'Whoomph!' All his hair, his beard, everything, went up in flames. He dived on the floor. I thought he was laughing, but he was screaming—and I was still pouring this stuff over him. He got third-degree burns. His mum phoned me and said, 'You barmy bastard! It's time you grew up. Our Bill might have to have his leg off.' I felt bad."

The British hard-rock band UFO recorded their 1982 album, *Mechanix*, at Richard Branson's famous Manor Studio in Oxfordshire. One night after a recording session, the band's drummer, Andy Parker, was driving his rental car down the M40 motorway when he was overwhelmed by a revolting, fishy smell. Then smoke started pouring from the car. He discovered that one of his bandmates had kindly attached a frozen kipper fillet to the exhaust pipe.

Luckily, like so many other drummers, Parker was blessed with a terrific sense of humor and could take a joke. And the fact that so many drummers are comedians, or at least genuinely funny people, may be linked to those old psychological stereotypes. When you sign up as a drummer, some people are going to assume automatically that you're either insane or stupid. So you have a choice: you can either keep protesting with a straight face that you are perfectly sane and intelligent, or you can take all the insults lightly—smile, shrug, and laugh them off. Which one of these options is more endearing, and is going to make you more friends?

2

WORKING-CLASS HEROES

Examined in the cold light of day, the idea that people choose to become drummers purely because they are nuts, screwy, or dim-witted doesn't stack up. For one thing, there are thousands of drummers out there who seem perfectly sensible, sane, and intelligent. I can personally vouch for dozens of these people, because I have spent many hours talking to them during my research for this book.

For another thing, there is little evidence that the most infamously insane people in history were able to lay down a funky groove with a bass drum, snare, a few toms, and some cymbals. Adolf Hitler was a house painter and a civil servant before he became a genocidal maniac, the emperor Caligula preferred sawing people in half to playing drum solos, and Charles Manson played the guitar. Yes, we can point to a small number of drummers who have definitely had psychological problems at one stage or another, but then we can also finger a number of painters, poets, actors, truck drivers, bankers, shoemakers, politicians, college students, housewives, and customer-service workers who have had their sanity called into question.

Good news for misunderstood drummers arrived in 2008 when a pair of scientists in Sweden announced that they seemed to have found a link between drumming and superior intelligence. Professor Frederic Ullen, from the Karolinska Institutet in Stockholm, and his colleague Guy Madison from Umea University, in northern Sweden, asked thirty-four men aged between nineteen and forty-nine to play a variety of rhythms as consistently as possible with a drumstick. These guinea pigs were then given an intelligence test consisting of sixty questions and problems. "We found that people with high general intelligence were also more stable on a very simple timing task," announced Ullen. "We also found that these participants had larger volumes of the white matter in the brain which contains connections between brain regions."

Of course, it would have been a more enlightening experiment if the guinea pigs had been actual working drummers. Plenty of people are good at keeping time, but they certainly don't all end up behind a set of drums. (Equally, some people who become drummers don't have a great sense of timing.)

But if insanity and stupidity are not the main qualifications for a life in percussion, what are? It was time, I decided, to move into the realm of socioeconomics.

When I began my love affair with rock music as a teenager in the 1970s, I formed the opinion that the drummer was often the most working-class member of the band. I think this idea was partly inspired by the physical effort that drumming requires, as opposed to singing or playing bass guitar or keyboards, for example. The drummer was usually the toughest-looking and sweatiest person in the band, and for practical reasons drummers tended to "dress down" much more than singers and guitarists, who would often be parading at the front of the stage in fancy clothing fashioned from the rarest silks, satins, and velvets.

In many cases, the working-class-drummer idea is confirmed by the former occupations of drummers, or their activities off the kit. John Bonham is a classic example. Bonham's future bandmate Jimmy Page was born in the sedate county of Surrey and regularly donned a snow-white surplice to sing as a choirboy in church. By contrast, Bonham was born in Redditch, in England's industrial Midlands, and as a boy spent hours fooling around on filthy building sites. His father, Jack, ran the construction firm JH Bonham & Son with Jack's father and brother Ernie, and John initially followed in their footsteps, joining the business as an apprentice carpenter. When he was drumming in various bands before he joined Led Zeppelin, he would do some bricklaying on the side to ensure he had an income. And even after he became a successful household name, he continued to roll up his sleeves and get his hands dirty. He bought a hundred-acre farm near Stourbridge, Worcestershire, where he bred Hereford cattle, planted trees, maintained agricultural outbuildings, and worked on the interior decoration of his farmhouse. At heart, he was a proud, salt-of-the-earth laborer who wanted a good, solid home for himself and his wife, Pat. "I was determined that when we had a house and garden of our own, I would keep them in wonderful shape," he once said. "I picked up quite a bit about house construction when I was working on the building sites."

When they started receiving serious attention from the UK media in 1972, it became clear that the art-rock band Roxy Music comprised an interesting collection of characters, most of them decidedly middle-class. The singer Bryan Ferry and the saxophonist Andy Mackay were both well-spoken aesthetes who had worked as teachers; the electronics wizard Eno was an articulate conceptual artist with a penchant for makeup and androgynous costumes; and the guitarist Phil Manzanera (born Philip Targett-Adams) was half Colombian and had grown up in a series of exotic locations including Hawaii, Cuba, and Venezuela. The drummer, Paul Thompson, on the other hand, was born to a working-class family, had retained his strong Geordie accent from the northeast of England (unlike Ferry), and had done a ton of work with his bare hands. In fact, the beginning of his career behind the kit with Roxy overlapped with the end of his career as a bricklayer and general laborer.

Even as the band was rehearsing and gigging, Thompson was living a Bonhamesque double life as a drummer/construction worker. This seems slightly absurd when you consider how important Thompson was to the early sound of this seminal band, which would influence artists as diverse as Talking Heads, Chic, and the Sex Pistols. Known as "the Great Paul Thompson" by fans—and one of the favorite drummers of the American producer Butch Vig, who plays drums in Garbage—his solid and persuasive drumming frequently served as an anchor for compositions that might otherwise have been dismissed as airy-fairy art-school electronica. Much of Thompson's work from the 1970s is still a delight to hear—highlights being the spine-tingling way he bursts into "The Thrill of It All" at the start of the *Country Life* album, and his majestic dynamics in "A Song for Europe" on *Stranded*.

Thompson hadn't been with Roxy Music for very long when he decided to leave construction work behind—and graduate to night work on London's subterranean rail network. "In the early Roxy days, we weren't getting any wages or anything," Thompson told me. "So I was working on a building site. But I was getting a bit sick of that, so I went for one of those night jobs on the London Underground, doing maintenance work and cleaning during the night. So I went to apply for a job; I had to go to a place off Marylebone Road in London, I think. The guy I saw was an ex-military type, and he gave me a look when I walked in with my long hair. I filled in a form and answered some questions. And his reply was 'Your application's failed.' I'm sure it was just because of the length of my hair."

Roxy had a novel approach for their early singles. Rather than shove album tracks on the B-sides, as many artists did, they indulged the individual members of the band with the opportunity to write experimental or frivolous instrumentals. It was this quirky B-side policy that gave Roxy's drummer the opportunity to enjoy some revenge on Colonel Blimp at the London Underground recruiting office. "I was a bit of a comedian at the time," recalled Thompson. "I used to make all the lads in the band laugh with my Geordie humor. I told them the story about going for the job, and at some point after that, somebody said, 'Oh, it's your turn to write a B-side,' so I was fiddling around with a guitar and I had this little idea. The Roxy B-sides were always fun things."

The band took Thompson's little idea into AIR Studios, the recording facility established on London's Oxford Street by a group of studio boffins including Beatles producer George Martin. "I think it was Bryan who said, 'Why don't you say, "Your application's failed" in the middle of the track?'" said Thompson. The recording, a funky little number with some nice Rototom work, duly became "Your Application's Failed"—a percussive anthem for struggling working-class drummers everywhere.

I recently watched Clem Burke, the drummer in Blondie, give a talk at the ICA (Institute of Contemporary Arts) in London as part of Blondiefest, the ICA's celebration of America's most successful new wave band. He talked about his origins in a "working-class New Jersey suburb," and it was clear from his continual wisecracking—and the strong residue of a Noo Joizey accent—that deep down inside he was still a streetwise kid from Bayonne.

I spoke to Burke after the talk, and he elaborated on his social background and his early motivations. "You hear about so many people who use sports or music to get out of the factory," he said. "I never really thought I was going to work in a factory, but I always wanted to get out of my working-class existence. I was fortunate: when I was in school, I was always drumming in bands, and it was always a way of earning money. I earned money as a musician from the time I was a teenager. I did other work as well sometimes. I remember at one point, I was playing in Blondie, I was going to college, and I was working in the post office, all at the same time. So that basically involved being up till three or four o'clock in the morning, going to work at about seven o'clock in the morning, and going to school around two or three o'clock in the afternoon. We had to do the photo shoot for the first Blondie album, but it was the Christmas rush at the post office, and they made an announcement: anybody who doesn't come in to work tomorrow is immediately fired. I went up to the boss and said, 'Sorry, I'm not gonna be able to make it in tomorrow.' I explained my dilemma, and he said he understood and let me take the day off. I did the photo shoot and went back to work the next day."

Another drummer who had to juggle drumming, school, and casual work is Nicko McBrain of Iron Maiden. "I grew up in Wood Green in north London, and I went to Wood-side secondary-modern school for boys. I was missing a lot of school, because I was playing gigs in the week with bands. I was going to stay and do my GCE exams, but I got the drumming bug, and I said to my mum, 'I don't want to stay at school: I want to go off and play in bands.' "

McBrain was granted his wish and left school, but gigging didn't cover his living expenses and he had to find extra income. His first job was also carpentry—or it was meant to be—and it didn't last for long. "They had me filling in cement foundations with slurry, and I said, 'Look, I'm here to do carpentry, not just laboring.' And they said, 'You do what you're fucking told.' And I said, 'You know what you can do with that—you can stuff it up your arse!' I lasted three days. I eventually ended up working in engineering; I worked for the Standard Bottle Company, a glass bottle manufacturer in Bounds Green, north London. They're not there anymore. They started me off on a day-release program, so for four years I went to college to study engineering, for one day and two nights a week." On the very day in the early 1970s when McBrain received his examination results, he turned professional as a drummer. "I only went to college because my mother insisted on it. My father knew I was good enough to turn pro."

Secondary-modern schools of the kind that McBrain attended existed in Britain until the 1970s, and were seen by many critics as a dumping ground for non-academic children who were not clever enough for grammar schools and were largely destined for menial jobs such as factory or building work. John Bonham attended Lodge Farm Secondary Modern, where the head teacher notoriously predicted in a report that "He will either end up a dustman or a millionaire."

Significantly, Keith Moon was the only original member of
the Who to have been educated at a secondary modern. He
went to Alperton Secondary Modern School for Boys in Wembley, northwest London, while Pete Townshend, Roger Daltrey, and John Entwistle were all considered bright enough to
attend Acton County Grammar School for Boys, situated a few
miles farther south. Like Clem Burke and Nicko McBrain, the
young Moon juggled casual work with his education. At one
time, he was employed by a greengrocer to wash and sort the
fruit and vegetables; for another period, he was employed by a
butcher to deliver cuts of meat to customers.

Many other drummers tell almost Dickensian stories of disastrous early jobs, with a musical opportunity finally arriving to provide a Cinderella-style happy ending. Paul Hester of
Crowded House once listed some of the many jobs he'd had
before he became famous, including working on a chicken
farm, rounding up shopping carts for a supermarket, working
in a timber yard, and making dental fillings. Travis Barker of
Blink-182 once worked as a trashman in the seaside resort town
of Laguna Beach, California.

Jobs like these may have been character-forming for the
boys who would later choose the sweatiest jobs in the music
business. While growing up in Los Angeles in the mid-1960s,
John Densmore, the future drummer with the Doors, found
himself folding a seemingly endless succession of shirts in a
Chinese laundry. Densmore later recalled that the temperature
of that shirt-folding room "never dipped below ninety-eight
degrees. And that was in winter. It was like taking a sauna every
day. I drank gallons of Orange Crush and ate Twinkies by the
box while singing the Sweatshop Blues . . ."

Steve White drummed for Paul Weller for twenty-five years, as well as enjoying short stints playing in Oasis and the Who. While in the sixth form at school, White applied to study at two colleges, and was successful. "But I come from a working-class family, and my parents couldn't afford for me to go to college," he explained. "So I left school, almost in protest. Once I'd left school, my mum said, 'You've got to get a job, then, haven't you?' And I remember doing one day working on a building site in Swanley in Kent, with a group of big, hard tunnel diggers from Newcastle. And I cut my hand on the first day and ended up in hospital, in Accident and Emergency. I thought, 'That's it! I'm not doing that again.'" Fortunately, he was rescued from a life of dangerous drudgery when a friend mentioned that Glenn Tilbrook and Chris Difford, formerly of the British band Squeeze, were looking for a drummer. White auditioned, got the job, and drummed with them for three months before receiving a call from Polydor Records, suggesting he try out for one of the label's new bands. He succeeded again, and joined Paul Weller in his post-Jam band, the Style Council.

Ross McFarlane worked in "a series of dead-end jobs" before he sat on the drum stool behind an impressive series of Scottish bands including the Proclaimers, Belle and Sebastian, and Texas. "I was a bit of a jack-the-lad at school and never really concentrated," the amiable dark-haired Scotsman told me. "So I left school at sixteen without many qualifications. I was seriously into drumming and I was playing gigs, but I had to find paying work as well. I worked in a stationery warehouse, but I was always turning up late for work, because I was going backwards and forwards from Glasgow to London and playing gigs. I'd leave work on Friday and go to London, then I wouldn't get back till the Tuesday. I was so tired, I used to sleep in the bubble wrap in the warehouse, and I was found out, because I had bubble marks on my face! So I got the sack from there. Then I got a job as a landscape gardener, but I knew nothing about either landscaping or gardening, and I got the sack from that as well."

Before he settled on the drum stool behind the Red Hot Chili Peppers, the young Chad Smith had brief, unsuccessful jobs at a paint company and a pancake house. "I had a few jobs, but nothing that I liked or was any good at," he told me. "I don't know what I'd be doing now if I wasn't a drummer. I'd be probably like, you know . . . I'd have to be a bank robber—I'd need money. And I'd be in jail!"

Even if drummers never have to endure a demeaning job or a spell in the penitentiary, they may still be regarded as inferior human beings. Drummers generally have long suffered from the fact that not all musicians respect the drum kit as a legitimate instrument; in the eyes of the doubters, drummers are therefore low-ranking musicians, if they are musicians at all. Throw in all the jokes about drummers, plus the myth that all drummers are either crazy or stupid, and you can see why Internet drum forums are frequently full of pain. Here is an extract from a rant about drumming that recently appeared online:

It's not a hard job, you just sit there on a stool smashing some sticks on the bongo things. Occasionally you might have to hit a cymbal. Big deal. Anyone can be a drummer so there is no excuse for being rubbish at it. If you are the drummer in a band you are probably an idiot and there is a good chance that the lead guitarist hates you. You should try having a bath once in a while.

While this was actually written in jest, it sums up some of the genuine negative attitudes that drummers have had to endure, and it was irresistible bait for some aggrieved drummers who took it seriously.

When drummers audition to join a band, they can suffer all kinds of humiliation even before they've played a beat. The Red Hot Chili Peppers held auditions for a new sticksman in 1988 after they had fired D. H. Peligro, formerly of the Dead Kennedys. Chad Smith was one of the last drummers to audition, and there were objections from the Los Angeles band as soon as he appeared. "I was wearing this Detroit rock 'n' roll leather jacket," he recalled, "and I had long hair and a bandana—at the time, it was the look of bands like Guns N' Roses, which was the antithesis of what the Chili Peppers were about. They were very much into this aggressive punk-rock look, with funny haircuts and 'What kind of tattoos do you have?' So when I walked in there, they were like, 'Oh, jeez, he's like some rocker dude,' and, 'Oh, God, let's get this guy outta here.' And then we started to play, and that all went out the window—we immediately connected musically. But they were like, 'You gotta shave your head,' and I was like, 'Fuck you, I won't shave my head for you.'" Fortunately for everyone, the band grew to tolerate the outsider's appearance and went on to shift tens of millions of records.

One very subtle indicator of the low esteem in which drummers have historically been held is the nickname. In countless cases, an ordinary name is not sufficient for a drummer, who traditionally requires an additional, jokey handle or an unnecessary first-name replacement. Sometimes these names are provided by fellow musicians, and sometimes they are self-created. Richard Starkey became Ringo Starr, the first name indicating his habit of wearing rings on his fingers, and Peter Baker became Ginger Baker because of the hair coloring he was born with. John Bonham became Bonzo, which is the sort of name you give to a dog. Keith Moon became Moon the Loon, with some justification, but he was also condescendingly addressed as Moonie—though his bandmates were never known as Townshendie, Entwistlie, and Daltreyie, no matter how catchy that might have been.

Musicians apparently need the tiniest excuse to find a catchy new name for their drummer. Ed Cassidy of the American psychedelic band Spirit was dubbed "Mr. Skin" simply because he shaved his head, as if nobody had ever seen a bald man before. The drummer in Dr. Feelgood, the 1970s band now regarded as a harbinger of British punk rock, was plain John Martin—but because of his impressive physical stature he was known as the Big Figure. Soon after joining the Clash, drummer Nick Headon became Topper Headon because bassist Paul Simonon thought he resembled a simian cartoon character called Mickey the Monkey, who appeared in a children's comic called *The Topper*. The drummer Brian Taylor, who played in the Tom Robinson Band (TRB), another notable ensemble in the British punk era, ended up with the nickname Dolphin.

The longtime drummer in Siouxsie and the Banshees was born Peter Clarke but is called Budgie—because when he was young, he saw somebody maltreating a budgerigar and intervened to stop them. Patrick Seacor, who played in the Scissor Sisters, answers to the percussive name of Paddy Boom. Ahmir Thompson, drummer in the Roots, is better known by his adopted alias, Questlove. Jimmy Sullivan was the drummer for the American metal band Avenged Sevenfold, but he is usually remembered now as Jimmy "the Rev" Sullivan, his pseudo-clerical handle deriving from a silly stage name he once adopted, the Reverend Tholomew Plague. When Carmine Appice played drums for Rod Stewart in the 1970s, the singer grew tired of Appice's fondness for bashing round the kit and started calling him the Dentist because of all the "fill-ins" he played.

Sometimes drummers receive their nicknames even before they become drummers. It's as if the people around them can sense their future occupation and want to give them a proper drummer's name in advance. Mott the Hoople were a highly enjoyable, hardworking British rock band that produced a string of UK hits and toured America in the 1970s. Brian May of Queen, who played on the same bill as Mott in 1973, once paid them this compliment: "On tour as support to Mott the Hoople (the only time Queen ever supported anyone), I was always conscious that we were in the presence of something great, something highly evolved, close to the centre of the Spirit of Rock 'n' Roll, something to breathe in and learn from." Mott's highly capable drummer was Terence Dale Griffin, who had attended the same school in Hereford as the bass player, Overend Watts. Watts explained how his bandmate had acquired a new name. "At school his name was Terry Griffin," said Watts, "and for some reason he got called Sniffin', and I didn't think that was good enough. I used to say, 'He's a bugger, that Sniffin',' and because I tend to change everything round backwards, I turned it round to 'He's a snigger, that Buffin.'" Henceforth, and for the vast majority of his career as Mott's drummer, he answered to Buffin or, because two syllables can be troublesome for rock musicians, just Buff.

There are many other examples of drummers having their names changed. One of the earliest is Warren Dodds, who acquired the patronizing name Baby, presumably because he was

younger than other members of his band. His name is still trotted out today as Warren "Baby" Dodds, as if he were an American assassin like Lee Harvey Oswald or John Wilkes Booth,
and despite the fact that he deserves more respect as a seminal
New Orleans jazz drummer.

Of course, other musicians are blessed with nicknames
as well, especially singers, but their handles are usually more
grandiose than those handed out to mere drummers. Bruce
Springsteen is the Boss, while many other vocalists have taken
on royal status: Nat Cole became Nat "King" Cole, Elvis Presley was the King of Rock 'n' Roll, Michael Jackson was the
King of Pop, and Aretha Franklin was crowned the Queen of
Soul. But only the occasional drummer is lucky enough to be
granted a complimentary nickname. Al Jackson Jr., who played
in Booker T. & the M.G.'s and laid down the immortal groove
of Al Green's "Let's Stay Together," was dubbed the Human
Timekeeper. Similarly, the American metal drummer Gene
Hoglan is so highly respected for his timekeeping abilities that
he is known as the Atomic Clock.

A substantial number of drummers may have been restless,
antsy, or hyperactive as children, and may even have been diagnosed as ADHD, which brings its own torrent of prejudice
from society. There has been a long-running tussle over the
causes of this complex condition, with some scientists blaming
faulty genetic coding or a deficiency in essential fatty acids,
some social commentators whining that ADHD is an imaginary complaint—a label for parents to stick on their naughty,
out-of-control children—and some people suggesting that
it is a genuine problem arising from lower-class lifestyles.
They point the finger at mothers who drink alcohol during
pregnancy, or mothers and fathers who fail to bring up their

children properly, are incapable of discipline, and allow their kids to live on junk food. Americans might use pejorative terms like "trailer trash" while snobbish Britons may mention "chavs," loosely defined as the inferior, lowlife element of society.

Unfortunately, it is within the social milieu of chavs and trailer trash that we find a particular practice that has been widely adopted by drummers. This is body decoration. Tattooing cuts across the musical community: many singers, guitarists, and other musicians have hearts, flowers, birds, cobwebs, or arcane Oriental symbols adorning their flesh. Even boy-band members who have never handled a grown-up musical instrument have it done now. But if it were possible to carry out a detailed, world-wide skin survey, it is my belief that drummers would emerge with the largest total surface area covered with permanent ink.

Some drummers settle for one or two designs, such as Nicko McBrain, who has one large, Oriental-themed tattoo on each arm. One of them resembles a dragon, and the other is an elaborate Samurai warrior. But many drummers take skin art much, much, further. Look at Tommy Lee of Mötley Crüe, who has had so many tattoos needled onto his body that he is said to have lost count of them. (And when a drummer loses count of something, you know they're in trouble.) He is estimated to have fifty of them, but now that there is so much overlapping and intermeshing of designs, he has said he prefers to see them as "one big work of art." His first design, acquired at the top of his right shoulder when he was seventeen, is a picture of the cartoon character Mighty Mouse flying through a bass drum. He has explained that "Mighty Mouse was my childhood hero. He always saved the day, he was a good guy, he was a role model who did the right thing, and at the end of every episode, he always got the chick."

Lee looked in the mirror after gaining that first piece of "art" and decided that he was artistically unbalanced, and he had to have more. Hanging around tattoo parlors became an inspiration, as he glimpsed some of the more exotic possibilities and acquired a taste for Oriental symbolism. Two dragons appeared on his chest, which also has the word MAYHEM on it, and an obscure "tribal" design was added to his back. In the early noughties, his fiancée Mayte Garcia—the singer and dancer formerly married to Prince—kissed Lee on the neck, and the drummer had her lip print turned into a tattoo as well. He had the self-referential word TATTOO tattooed on his wrist, and he had two designs resembling electric switches added to the inside of one elbow, marked RESET and KILL, which have been pressed at stressful moments for a form of personal therapy. Perusers of other parts of his body may find a koi carp, a cheetah, and a skull wearing a top hat, unless these have recently been obliterated by fresh new layers of designs.

Travis Barker is another hot contender for rock's most illustrated man. His first tattoo was the word BONES in honor of a childhood nickname. He had a Cadillac emblem emblazoned on his chest, and a checkered racing flag on his neck, and just to remind you that he is a rock musician rather than a racing driver, he had a little bit of musical notation added to his neck as well, along with a boom box on his stomach. Barker added glamour and drama with some sexy women, flames, and smoke.

Compared with Lee and Barker, Dave Grohl is the personification of tattoo restraint. But Grohl does have some of those miscellaneous "tribal designs" on his arms and shoulders, FF (for his band Foo Fighters) on the back of his neck, and a

symbol—tattooed in three places, so you know he means it—
that will be very familiar to Led Zeppelin fans. This is the mys-
tical three-circle symbol that represents John Bonham on the
Led Zeppelin IV album.

Tattoos still create an unfavorable impression in certain
places, branding drummers as unwelcome lower-class types. In
2013, Jeff Fabb, the drummer in the American rock band Filter,
tried to enter an eatery in Denver after playing a show in the
city, but was stopped by the doorman because of the large mul-
ticolored tattoo on his neck. "I was kind of hurt," he told the
Hollywood Reporter after the incident, "since most of the people
who were in there at the time were from our show," and he had
been eager to join them.

Some drummers have become so enchanted by the world
of tattoos that they have crossed the line. Corey Miller was an
American punk drummer who became so enchanted with the
art form that he started working as a tattoo artist himself at the
age of twenty, needling customers' flesh at Fat George's Tattoo
Gallery in La Puente, California. In 1997 he set up his own
parlor, Six Feet Under, in Upland, California.

Nobody knows who was the first drummer to stumble into
a tattoo parlor and lay down cash for body art, but it's tempt-
ing to believe that it all started because of a linguistic misun-
derstanding. There are two different words with the spelling
tattoo in English. The one meaning "pigment design on skin"
was mentioned by Captain Cook back in 1769, and comes from
the Polynesian word *tatau* or *tatu*. The other *tattoo* is an earlier word, meaning a military drumbeat—originally a signal
calling troops back to their quarters—which has Dutch origins. Is it just extreme coincidence that both *tattoos* have strong
drumming connections? Perhaps a drummer was out strolling

one day, centuries ago, when he saw a sign offering TATTOOS, thought it was something to do with drumming, wandered in, liked what he saw, and started the whole drum-needle connection there and then. Stranger things have happened.

Drummers' tattooing tendencies have got so out of hand now, the tattoos have taken on a life away from their bodies. They've been celebrated by the manufacturers of the drums and drumsticks that they use. Ludwig's Corey Miller Tattoo Drum Set, designed by Miller himself, is covered in Miller's trademark black-and-gray tattoo art. (A drummer with all-over tattoos could appear to be invisible behind this kit, as the audience sees only a vague mass of merging designs.) Chad Smith once had a kit painted with octopus and whale designs that were based on tattoos on his body. And Zildjian's Dave Grohl Artist Series Drumsticks are decorated with replicas of the tattoos up Grohl's arms.

Even drummers you wouldn't expect to have tattoos have been inked. Steve Gadd isn't a lank-haired, dead-eyed heavy-metal basher but a highly respected master of his art, a drummer who has graced innumerable recording sessions and gigs with some of the biggest music stars of all time. He is Dr. Steve Gadd now, having had an honorary doctorate bestowed on him by the Berklee College of Music in Boston, Massachusetts. The British drummer Bill Bruford, no slouch himself in the percussion department, has given Gadd this glowing encomium: "Steve is a veteran of thousands of sessions, during which he can assess and provide exactly what is required to lift the music, in countless different styles. He is the interpreter without parallel. From the lilt of Paul Simon, to the blues of Eric Clapton, the jazz of Chick Corea, or the laidback vocal style of James Taylor, Steve does detail in one take. His encyclopedic knowledge of the appropriateness of a given rhythmic feel is born from his voluminous experience. No matter how dismal your little of-fering, if you have Steve Gadd on it, it'll shine."

But look at Gadd's lean, pink arms and you'll find some ex-tensive dark-blue decoration, which he discussed at length in a recent interview. The first tattoo he ever had, in the early 1970s, is an animal design near his right shoulder (very close to where Tommy Lee had his first one). Gadd said it now reminded him of a dog he used to have, an old English bulldog—although, confusingly, he had the tattoo done years before he had the pooch. The other tattoos followed more recently, many of them "shared" with his wife, Carol—meaning that he has the same de-signs that she has on her body, including an Oriental om symbol on his right hand, a chi symbol on his left wrist, and "a tribal thing" adorning his right arm. He also has a Japanese version of the number thirteen on his left hand, "because I like the number thirteen." When his wife had some tattoos done, "something happened, and I just felt the need to decorate myself," he said.

Lovers of Gadd's exquisite drum skills have been disap-pointed and horrified by the low-rent appearance of all this self-decoration. One fan from Arizona has complained online: "I really wish Steve was a tux-and-tails kind of drummer . . . When you are at the top o' the heap you should also look like you belong there . . . his artistry and skill set deserve better."

When I met Russ Miller, another prolific and skillful Amer-ican session drummer, I noticed that he had writing on both arms. One has his wife's name in Japanese, and the other has his daughter's name, also in Japanese. He lifted the left sleeve of his T-shirt to reveal another tattoo, a drawing of a drum kit. "I think it's my ongoing midlife crisis," said the forty-four-year-old, "because I got them later on in life."

I asked Roger Taylor of Queen why he thought so many drummers acquired tattoos. "Well, of course, they have the most beautiful bodies to put them on," he laughed. I was un-surprised to learn that Taylor, too, had crossed the threshold of the tattoo parlor. "I have a few, mostly on the legs," he said. However, what was surprising was that, like Miller, he was a late starter: his tattoos weren't acquired in his 1970s heyday, when he was bashing away behind Freddie Mercury to make exciting records like "Bohemian Rhapsody," "I Want to Break Free," and "We Will Rock You," but much more recently, in his sixties. He is known to have a fondness for dragons, and a recent photograph shows him with a big dragon tattoo slither-ing up his right leg. When I asked Taylor why he had acquired the tattoos—was it because drummers were generally under some kind of pressure to have them?—he seemed to dislike the question. He started muttering, before terminating the con-versation. "I just thought . . ." he said, "I really don't . . . It's my choice . . . I don't give a fuck . . . I tell you what—I'm gonna have to go, because I've got to take my wife to the airport."

Chad Smith blames his bandmates Anthony Kiedis and Flea for his tattoos, which now honor his chosen instrument, his zodiac sign (Scorpio), and his children, as well as some of the sea creatures he has spotted while scuba diving. "I didn't have any tattoos when I came out to California and started playing with the Chili Peppers," he told me. "But then I went to Europe for the first time in my life, and we played to three hundred thousand people in Amsterdam. Anthony and Flea had gotten tattoos from this famous artist there, Henk Schiffmacher, and I think at the time it was sort of a band thing—'Let's all go get tattoos from Henk.' And after my first experience of getting a tattoo, it became kind of addictive. You kind of want to get another one, and then another one."

If clothes maketh the man, then they can also—like tattoos—give drummers the impression of belonging to an inferior social bracket. The British drummer Robert Wyatt is an interesting case in point. The Canterbury Scene of the late 1960s and early 1970s was very much a middle-class affair, based loosely around the historic cathedral city—the center of Christianity in Britain since the sixth century—that gave the movement its name. Nicely educated musicians from relatively affluent families formed bands such as Soft Machine, Caravan, and Gong to explore the furthest reaches of experimental rock and pop, throwing jazz, classical, and literary influences into the mix. Robert Wyatt was certainly not an ordinary working-class prole: his mother was a BBC journalist, he went to grammar school, and he was privileged enough to have lessons from an American jazz drummer. But Wyatt's social status was apparently downgraded by the fact that he sat behind the drums in Soft Machine. He has since described himself as "the only lout in the group" and has said that he sometimes saw his bandmates' eyes "raised to heaven" at his behavior and utterances. It probably didn't help that while the other players were usually dressed to the nines in the latest psychedelic finery, Wyatt often played the drums shirtless like a sweaty builder, roustabout, or fairground worker.

If you're a drummer who tends to perspire a lot, it's probably a bad idea to wear a three-piece velvet suit with a fur coat over it. There is the shirtless option, but there is also a variety of sports clothing that does the job—at the expense of your position in the social hierarchy. "Why is it that drummers have a habit of wearing basketball jerseys on stage?" asks one perceptive commentator, Vince Neilstein of the MetalSucks website. "Tool's Danny Carey constantly rocks his Lakers jersey (though dude, [what's] with the t-shirt underneath? That's like wearing socks with sandals)." According to Neilstein, other offenders have been Zoltan Chaney, drummer for the solo band of Vince Neil of Mötley Crüe, and Mike Portnoy, who "is rarely seen on stage without a jersey of some kind (though to be fair, he also sports baseball and hockey jerseys) . . . Think about the utter ridiculousness of a guitarist or bass player wearing a basketball jersey as their stage outfit . . . they'd be laughed off the stage . . . Is it the comfort? The pure athleticism of being a metal drummer is certainly demanding, and I've known drummers to be completely soaked in sweat from head to toe after a performance. But I'd think a plain old cotton t-shirt with the sleeves cut off would absorb the sweat way better than the mesh of a jersey, and I'd think it would be more comfortable/less itchy to boot."

It's not just online ranters who disapprove of what drummers wear. In the summer of 2009, Matt Helders, drummer with Arctic Monkeys, was attempting to buy a camera at a store in the British band's home city of Sheffield when he was asked to leave the premises by security staff who didn't like the cut of his jib. The drummer—reportedly a multimillionaire—was wearing casual, sporty clothing, including a hoodie. According to one British newspaper, he had been mistaken for "a chav shoplifter." Helders would get on well with Questlove, who loves hoodies so much that he cofounded a store to sell them on the Lower East Side of New York City, with the imaginative name of the Hoodie Shop.

Many drummers have acquired an undesirable reputation in quiet neighborhoods simply because their chosen instrument is so loud and lacks a volume control. Jack Bevan is the energetic drummer in the British band Foals, whose album *Holy Fire* was voted the best album of 2013 by readers of the UK music bible *NME*. Bevan told me about the problems he suffered as an aspiring drummer growing up in Oxfordshire in the late 1990s and early 2000s. "It was all right in the beginning," he said. "A lot of the time, I'd play after I got home from school and before my parents got home from work. But then one of the neighbors started complaining. Then it felt like treading on eggshells when I was practicing. Eventually they took it to the local council, they did a volume test in the adjoining garden, and I was basically told that I couldn't play anymore. I had to buy an electronic drum kit, which I hated: it sounded so synthetic, and you don't have the feel of playing a real drum kit. But then I joined a band, and then I only really played when the band was rehearsing."

Steve White, who has given many lessons to young drummers, told me he had seen a change in attitude toward drumming over the years in England. "When I was a boy living in south London, " he said, "my dad built a practice room in the loft, which wasn't particularly soundproof, but I could go up there. I played in there from when I was eight until I left home years later. And we handled it really well: when I decided that I wanted to do it, we went and spoke to all the neighbors and said, 'If there's a problem, let us know.' We told them that I wouldn't practice at particular times, and all the neighbors were so supportive—people said things like, 'Oh, drumming— that's a really good hobby.'

"But these days, practicing is a real problem for young drummers. The trouble is, people are ultrasensitive to any kind of invasion of their own space. They'll happily put up with somebody revving their Range Rover up at nine o'clock in the morning, but if a kid gets up and plays the drums, immediately it's taken as an antisocial act. I get a lot of students who come up against all this intolerance the minute they start to play the drums. There's not a lot of give-and-take with people now. They take it as an offense. Well, there are electronic kits that you can play with headphones. It's not the same, but I would say it's better to be playing in some way than not at all. You have to deal with your own set of circumstances and find a way round it."

Even before you achieve the tricky task of winning over Sid and Vera next door, you have to avoid upsetting the people you live with, such as your parents. "Playing the drums caused a lot of grief in my house, I have to say," Ross McFarlane told me, "a lot of hassle. We didn't live in a stately home—there wasn't a B-wing to the house where the drum kit was! It was in the bedroom above the living room, in a semidetached house in Glasgow. My parents would go out and they'd say, 'Don't play your drums,' and then I'd play them. And I wouldn't hear them coming in, because I was playing, and the door would swing open and my old man would be very angry."

If you want to become a drummer nowadays, you've got to have a perfect storm of good things happening," said Steve White. "You need the support. If you're lucky enough to have a tolerant family and neighbors, you can practice. If you don't, you're screwed."

Joey Kramer, the drummer in Aerosmith since the band's formation in 1970, grew up in Yonkers, New York, where his drumming was anathema to his parents. "My mother never used to allow me to practice," he said, "so I would wait until she went out. Whenever she was leaving, I would get downstairs and practice." One day, when he brought home a bad report card from school, Kramer's father punished him by confiscating his drum kit, dismantling it, and stashing all the pieces in the attic—"because he knew my determination, and he knew that if he didn't take the drums apart, I'd sneak up there and use them." Kramer ended up borrowing a set from a young man he would later come to know very well: Steven Tallarico, who would become Steven Tyler, lead singer of Aerosmith.

"My parents discouraged me the whole way," said Kramer. "But if not for my parents' discouragement, I probably wouldn't be where I am today. Whereas if they had encouraged me and said, 'Yeah! Go ahead! That's what you should do,' I probably would've canned it long ago. I thank my mom for it now, and she thinks it's funny." Kramer's insight is revealing. The big attraction of the drums for him, initially, was a powerful urge to rebel against the authority of his parents. It might explain why many of the people who are drawn to this often antisocial instrument are rebellious in their nature—the kind of people who like to cover themselves with tattoos, misbehave like Keith Moon, and get wasted like John Bonham.

On one level, drumming is a form of physical exercise, and because its practitioners need to be reasonably fit, many of them participate in one sport or another. As sports are an important element of working-class life, this provides another link between drumming and chavvy, plebeian life. The street sport of skateboarding has been an attraction for many drummers, including Travis Barker, who lived for both drums and skateboards when he was a boy. Barker has said that skateboarding actually gave him the incentive to become a better drummer. He was envious of the older boys in his neighborhood in Fontana, California, who skated on a very special mini-ramp, and said they would only allow him to use it if he learned to play all the drum parts for the song "Master of Puppets" by Metallica—a stop-start rock epic that has been dubbed "the metal Bohemian Rhapsody." It took Barker a week or so to learn the song, pounding away on his kit, but he got his wish.

Jack Bevan said that skateboarding, like drumming, helped him use up excess energy when he was younger: "I can't remember if I was diagnosed or not, but I was definitely hyperactive. I think I used to drive my parents nuts as a kid—I'd always be running around. When I was a teenager, I started skateboarding at the same time that I started drumming. And that was good because skateboarding was a huge energy release, and so was drumming, so I actually tired myself out."

Aaron Beamish was the drummer in the Canadian rock band Slow Motion Victory, based in Toronto. Like many drummers, he had an alternative name—Aaron Arsenic—and he was fond of skateboards. Unfortunately, his hobby led to tragedy. In the early hours of October 21, 2011, the twenty-five-year-old drummer was skating on his long board when he was hit by a garbage truck and killed.

Had his life worked out differently, Ginger Baker might have earned his living on a pair of wheels. "I was obsessed with the idea of being a professional cyclist when I was a kid, and I rode everywhere," he once recalled. "I worked in the art department of an ad agency, and I used to ride in on my bike every morning." One day he was cycling in Duke Street, in the St. James's district of London, when he had an accident and wrote off his bike. It was around this time that a friend suggested he start playing the drums, having noticed that he seemed to have an aptitude for it, and the professional-cycling ambition was left behind.

When the worlds of sports and music are scrutinized, it becomes clear that there are parallels between drummers and goalkeepers. In soccer or hockey, the goalkeeper may not receive his fair share of respect from his teammates, despite the fact that he plays an essential role on the team. "When I played football as a kid, I was always a goalkeeper," said Richard Jupp of Elbow. "And it's just like being a drummer. You're the man at the back, and you're there when you need to be. But if you cock up, people really notice it. You're holding the beat, and if you drop a beat, or miss that fill going into the chorus, everybody knows about it. But when you get it right, when you save the penalty, you've done your job." Roger Taylor of Duran Duran (not to be confused with Roger Taylor of Queen) actually had a burning ambition to be a goalkeeper for his favorite British soccer team, Aston Villa, but never grew tall enough to make the grade and had to settle for keeping time in a 1980s New Romantic band.

The legendary soccer goalkeeper Peter Schmeichel, who played for Manchester United and Denmark, has said that his heroes are drummers, "and specifically drummers who have played with Sting since he left the Police. Guys like Omar Hakim, Manu Katché, and Vinnie Colaiuta. I would go and buy videos of these guys and watch them. I have always felt a lot of empathy with drummers, because it's a bit like being a goalkeeper: you're behind the rest of your team."

But some drummers are drawn to more glamorous and exotic sports. In the 1970s, when Carl Palmer played behind the kit in the prog-rock supergroup Emerson, Lake & Palmer, he studied Oriental martial arts and even had a personal karate instructor accompanying him on the road with the band for a while. And on at least one occasion, karate has helped a drummer land an important gig. The British skin basher Geoff Britton studied the martial art and became a part-time karate teacher in the early 1970s. One day, Britton was informed by one of his pupils—Clifford Davis, who had managed Fleetwood Mac—that Paul McCartney needed a new drummer for his band Wings. Britton went along to audition and got the job.

Ralph Johnson of Earth, Wind & Fire is another drummer with martial-arts skills. "I'm a double black belt," Johnson told me. "I have a black belt in Kong Soo Do, which is a kind of karate, and I also have a black belt in Kung Fu San Soo. I love the martial arts, and I noticed that after I got into the martial arts I got stronger on the drum set. But I'm not in the dojo as much as I used to be. These days, I gotta tell you, my real love is tennis. I'm on the court once a week with my instructor for two hours, and I've been working with him for the past six years."

Two other important American drummers used to meet regularly to smash a rubber ball around with a pair of racquets. These are the fusion legend Billy Cobham, who has played with Miles Davis and the Mahavishnu Orchestra, and the top session drummer Ndugu Chancler, who has also drummed behind Miles Davis, as well as performing with acts such as Michael Jackson, Frank Sinatra, Santana, Donna Summer, Patrice Rushen, George Duke, Thelonious Monk, Herbie Hancock, and Weather Report. "Billy and I used to play racquetball together a lot," Chancler told me. "You guys in Britain play squash, but we play racquetball. Billy's now a squash player as well, because when he was living over in Switzerland, there was more squash than racquetball. He's moved to Panama now, so we don't see each other as much. Billy would beat me at racquetball most of the time."

One way of elevating your social status might be to choose a sport with high-society connections. At least two famous drummers have done this by racing around fields on horseback in pursuit of a 3¼-inch-diameter ball. Ginger Baker's travels took him to Nigeria in the 1970s, and it was there that he first threw himself into the sport of polo—a pastime more usually associated with the British aristocracy, the Raj in India, and the British Royal Family. After returning to England, Baker continued to play, plowing much of his money into the upkeep of dozens of horses. His daughter Ginette, who began working with him as a groom, taking care of the horses, recalled: "We traveled up and down the country and met all these members of the aristocracy, which was great fun. I thought I'd marry a polo player. I was really getting into the polo when the money went."

Years later, Ginger Baker indulged his passion for polo in California and was soon swinging a mallet again when he went to live in South Africa in the 1990s. "It was always his dream to have his own polo farm," said Ginette, "and he achieved it in South Africa, where it was much cheaper. He couldn't live the polo life in Britain, because it absolutely breaks you."

When I spoke to Ginger Baker, he gave me the impression that he had thrown himself headlong into polo, not unlike his approach to drumming. "A lot of my favorite polo ponies have been horses that not many people could play," he said. "I tend to find a crazy horse very enjoyable. It's because of the horses that I love polo so much. You have to get into the horse's brain so it will do what you're thinking: you don't have to tell it what to do all the time."

In 1987, when he lived in the English countryside, Stewart Copeland flung himself into the same sport with a Bakeresque enthusiasm. But he discovered that despite being a posh activity, polo was not without its hazards. As he recounted in his autobiography, *Strange Things Happen*, "One day, in the semifinal of the County Cup at Cirencester, having a great game on a hot day, I ask my horse to turn right when he's just about to turn left. He crosses his front legs, trips, and is suddenly somersaulting . . . Even though I roll like a ninja and am back on my feet before the horse is, there is something wrong with my shoulder. My collarbone has a new flexibility in a place that it shouldn't. Damn! It's broken. The horse is fine, but there is no more polo for me this summer. Pity also about that Police album that we were just about to record."

One recent incident in London provided a wonderfully cartoonish picture of drummers' place in British society. On the evening of Saturday, May 4, 2013, Dame Helen Mirren was on stage at the Gielgud Theatre. The world-famous actress was performing in *The Audience*, a play by Peter Morgan in which she played the reigning British monarch, Queen Elizabeth II—reprising her Oscar-winning role in the 2006 movie *The Queen*—when suddenly she became aware of a loud drumming sound outside the theater. The noise increased in volume until it became impossible for her to deliver her lines audibly and effectively to the audience. Mirren then blew her top; she stomped off the stage, up some stairs, and walked out the stage door to confront the noisemakers in person.

She found a group of about twenty-five people beating drums, who were surprised to see a woman looking remarkably like Her Majesty, wearing a string of pearls. The drummers—who were parading through the West End of London to promote a gay music festival, One in the Park—carried on drumming. "Shut the fuck up!" shrieked Mirren, who launched into a rant about how she was trying to perform a play, and how much money people had paid for tickets to see it. If any drummers had doubted it, here was an extraordinary tableau illustrating the contempt with which they were regarded by the British Establishment.

Speaking after the incident, as herself rather than the British monarch, Mirren said: "The irony is, I love drumming and I love drummers. In another situation, I would have been out here enjoying it with all the punters. Unfortunately, I was having to do a play at the same time."

Suddenly, it looked as if my quest for the truth—why would anybody become a drummer?—might be near to its conclusion. Drummers are drawn from one of the lowest classes of society, and drumming is an escape from poverty and demeaning, unskilled manual work. And that's why drummers dress badly, have horrible tattoos all over their bodies, play all kinds of rough sports, and regularly thank their lucky stars that they have been rescued from a life of drudgery and anonymity by the magic of music.

But the more I examined my research, the more I realized that there were serious problems with this conclusion. I might have to tear that whole idea up and start again. But I did have another theory that was seriously worthy of investigation.

3

ROCK 'N' ROLL
SHOW-OFFS

So it could be argued that drummers are the panel beaters of rock 'n' roll: working-class types for whom manual labor comes perfectly naturally; blue-collar dudes who might today be sweating in factories and workshops, or heaving hods of bricks on building sites, if they hadn't lucked into the rock 'n' roll life and found a more glamorous outlet for all that muscle power.

Unfortunately, while this rule often rings true, there are far too many exceptions. What about Max Weinberg, who has kept the beat in Bruce Springsteen's E Street Band since 1974? Weinberg was born into a well-off family in the suburbs of New Jersey. His father was a lawyer and his mother was a high school PE teacher, and Max was planning to become a legal eagle himself before fate intervened. As a child he could regularly afford to watch Broadway shows, and as a precocious young drummer he would perform onstage in a swanky three-piece mohair suit. And what about Stewart Copeland of the Police, who was born to a high-ranking CIA officer and an archaeologist in the picturesque riverside city of Alexandria, Virginia, and attended a posh school in England and smart American colleges before opting to wield a pair of drumsticks for a living?

There are plenty of exceptions from the famously class-obsessed United Kingdom as well. Philip James Selway was born in the royal county of Berkshire and studied literature and worked as an English teacher before finding fame with Radiohead. Will Champion of Coldplay was a churchgoing child of leafy Hampshire, whose father was a professor of archaeology. And you won't hear any low-born glottal stops from Bill Bruford, either: this jazzy and cerebral drummer, who has powered such prog-rock legends as Yes, King Crimson, and Genesis, grew up in Kent (the Garden of England, no less), studied at public school, and had the privilege of drumming lessons from a percussionist with the Royal Philharmonic Orchestra.

So if working-class roots aren't the answer, the single defining characteristic of drummers everywhere, what is? Maybe it's time to step back and take a harder look at the personalities of these extraordinary people. Perhaps we have missed the point by labeling drummers as "mad" or "insane"; maybe the wild-eyed rock drummer, with his arms flailing as he beats the hell out of his kit, only appears to be unhinged but is simply showing off.

One word often associated with drummers is *flashy*, and many of the greatest drumming performances can be summed up using the f-word. Drummers through the ages, from jazz giants Buddy Rich and Gene Krupa to modern rock players like Terry Bozzio and Virgil Donati, have been exceptionally flamboyant, cocky, ostentatious, and theatrical. Audiences encourage them to show off, too: people love to see a drummer showing what he can do, whacking everything in sight at terrific speed. It's a quality that other musicians appreciate as well. BAND SEEKS FLASHY DRUMMER, said an online advertisement placed by musicians in Massachusetts in 2012—though you wonder if they might later come to regret their impetuous request. My late mother, a naturally gifted pianist, would reminisce fondly about the "jam sessions" she watched in the 1930s and '40s, when sharp-suited jazzmen launched into complex improvisations and, in her words, "the drummer went absolutely mad."

So there is an important distinction here: drummers are not necessarily "mad" in the certifiable sense, but they often "go mad" during a performance. We could argue, therefore, that drummers are basically childish show-offs. Just as children resort to the primal activity of banging household objects to gain attention and respect, these puerile adults acquire an admiring audience simply by hitting things and making a racket. All they are saying, basically, is "Look at me!" And over the years, drummers have discovered and invented an astonishing variety of ways to get people to look at them.

A few years ago, Stewart Copeland argued—tongue slightly in cheek—that drumming, exhibitionism, and testosterone are closely related. "I think the physicality of drums, and the fitness of drummers, has given them a physical confidence in terms of mano-a-mano confrontation," he said. "If you look at the nature movies, you'll see the correlation between noise and male dominance amongst primates. You see the big hairy silverback banging the trees, and he's the big bad guy and he makes the most noise, and that's what we humans do as well. So drummers are absolutely the alpha males of our species."

The most obvious showcase for a show-off drummer is the drum solo. It was the jazz drummers of the twentieth century, such as Rich and Krupa, who first turned unaccompanied drumming showcases into a fine art. They entertained crowds with "drum battles," live performances in which two or more drummers played competitively and traded complex patterns of beats. When rock bands came along, many of their drummers were directly influenced by their jazz forebears, so it was only natural for them to start playing solos onstage.

When Cream performed their instrumental "Toad" onstage in the late 1960s, Eric Clapton and Jack Bruce indulged their famous drummer, Ginger Baker, with a solo spot that could extend from several minutes to a quarter of an hour, in which Baker—who had originally played in jazz bands—created a controlled storm of elaborate, evolving patterns around his kit. The version of "Toad" from Cream's 1968 farewell concert at London's Royal Albert Hall showed him at his blistering best. Baker was famous for using two bass drums rather than just the usual one, and his 2009 memoirs were subtitled *The Autobiography of the World's Greatest Drummer*, and if that's not flashy and egotistical, I don't know what is.

As the ultimate late-1960s rock spectacular, Woodstock might have seemed incomplete without a jaw-dropping drum solo. It was provided on the afternoon of the festival's second day—Saturday, August 16, 1969—by Michael Shrieve of Santana. Carlos Santana's band was based on the West Coast and had yet to release its first album, but the set captivated many of the 500,000-strong East Coast crowd. Shrieve's solo, an interlude of just two minutes in their closing number, "Soul Sacrifice," is a tasty piece of improvisation that drops from a storm to a whisper, rises to a tempest again, slows down, and then speeds up as the rest of the band comes back in. The mythology of the day suggested that Shrieve was a mere fifteen or sixteen years old at the time, when in fact he was a youthful-looking twenty. In an interview years later, he said he found it difficult watching footage of his solo, which appears in the Woodstock movie: "Every time I see it, I cringe when I get to playing really softly on that Woodstock solo. I keep saying to myself, 'What were you thinking? There's a half million people out there—keep the groove going!'"

There was clearly a trend for naming drum solos after animals, because shortly after Baker's "Toad" came Led Zeppelin's "Moby Dick" and Deep Purple's "The Mule," in which the drummers John Bonham and Ian Paice respectively showed off their chops. Neither Bonham nor Paice can be dismissed as an everyday hard-rock basher: these two British players elevated the music they played with their considerable technical skills.

Before he joined Zeppelin in 1968, Bonham drummed in various rock bands in the Midlands, with the volume of his playing causing him to be banned from many venues. But behind that kit, Bonzo combined sheer power with a highly innovative approach to drum patterns. To this day, decades after his death, many novice drummers still struggle to replicate many of his licks, such as the legendary "Bonham triplets"—thunderous fills created by rapid alternation between various parts of the kit, such as the bass drum, floor tom, and rack toms. These were played to great effect on tracks such as "Dazed and Confused" and "Good Times Bad Times," both on Led Zeppelin's 1969 debut album. (Sadly, he wasn't always 100 percent original. Another of his flashiest moments, the spine-tingling snare-and-hi-hat intro to "Rock and Roll" on *Led Zeppelin IV*, sounds like a direct lift from the start of the 1957 recording of "Keep a-Knockin'" by Little Richard.) Bonham remains an inspiration for many famous modern drummers. Dave Grohl, who has whacked the drums in Nirvana and Queens of the Stone Age, has encapsulated the sense of excitement, and even danger, in Bonham's playing. According to Grohl, he "played the drums like someone who didn't know what was going to happen next—like he was teetering on the edge of a cliff."

The drummer Steve White, who has worked extensively with Paul Weller, said that Bonham took the art and craft of drumming very seriously. "From what I can gather from people who knew him, he was a hard hitter, but he also knew how to tune his drums really well," says White. "And when you tune the drums really well, they sing; you get the most out of them."

When BBC television asked the British public to vote for their favorite rock drummer in 2010, they chose Bonham (with Keith Moon and Dave Grohl in second and third places). One waggish fan recently claimed online that "John Bonham died because God wanted drumming lessons."

Ian Paice is another drummer's drummer, highly respected by his percussive peers. "Ian Paice was one of my heroes when I was growing up," said Chad Smith. "I loved his drumming, and I still do. When we met and had a chance to play together in London years ago, it was an incredible honor. And he was very nice and complimentary—he said he liked my drumming, which was fantastic."

Paice has long been a big draw at "drum clinics" (live shows at which drummers play for fans and fellow drummers), and for good reason: his flashiness comes from an exceptional mastery of the traditional rudiments of drumming. He can play a rapid drum roll using just a single drumstick held in one hand, which looks like a conjuring trick. He is also a highly proficient para-diddler. A paradiddle is not, as some non-drummers believe, an ordinary left-right-left-right drum roll: it is a more complex pattern involving multiple left and right beats. For example, the basic "single paradiddle" usually follows the repeating pattern right-left-right-right, left-right-left-left. If you're not a drummer, try sitting down and playing this "RLRR-LRLL" pattern on your knees (with each beat ideally having the same length) and see how fast you can go. It can take a very long time to master; some people find it easier to rub their stomach while tapping their head and reciting the Lord's Prayer while drinking cider through a straw. But Paice has often used paradiddles to create rapid, sophisticated rhythms all round the kit as if it's the most natural thing in the world.

Potentially, a drum solo is an event that straddles several fields of human endeavor. At its very best, it can resemble a sporting event, a magic show, an endurance test, a dance routine, and the creation of an abstract expressionist painting all rolled into one. Thus a drummer performing a great solo can become a hugely charismatic Muhammad Ali/Harry Houdini/Rudolf Nureyev/Jackson Pollock figure, if only for a few minutes. Expert drumming uses all four limbs at once, like a circus acrobat juggling balls while riding a unicycle.

So why do drum solos have such an image problem? Well, I blame the reviewers. Concert reviews from the 1960s and '70s show that while drum solos could captivate an audience, they were often dismissed and even despised by critics. The reviewer from the pop newssheet *Record Mirror* who attended Cream's 1968 farewell gig noted, scathingly: "The only drag (to my ears) at the Albert Hall was Ginger's long, long drum solo on 'The Toad' [*sic*]. It was undoubtedly a tour de force, a reckless display of violent virtuosity. Predictably enough, the crowd went wild with delight. But then drum solos always have that effect. I was reminded of those cynical drum features we always used to have to suffer from the great jazz bands. Cynical because a mass audience of young people can be relied upon to get ecstatic over crude, brutal, tasteless noise."

Fast-forward seven years to 1975, and we find the rock monthly *Phonograph Record* making similar points in a review of a very different event across the Atlantic Ocean—a show-off drum spot by Mick Tucker of the Sweet, the British glam-rock band, at the Santa Monica Civic Auditorium: "First he pranced around the stage spinning sticks, tossing them to the crowd, setting off fireworks—everything in fact, but actually performing a solo, so for a while I was quite encouraged. But then the band came back, played a snippet of 'Man with the Golden Arm,' and then he went into the damn solo, and it was a brain-number . . . the drum solo went on for apparent ages, destroying all previously built-up momentum, as always. And as always, the crowd ate it up with blank, Zombie-like adoration, indicating that such gim-micky showcases may not harm the Sweet's case at all (except with regard to jaundiced writers lacking the esthetic sensibilities to appreciate the intrinsic worth of drum solos)."

In the same year, the rock critic Max Bell poured scorn on a drum solo played by the great Ndugu Chancler during a con-cert by Santana at London's Hammersmith Odeon. "For their encore Chancler hauled out his party piece, one of the most boring elongated drum solos yet seen on an English stage," he wrote. "God knows how drummers get away with it really; if any other musician played such an arbitrary series of notes, chords or scales he'd be given the elbow."

As you might expect, many drummers are much more ap-preciative of the art of drum soloing. As well as being an enter-taining soloist himself, Neil Peart, drummer in the Canadian prog band Rush, is a longtime connoisseur of the tradition.

While growing up in Canada in the 1960s, he enjoyed watching local bands play live and paid particular attention when the spotlight fell on the drummer. "In a way, I think it was good for me to learn about drum solos from being in the audience, rather than from records and from being behind the drum set," he has said. "As a young music fan watching from the crowd, I picked up on what was exciting, what was dynamically effective and what was musical." His own performing career actually "began with a drum solo." At a high school variety show in 1967, a fifteen-year-old Peart played the kit in a fledgling band called the Eternal Triangle while seated on a wooden kitchen stool. One of the band's numbers, "LSD Forever," required him to play his first ever public solo. Shortly afterward, after joining his first proper rock band, Peart had the audacity to cover Ginger Baker's "Toad" in front of an audience. And he has been playing intricate drum solos ever since, diligently adapting and transforming his performances for each successive Rush tour. On his own commercially released DVD, *Anatomy of a Drum Solo*, he talks articulately about his approach to drum soloing and about the qualities of the many drummers who have influenced him over the years, from the "driving snare work" of Buddy Rich to the "explosive fluidity" of Keith Moon. "In many ways, my drum solo remains an ever-changing tribute to all of the drummers I have ever appreciated," he explains. In Peart's opinion, the drummer's solo spot is not just an opportunity to show off, but a vital musical legacy: "A drum solo can be an enjoyable and demanding performance for the drummer, an enjoyable and not-too-demanding experience for the audience, and a nice break for the other guys in the band."

Of course, drum solos are not always planned and meticulously rehearsed. In fact, whenever there are sudden amplification problems at a gig, it has become almost traditional for the musician with the loudest acoustic instrument to launch into a solo to keep the audience entertained until the problem is sorted. "You can guarantee that sooner or later, the back line will get kicked off, or there'll be a power cut," said Nicko McBrain of Iron Maiden. He remembered that when the band played Wembley one night, the guitarist Janick Gers's equipment malfunctioned. "Jan's guitar amp blew up. So they put another amp up, and that blew up as well!" Lead singer Bruce Dickinson reacted at lightning speed. "Bruce turned round to me and said, 'Okay, you know what's coming now: drum solo!' So off I went for about five minutes, until it was fixed and I'd run out of ideas!"

Omar Hakim is an extremely skilled drummer who has played for artists including Madonna, David Bowie, Mariah Carey, and Kate Bush and has occupied the drum stool behind bands such as Chic and Weather Report. But it was when he was a mere boy, growing up in New York, that he got to play his first emergency solo. "I was a young kid playing in a local band," he said. "It was an amazing little band, but I had stepped in when their regular drummer had a family incident and couldn't play a particular gig. It was a talent show, and we were playing onstage when one of the rival bands suddenly pulled the plug on us, because we were doing so well. But when they did that, I instinctively kept going and played a drum solo. I remember the crowd getting into it. Someone finally found the plug and switched us back on, and we ended up winning the talent show anyway."

In the early 1970s, the British band Procol Harum, famous for their megahit "A Whiter Shade of Pale," would allow their drummer, B. J. Wilson, to launch into an intricate solo in a song that they actually named "Power Failure" in honor of these electrical crises. But power outages aren't the only problems that require the drummer to do unexpected voluntary work. When Led Zeppelin toured the USA in early 1975, they were hampered by illness and injury: Robert Plant's voice was suffering because of a flu bug, and guitarist Jimmy Page had broken a finger. The considerate John Bonham helped out by lengthening his "Moby Dick" solo "so that the lads can have a rest," he said. Plant later described the solo as "the life preserver that kept the show afloat."

By this time, the old-fashioned drum solo was beginning to evolve with the addition of electronic gimmickry. The great pretender to the throne of show-off drumming in the 1970s, when progressive rock reached its zenith of complexity and absurdity, was Carl Palmer of Emerson, Lake & Palmer. On ELP's 1973–74 tour of the US, Canada, and Europe to promote the album *Brain Salad Surgery*, the supergroup was accompanied by twenty tons of equipment and a retinue of forty roadies. Palmer had teamed up with the British Steel Corporation to create his own stainless-steel drum kit. "And they said, 'Did you want the shells a quarter of an inch thick, or half an inch thick?'" he later recalled. "I said, 'What's the difference in the price?' 'Basically the same.' I said, 'I'll have half an inch' . . . not thinking it'd take two guys to lift the bass drum." The kit and its rostrum weighed about two and a half tons, which meant that ELP's stages had to be reinforced in case Palmer crashed through them. "Each drum was suspended by a rod that was angled at the exact position I wanted it. I would make a template out of cardboard and take it to the steel manufacturers with my specifications."

This extraordinary kit could rotate either clockwise or counterclockwise as Palmer played—an idea that wasn't entirely original. As a thirteen-year-old boy he had enjoyed watching a British performer named Eric Delaney. "He was a popular big-band swing drummer, and he would play a set of red-and-silver glitter drums on a revolving drum riser, dressed in a gold lamé jacket. When you're thirteen you get influenced by things like that."

Palmer's 1970s drum solos were steeped in machismo. As he assaulted his extensive battery of equipment, which included orchestral timpani and thirty-eight-inch- and fifty-inch-diameter gongs, he would perform the feat of stripping off his T-shirt while continuing to play. And the decorations he chose for his highly personalized kit were redolent of the masculine tastes of an imperialist ruler of ages past. Having seen some handsome hunting scenes incised on rifles made by James Purdey & Sons of London, Palmer commissioned a jeweler to engrave similar images on the shells of the drums, using a dentist's drill. His two gongs were painted with dragons copied from an Oriental vase.

Palmer's kit was also proclaimed to be the first electronic drum kit in existence. "I just have this thing in me that I like to do things first," he explained at the time. However, while "electronic drum kit" sounded futuristic, in practice this was still the 1970s—the era of chunky electronic calculators and cassette players—and it meant that Palmer would bash something and trigger a cacophony of seemingly random analog sounds. "And everyone thought it was keyboards, but they were drums." The results, which haven't aged well, can be heard today in "Toccata" and "Karn Evil 9" from *Brain Salad Surgery*. "It's the seventies, isn't it?" Palmer reflected decades later. "You do it. The bigger the better. If there was something that was available, from the technology point of view, that would enhance the sound of the band, we wanted it yesterday."

When the British drummer Cozy Powell became the drummer in the Deep Purple spin-off band Rainbow, featuring Ritchie Blackmore on guitar, he was given his own live solo spot toward the end of their gigs. This was full-on mid-1970s theatrical bombast, with Powell bashing along to a recording of Tchaikovsky's "1812 Overture," flash bombs and strobe lighting adding to the drama.

In 1974 the pantomime-rock band Kiss found a primitive way to raise the drumming stakes in concert. Peter Criss had chains bolted to his drum riser so that members of the road crew could haul him several feet in the air on pulleys. Criss's "levitation" was often an amateurish affair, however: the roadies were known to lift the riser unevenly, causing the drums to slip and slide, and when the band supported the British rocker Rory Gallagher at the Cleveland Agora in August 1974, Criss wobbled into the air and found himself engulfed in smoke in a tight space below the venue's low ceiling. He passed out and required hospital treatment.

But a very different American outfit had already been experimenting with more sophisticated special effects. In the early 1970s, the American soul-funk megaband Earth, Wind & Fire had begun to incorporate the trappings of arena rock into their live shows. Guided by their visionary leader, Maurice White, EWF used dazzling light shows and pyrotechnics and fused Egyptian mysticism with elaborate stage magic, courtesy of the Canadian illusionist Doug Henning and his then little-known assistant, David Copperfield. In one memorable illusion, the band members would enter a pyramid, one by one. The pyramid would then rise above the stage and suddenly fall apart, with the musicians having apparently vanished without trace. Back down on the stage, a group of mysterious "androids" would then remove their metallic helmets and reveal themselves to be the members of the band.

During many of EWF's concerts in 1975, audiences were amazed by a stunt during the song "Mighty Mighty." The drummer Ralph Johnson would continue to play as his drum kit rose up off the stage, spun round in both directions, and turned upside down. "That idea didn't actually come from Doug Henning," recalls Ralph Johnson four decades later. "It came from a special-effects guy around the Hollywood area. We were trying to figure out a way to take the show up a notch, if you will. And we called on this guy to see what he had and what he could produce, and he came up with the spinning drum set. And I kinda volunteered for it: I said, 'That looks interesting. Let's check this out—let's do it!' "

Invisibly lifting the drum platform was a huge scissor jack, a gigantic version of the expanding apparatus you might use to lift a car to change a tire. "I was strapped in with a seat belt behind the drums, and the drums were wired down. And there was a steering wheel that was attached to a giant post that went straight up to my platform and my seat, and I could be turned any way they wanted me to go." The steering-wheel operator, out of sight, would have some fun with Johnson and his kit. "They would tease the audience: they would move me from side to side, and then they just dropped me and turned me over, and I would play the song for a few bars upside down. Then they might spin me a couple of times one way and then a couple of times the other way, and that was it—they'd bring me back down."

Playing the drums topsy-turvy brought its own challenges, says Johnson. "I have to tell you, Tony, that I was never frightened of doing it: after I saw the construction and the engineering of the apparatus, I said, 'Well, okay, this'll be fun!' But it's quite interesting trying to play inverted, because gravity is now working against your legs, especially, as they're heavier than your arms. So if you're playing your hi-hat and your kick drum, you're really feeling it."

Sadly, Ralph Johnson's pioneering drum aeronautics are much less celebrated today than they should be, because hardly anybody seems to have pointed a camera in 1975 as the drum kit flew through the air. "You know what? I have never seen any footage of me spinning. There are some still photographs, some of which can be seen on the inside cover of our double album *Gratitude*. But that's about it."

Joey Kramer discovered the joys of the live drum solo in 1976, when Aerosmith played the eighty-thousand-capacity Silverdome in Pontiac, Michigan. "No drug has a rush like that," he later enthused. "When the audience responded to me, I could feel the joy in every cell in my body." Thus began the long tradition of the Joey Kramer solo: ever since then, he has delivered many exciting and creative percussion workouts, including routines in which he hits the drums with his bare hands, like his hero John Bonham. Witnesses to Aerosmith shows have reported seeing him strike the drums with other parts of his body, too, such as his head—but when I met Kramer in his dressing room on Aerosmith's European tour in 2014, he laid this myth to rest. "It's really just my hands," he said. "But out in the audience, when I do what I do, it has a tendency to look like I'm using my head." He mimed playing a solo, with his upper body bent forward and his face virtually in his lap. "Because when I'm doing it, I hump over the drums to get more accuracy and more speed, and I put my face right up to the snare drum."

Kramer took the drum solo to a new dimension during Aerosmith's Permanent Vacation tour of 1987–88, when he came out from behind his kit and produced sampled drum sounds by hitting a pair of drumsticks on his own body, on the floor of the stage, on the outstretched hands of members of the audience, and even on the head of a bemused security guard. He achieved this flashy feat using specially rigged sticks that were wired to electronics fitted in a neoprene belt around his body. Kramer has been modest about these stunts, recalling: "We had an applause meter to measure crowd reaction to this or that, and the drum solo was always the thing that got people fired up the most."

But elsewhere, it was time for the drum kit to become airborne once again. During Mötley Crüe's Girls Girls Girls world tour of 1987–88, the band's drummer Tommy Lee started wowing audiences by bashing his drums in a cuboid cage suspended above the stage. His solo began with him hollering to the crowd about having had "this sick motherfucking dream," and he would then demonstrate what had happened in the dream. It was at this point that the extreme mobility of his cage, controlled by some clever and largely invisible engineering, became evident. As he carried on playing, the side of the cage to his right began swiveling down, so he was drumming diagonally. Then it lifted up again, and the opposite side dipped down. Then the cage righted itself, before tipping forward and doing a full 90-degree turn, so Lee was now facing down at the stage. Within seconds, the cage was spinning forward all the way round, with Lee defying gravity and continuing to play the drums. This was followed by some backward rotations, and then Lee gave the command to "turn this motherfucker upside down"—whereupon the left-hand side started dipping again and the whole caboodle went topsy-turvy, with Lee still beating those skins. Lee's experience was similar to that of Ralph Johnson's: he later admitted that playing upside down was "actually a nightmare," with his arms being dragged down by gravity and his feet slipping off the pedals.

Lee's cage stunt came about after he met a hydraulics expert named Chris Dieter who agreed to create it for him. In his autobiography, *Tommy Land*, Lee explained that the drum cage "was welded to a fork-lift" and "connected with a ton of cables and pumped up into flight by some crazy hydraulic fluids . . . I could only make five revolutions because there was only enough slack in the microphone cables to turn that many times before we had to rotate me backwards to unwind them. If we did it today we could do the whole thing wireless. Damn, if we did it today I could turn 360s until I puked."

Lee had, in fact, been having a real recurring dream about flying with his kit through an arena, right above the crowd. Dieter fulfilled that ambition for him as well, and the feat became a feature of the band's Dr. Feelgood tour of 1989–90. Then, in the noughties, Lee started talking about an idea that would top his previous stunts. "My dream and goal—and I will do it—is to build a roller coaster that can pack up and travel from city to city," he said in 2010. "It will have all the workings of a roller coaster, but I'll get rid of the car and replace it with a drum riser with two seats in the back. I'll run out into the audience, grab a couple of fans, strap them in and go." Within a year, the tattooed daredevil's drum roller coaster had become a reality, doing full 360-degree circuits at the Crüe's concerts. "Now everybody expects you to come up with something more over-the-top than the last one," he told an interviewer. "I'll sit around and come up with some insane idea, and people go,

'Dude, you're on crack! There's no way to do that.' Then we massage it into something that's actually doable and that you can put in a truck and ship around from city to city."

Tommy Lee and Ralph Johnson have been rewarded over and over with the sincerest form of flattery, as their aeronautical stunts have since been imitated and adapted by drummers including Joey Jordison in Slipknot and Travis Barker in Blink-182. Recently, the Detroit-born drummer Tommy Clufetos levitated with his kit while playing in Ozzy Osbourne's live band.

These days, the Internet has the power to turn unknown flashy drummers into stars overnight. In 2010, a laugh-out-loud video of a flamboyant drummer became an online sensation. It was entitled "This Drummer Is at the Wrong Gig" and showed a gold-jacketed Vegas-style band churning out a cover of ZZ Top's "Sharp Dressed Man." The man behind the kit steals most of the attention with hilarious thrashing arm movements, stick twirling, and ridiculous facial expressions. The group was the little-known variety show band Rick K and the Allnighters, with Steve Moore on drums, and the clip is from a 2008 show they played at Knoebels Amusement Resort in Elysburg, Pennsylvania. Two years later it was posted on YouTube by a fan and soon went viral, receiving millions of hits in a few weeks. Moore, who was dubbed "the Mad Drummer," suddenly became the hot subject of drum magazines and online drum forums, and was even invited to guest in the American version of the comedy show *The Office*, on which he traded beats with Brian Baumgartner, who played Kevin Malone.

When they're not spinning round or flying through the air, flashy drummers are rarely content with a basic drum kit: a bass drum, floor tom, snare, and a couple of cymbals. The kit is not really a single instrument but a collection of instruments—various drums, cymbals, and other items of percussion—and drummers do seem to enjoy collecting. They may claim that they continually need new equipment to enhance their sound—a gorgeous upside-down China crash cymbal, say, or a nice set of temple blocks. Bill Bruford has compared his kit assembly to that of a "European percussionist" who works with different bits and pieces according to the music he is playing. "The kit is a function of the music that's being played."

These are the grown-up justifications and excuses for buying more gear, but there is another way of looking at it. If, as I suggested earlier, drummers are basically big kids, then these toms and cymbals and gadgets and gewgaws are their toys. And just as kids love to amass a big collection of toys to impress and compete with their friends and rivals, so flashy drummers love to have a lot of different things to hit. It may also be compensation for that ever-present chip on the drummer's shoulder, the perception among guitarists and keyboard players that the bloke behind the kit isn't really a proper musician. "Look!" the absurdly well-equipped drummer seems to be saying. "I've got all this gear. I must be a virtuoso."

Terry Bozzio, famous for his work with Frank Zappa and the US bands Missing Persons and Korn, is a classic collector-drummer. As of 2012, Bozzio's box of toys included a xylophone, a glockenspiel, thirteen Thai gongs tuned to a chromatic scale, and a metal "thunder sheet" simulating the sound of terrible weather. Bozzio's pride and joy is his "Big Kit," a leviathan of curvilinear metal bars containing eight bass drums, twenty-six toms, fifty-three cymbals, and twenty-two pedal-operated doo-dahs. When he sits behind this monster and plays it, he resembles a hyperactive leprechaun. "It's hard to get past the overwhelming impression that that kit makes," Bozzio once explained. "But it really isn't about being big, or trying to get attention by having more drums than most people. It's really about . . . I'm trying to play music on the drums, and so if you're playing melodies, you need notes. And you can't just have two toms, because you can only make two-note melodies. So it's built up to the point where it's half chromatic and half diatonic."

Bozzio was flashy enough to play some extremely complicated pieces of music with Zappa, the most notorious of which is called "The Black Page," owing to the alarming number of notes written on the sheet music. Zappa brought it to the drummer in a rehearsal one day, and Bozzio spent every day working on it for about a week, until he had mastered its intricacies.

Chad Smith has owned and played many flashy kits, including the stunning giant custom Pearl set that he played at the 2014 Super Bowl halftime show, which lit up and was decorated with the logos of all the US professional football teams. After Smith played it, the kit was divided into two kits and auctioned, raising nearly $37,000 for the Make-A-Wish Foundation to spend on unforgettable experiences for children with life-threatening medical conditions.

Back in 1994, Smith got to play a ridiculously large collection of drums in Pontiac, Michigan, which was officially declared the biggest kit on the planet. "An old friend from high school owned a music store," he explained, "and I would see him from time to time, and one day he said, 'Chad, I think I'm going to put together the world's biggest drum set.' I said, 'Oh. Good for you. Great!' And he said, 'I think it'll be, like, three hundred pieces. If I put it together, would you come in and play it?' And I'm like, 'Sure'—like he's ever going to do that. And, lo and behold, six months later he calls me up and says, 'Yep, I've got that world's biggest drum set. Will you come in?' So it was all set up, and there were three hundred and eight pieces, and the challenge was for me to hit every piece while the Guinness World Records person who was there ticked each one off. It was really like walking through a giant drum shop, full of all these drums and cymbals and other things—there was nothing musical about the performance at all. At the time, in the band we all had these flaming helmets to wear onstage, so I put on my flaming helmet and went round and hit everything. It was kind of a goof. But I don't know if somebody's broken the record since then."

They have, Chad. Seventeen years on, in October 2011, a new Guinness World Record for kit size was established by an American pastor, Dr. Mark Temperato, in Lakeville, New York. He had been gathering and custom-building the 340-piece drum set for "about thirty-five years." It routinely took about fifteen hours to put the whole kit together, "with four of us working diligently." But, praise be to God, the kit refused to stop growing. Two years later, it had 813 pieces—drums, cymbals, and bells—weighed about five thousand pounds, and required an eighteen-wheeler truck to take it out on the road.

The ramshackle, agglomerative essence of a drum kit—the fact that the basic setup is historically cobbled together from bits and bobs, and that kits are usually customized extensively by their players—means that one drum set can be vastly different from the next. In fact, comparing two kits can be like comparing a Gibson Flying V guitar to a Hawaiian soprano ukulele. It is fascinating to examine some of the unique kit layouts used by the big players. A 1994 inventory of a kit belonging to Airto Moreira, the Latin-jazz virtuoso from Brazil who played with Miles Davis and Weather Report, includes such exotic playthings as a "Brazilian noise maker," some "Chinese wooden toys," and a length of "refrigerator hose."

Kit customization provides boundless opportunities for flashy drummers to develop their own unique, attention-grabbing styles. "When you look at the difference in drummers and their kits," said Nicko McBrain, "the analogy I like to use is: say you've got a Jaguar XK sports car and I've got a Jaguar XK sports car—exactly the same motor—and say I get in yours. I'm gonna go, 'Ooh, I don't like that, I can't drive this,' and I've got to move the seat up or down. That's exactly the same vibe as a drum set, because we all have our own template. I sit low and have my drums high, whereas somebody like Mike Portnoy sits quite high and his drums are lower down. If I sat on his kit, I could play it—we could all play each other's drums—but not as comfortably and not as well as my own. It's like a fingerprint. Take Mike Mangini, who's a phenomenal player. He's got these octobans [small tubelike toms] in front of him, up above him, and when I saw them recently I thought, 'How's he gonna hit them?' It looks impossible. But when you actually sit behind his kit, you can reach them, because of the way he's got it set up. And people look at my set and go, 'How the heck do you hit that little cymbal over there?' or 'How do you hit that little drum up there?' But you sit behind my kit and you can do it."

Drummers don't always restrict themselves to a single kit, of course. The longtime drummer with Beck, Joey Waronker, who has also drummed in R.E.M. and in the supergroup Atoms for Peace with Thom Yorke of Radiohead and Flea of the Red Hot Chili Peppers, told me he owns "maybe thousands" of items of percussion. "One of my goals is to thin out my collection of stuff, because I don't even know what I have anymore," he said. "A lot of it is found objects and metal scraps. I know that part of the collection, when I have it in storage, goes three stories high and about twenty feet across. And then I have one smaller collection in an old studio, another small collection somewhere else, and a small collection at home. I did a record with Neil Diamond recently, and they wanted me to be prepared to make some unusual percussion sounds. One of the producers said, 'Bring everything you have,' but that just wasn't possible. The drum-haulage people who work with me said they didn't have enough vehicles to get even close! It's silly."

When I spoke to Clem Burke in the back of a car hurtling to a Blondie sound check at the Roundhouse in London in 2013, he admitted to owning hundreds of drums. "I have maybe forty drum sets, which is about thirty-nine too many," he said. "There's some in storage in New York, there's some in my house in New Jersey, and there's a load in my house in LA. And there's a few that were left behind here and there. There's a couple in London that I never got back." He peered for a moment out of the right-hand passenger window, as if he might catch sight of some familiar old Premier drums sitting outside Euston railway station or plonked on the curb in Mornington Crescent. "And I've got some collectible stuff that I've acquired along the way. I've got a replica of a Ringo Starr Beatles kit. And I've got a kit from the 1950s—a lovely kit, the kind that maybe somebody like the Crickets would have used. I like vintage equipment in general."

It is unsurprising that the Jaguar-loving Nicko McBrain seized on cars as an analogy for drum kits, because many rock drummers have diversified from collecting drums to buying flashy road vehicles. It seems that they can be just as tempted by a beautiful set of wheels as they are by a lovely, sparkly-shelled set of drums. "It's true," agrees Steve White. "Drummers tend to be the ones who go off and buy silly cars, and fall in love with motorbikes and things like that." High-end automobiles are not unlike expensive drum kits, in that they are gleaming, lovingly manufactured objects with shiny metal parts. Drum kits even have a driving seat, commonly known as the drum stool. Nick Mason of Pink Floyd is a famous car collector, with a love of classic motors by Aston Martin, Bentley, Bugatti, Ferrari, Jaguar, Maserati, and Porsche. He has entered many races and rallies, and has even published a handsome book for auto maniacs—*Into the Red: 22 Classic Cars That Shaped a Century*.

But when I suggested to Mason that he seemed to have an eye for "shiny things" such as nice drums and fast cars, he almost exploded. "I'm not a jackdaw!" he protested. And he quibbled with my description of him as a collector. "It's actually not collecting," he said. "It's accumulating. That's rather different. 'Collecting' suggests a slightly more measured approach, whereas what I do is, you collect stuff because . . . or you accumulate stuff because you think you need it, or it would be good to have, and then you have a big problem parting with it. So all my cars, I didn't buy because I wanted to become a car collector: I bought my cars because I wanted to go motor racing, and then couldn't bear to get rid of them, and ended up being perceived as a collector. But it wasn't like stamp collecting, where you think, 'I must get that orange threepenny George V.'"

In January 2013, Mick Fleetwood, the drummer in Fleetwood Mac since 1967, appeared on BBC TV's *Top Gear* to discuss his love of cars with the gasoline-guzzling broadcaster Jeremy Clarkson (who also plays the drums in his spare time). Proof of the drummer-automobile connection forms a long tailback into the past. Dennis Wilson of the Beach Boys also loved fast cars, enjoyed racing them, and even played a drag-racing mechanic in the cult 1971 movie *Two-Lane Blacktop*. Though he wasn't licensed to drive, Keith Moon started collecting cars with characteristic zeal in the 1970s, including a Mercedes 300 SEL saloon and a Ferrari Dino 426. At one point, he was said to have no fewer than a dozen vehicles. In the Led Zeppelin movie *The Song Remains the Same*, a John Bonham drum solo is accompanied by footage of the drummer tearing along in a fast car. Other drummers with a passion for speedy, competitive driving include Frank Beard of ZZ Top, Phil Rudd of AC/DC, and Nigel Olsson, who has often played in Sir Elton John's backing band.

"I'm not a big collector," said Roger Taylor of Queen over the telephone from his house in Surrey, before admitting: "I've got about ten or twelve drum kits here in my studio from over the years." A multi-instrumentalist, Taylor also revealed that he had "a decent collection of about forty guitars. I love guitars—they are beautiful things." Lest we forget, this is the man who wrote the song "I'm in Love with My Car," and he once had a decent automobile collection as well. "I've always liked cars, but I decided to get rid of them. I had a beautiful old Bentley and a beautiful old Aston Martin, but I decided they weren't very safe anymore. Modern cars are fantastic, and the old cars are lovely, but simply not as good."

When I met Joey Kramer, he was wearing a Lamborghini T-shirt, and he explained how he had been trying to rein in his automobile collection. "At the moment I have only four cars," he said. "I have limited garage space where I live in Texas. I'm actually entertaining the idea of building another garage. But I have found over the years that to have more than four or five cars on the road at the same time is a waste of time and energy. Because when I get into a particular car, I enjoy driving it and I like to have a relationship with that car. And while I'm having a relationship with that car, the others sit idle. I have a relationship with a car for maybe a year and a half, sometimes maybe two years, and then it's off to the next thing." Does he have a similar attitude toward drum kits? "Yeah. There are too many different things to do, and too short a time to do it all in."

Neil Peart not only adores full-size cars but has a passion for miniatures as well. Peart accumulated toy cars as a boy, before graduating to elaborate models of his favorite Ferraris and Bugattis. Ndugu Chancler told me he collects miniatures of a different kind—models of drums and other percussion instruments. "I've probably got a hundred and fifty of them," he said. "I bought another one the other day, a nice little bronze piece."

"I collect antique snare drums," Phil Collins told me. "When I've done recording sessions, I tend to bring out the stuff that's not necessarily hardy, that wouldn't like life on the road too much, because it might fall apart. I bring those old cymbals and other things that are now collector's items, and I might use them in a studio, but I wouldn't use them anywhere else."

In addition to acquiring drums and cymbals, Collins has amassed an impressive collection of memorabilia from the Alamo, the pivotal 1836 battle of the Texas Revolution. In 2010, Collins gave a talk at the Dallas Historical Society in which he discussed some of his prized possessions. His interest goes back to watching the Davy Crockett television series as a child, but his acquisition of Alamobilia only began in earnest after he became a drummer. "That's what I spend my money on—no Ferraris," he told the assembled Texans. Collins's collection includes hundreds of cannonballs from the conflict; an item "purported to be Crockett's pouch," with two musket balls still inside; a receipt for a saddle, signed by an Alamo defender; and a receipt signed by an Alamo commander for thirty-two head of cattle for the feeding of Alamo defenders. Collins's luxury book on the subject, *The Alamo and Beyond: A Collector's Journey*, was published in 2012.

The collection has now expanded beyond the Alamo, said Collins. "I recently bought something from a little later than that period, from around 1847," he said. "It's a tenor drum from the Mexican-American War, in which there were Irish regiments fighting. These Irishmen started fighting for the Texans, but they were treated so badly that they went over to the Mexican side. This drum would have been used like their marching bass drum."

In June 2014, Collins announced that he was donating his Alamo collection, thought to be worth tens of millions of dollars, to the state of Texas. Addressing a crowd in San Antonio, he said he thought his private collection deserved a wider audience. "It's at my home, in my basement in Switzerland," he explained. "I look at it every day, but no one else was enjoying it."

One of the flashiest things that you can do, as a famous drummer, is work with a big manufacturer such as Premier, Pearl, or Ludwig to create your own drums, or maybe even a whole "signature kit" for fans to buy if they want to replicate your sound. The manufacturer Tama recently made a limited edition of fifty Stewart Copeland signature kits, based on the kit that Copeland played on the 2007 Police reunion tour. The drums have a stunning blue sparkle finish and feature four octobans (long, small-diameter toms), and the full fourteen-piece set cost $12,800—cymbals not included. In 2012, for the fortieth anniversary of Deep Purple's classic *Machine Head* album, Pearl launched its signature Ian Paice kit. Limited to just twelve sets, its nine silvery-shelled drums cost more than $7,650, with the Paiste cymbals to go with it priced at around $2,600.

Vintage kits have commanded much flashier prices. When five silver-shelled Premier drums played by Keith Moon in the late 1960s were auctioned in London in 1991, an anonymous buyer snapped them up for around $16,000. When the drums came onto the market again in 2004, they went under the hammer for more than $250,000. These five drums have been widely described as "the world's most expensive drum kit," but they are only a portion of the original kit that Moon played, which included nine drums and three cymbals.

Of course, it's no good having fantastic gear if you don't have the chops to use it. And the number-one skill that people look for in a flashy drummer is, of course, speed. Famous modern thumpers known for the rapidity of their beats include Mike Portnoy, Mike Mangini, and the Australian virtuoso Virgil Donati, who has been called "one of the most startlingly quick drummers alive" and played to a capacity audience of open-mouthed fans at the 2012 London Drum Show. Donati's drumming can be heard in all its jaw-dropping, beautiful complexity on his 2013 solo album, *In This Life*, on which he trades prog-fusion beats with a small army of brilliant bassists, guitarists, and keyboard players.

Critics complain that speed does not equal musicianship, and that the quest for speed trivializes and infantilizes the serious business of percussion, but Donati is unapologetic. "It's the nature of mankind to want to be faster, stronger," he once explained. "What are the Olympics all about? What do we want to do when we get behind the wheel of a car, or on a bike? Why should drummers be any different? Here's an instrument that we have the potential to drive fast—although with a lot of effort. I think it's unhealthy to deny that instinct."

Drummers in thrash-metal, death-metal, and hardcore

punk bands have found their own way of impressing with speed. They use "blast beats," which are basically loud and fast coordinated beats on the bass drum, snare, and cymbals, but which encompass a growing number of variations. Blast beats are not subtle; they make you sit up and take notice, or scare you out of your wits, as if someone has just fired a machine gun. Typical examples can be heard on records by bands with ugly names such as Napalm Death, Dying Fetus, and Dark Funeral.

Today, fast drumming has burst out of the music world to become an international sport and an industry in itself. "The World's Fastest Drummer" (WFD) is not a phrase that can be used casually now, because it is a trademark of a Nashville-based electronics corporation called McAfee Enterprises Inc. For decades, drummers and their fans would argue endlessly about who was the fastest behind a kit, with no way of proving their arguments conclusively. But that all changed in 1999 when two American inventors, Boo McAfee and Craig Alan, came up with the Drumometer, a compact device that counts drum strokes played by both the hands and the feet. McAfee Enterprises' invention was inspired by an incident at a Chicago drum clinic twenty-four years before, in 1975. McAfee was there when the swing-jazz player Barrett Deems declared himself to be the fastest drummer in the world, before being heckled imaginatively from the crowd. "Oh yeah? What machine did you use?" asked the heckler, who turned out to be the legendary Buddy Rich.

The invention of the Drumometer has led to regular WFD competitions at which the machine is employed to sort the men from the boys (and the women from the girls). Triumphant drummers at these contests have clocked up some amazing statistics. A Canadian drummer, Mike "Machine" Mallais, somehow managed to play 978 beats with his feet in a minute in 2007. Six years later, another Canadian, twenty-two-year-old Tom Grosset, became the world champion in Nashville when he scored a record-breaking 1,208 beats within a minute with his hands—more than twenty beats per second. "I was quite stunned when I broke the record," Grosset told me. "There were all these people staring at me and cheering, and I was just standing there, thinking, What just happened?"

Straight after his win, Tom Grosset was congratulated in person by Bernard Purdie, legendary inventor of "the Purdie shuffle," who has recorded with a galaxy of stars including Aretha Franklin, James Brown, Simon & Garfunkel, and Steely Dan. But some other drummers are unhappy about WFD: they complain that all this superfast stick-smacking is a soulless business that has nothing to do with music. One online critic has said it encourages "the mentality where every little kid thinks he or she can become a rock star if they can just play fast."

"There's this whole genre of drumming now, which is drumming for drumming's sake, rather than drumming for music's sake," argued Steve White. "You're getting all these drummers that just compete, and never play in bands. It's like dragster racing, as opposed to ordinary driving. Or it's like ball tricks in soccer: sometimes at halftime during a big football game, they'll have somebody come out and do all kinds of tricks with the ball. But when the referee blows the whistle for the game to start again, they disappear. They're not footballers, just tricksters."

"For some reason," said McAfee, "the haters of WFD think we have some hidden agenda to change music. We don't: it's just good, clean fun, and we simply want to entertain people." Grosset said he has been targeted by some of those haters: "I

get messages all the time, telling me to 'learn to drum properly,' when they don't even know anything about me," he said.
Grosset is actually a talented drummer who plays in a Canadian
jazz fusion band and performs drum-based covers of movie
soundtracks; he has made videos in which he brings extra percussive power to music from films such as *Man of Steel*, *Skyfall*,
and *Pirates of the Caribbean*. "I've noticed that WFD has helped
my endurance as a drummer," he said. "I've built up all this
strength in my forearms, and I've been able to handle six-hour
recording sessions."

Flashy drumming isn't always a direct route to fame. Some
of the greatest feats in the history of drumming have been
achieved by people whose names are still unknown to the general public. In August 2011, the little-known Canadian drummer Steve Gaul set a record by drumming solidly for 121 hours
in Burlington, Ontario, raising over $18,000 for the Canadian
Cancer Society. In February 2012 an American sticksman
named Christopher Anthon, similarly raising funds for the
National Multiple Sclerosis Society, performed a single roll on
a snare drum that continued for an incredible eight hours, one
minute, and seventeen seconds in San Mateo, California.

One night in 2006, a thirty-one-year-old Australian drummer called Col Hatchman was idly surfing the Internet, looking at the records set by various drummers, when he noticed
that the "world's loudest drummer" had achieved a record
noise power of 109.1 decibels. This wasn't terribly impressive
to Hatchman, who had once been told that he had reached 120
decibels with his snare drum onstage, without the benefit of
any amplification. He decided that he would try to beat the
record, "just as something fun to do." He went on to play a gig
in Newcastle, New South Wales, with his band at the time,

Dirty Skanks. During the event, organized to raise awareness of the Australian Jeans for Genes scheme (which raises money to help children with genetic disorders), Hatchman hit a high of 137.2 decibels during a drum solo. Guinness World Records officials were in attendance, and their rules were strictly adhered to: he had to play a standard-size kit, and it had to be an acoustic drum sound. He later received a certificate declaring him to be the world's loudest drummer.

When I spoke to him, Hatchman was still the proud holder of the title, with the certificate displayed on his wall, and said he hadn't heard of any attempts to break his record. "I've always been a hard player," he said. "I was always inspired by really hard drummers like Dave Grohl and Tommy Lee." He recalled that many years before, when he lived with his parents in Mango Hill, north of Brisbane, his weekend drum practice was regularly interrupted by the local police—despite the fact that the Hatchmans had half an acre of grounds and were surrounded by bush.

As the biggest, flashiest titles are gradually taken—world's fastest drummer, world's loudest drummer—sneaky drummers are looking to find specific, niche drumming records they can claim for their own. In 2013, Andrew WK broke the record for the longest drumming session in a retail store when the American singer and multi-instrumentalist played at the big Oakley store in Times Square, New York City, for twenty-four hours. During the ordeal, fellow drummers, including Questlove, came by to offer moral support. "I actually never got tired," he told MTV afterward, "because there was so much adrenalin and so many people that were especially giving so much energy, it really felt like a team effort."

Another way of proving yourself as a flashy drummer is to master the mathematics of difficult rhythms. Most straightforward rock is in common time, also known as 4/4 (where the first 4 is the number of beats in the bar, and the second 4 signifies that the beat length is a crotchet), but there are plenty of other, more difficult time signatures for adventurous musicians. Early examples appear in African polyrhythmic tribal drumming, and in jazz—"Take Five" by the Dave Brubeck Quartet being the most famous 5/4 number ever written. "Spanish Moss" by the drummer Billy Cobham is in a mind-blowing 17/16—built on a pattern of seventeen sixteenth notes. And many examples can be found in mainstream popular music. The irresistible, infectious quality of the 2003 hit song "Hey Ya!" by the hip-hop band Outkast (which propelled it to the top of the Billboard Hot 100 for a nine-week residency) is partly down to its use of a peculiar 4/4, 4/4, 4/4, 2/4, 4/4, 4/4 cycle.

One of the hallmarks of prog rock is the use of tricksy time signatures, and modern bands who love them include the US prog-metal rockers Dream Theater, whose 1999 song "The Dance of Eternity" switches time signatures more than a hundred times. And this was the band that presided over one of the greatest-ever showcases for flashy drummers when they held auditions after the departure of the formidable Mike Portnoy. In April 2011, Dream Theater invited seven dazzling drummers to SIR Studios in New York City, where they spent three days trying them out individually with the rest of the band. We know these were "The World's Greatest Drummers" because that is how they were collectively addressed in seven identical letters from the "Dream Theater Audition Team." The magnificent seven were Virgil Donati, the German-born Marco

Minnemann, the American Derek Roddy, the Swede Peter Wildoer, Aquiles Priester (of the Brazilian power-metal band Hangar), Thomas Lang (the Austrian drummer with the LA-based prog-metal band stOrk), and Mike Mangini. The task was to play some especially difficult Dream Theater material and to jam with the band. Mangini later revealed that his grueling audition included "time-signature tests to play on the spot," with bar sequences such as "2/4, 7/16, 3/4, 4/4, 5/8, et cetera." Skilled enough to translate all those numbers into solid rhythms, he got the job.

Earlier prog bands have enjoyed the occasional nice, challenging time signature. "Money" by Pink Floyd, from *The Dark Side of the Moon*, managed to be a hit in America in 1973 in spite of the fact that the song is mostly in 7/4 time (it switches to a straight rock 4/4 for David Gilmour's guitar solo). And the real challenge for prog drummers is to make a strange time signature come alive: if the beat is 23/16, it's not impressive enough to just hit the bass drum and snare twenty-three times to keep the band in time. As far back as 1973, Phil Collins put in a particularly good performance in the instrumental end sequence of "The Cinema Show" on the Genesis album *Selling England by the Pound*, making 7/8 time sound almost danceable. The storming "Apocalypse in 9/8" section of Genesis's famous prog epic of 1973, "Supper's Ready," has bars of nine quavers, as its title suggests—the same signature as Wagner's apocalyptic "Ride of the Valkyries." After Genesis parted ways with its original lead singer, Peter Gabriel, both parties continued to flirt with unusual rhythms. Gabriel's "Solsbury Hill" (1977) was mostly in 7/4, and "Turn It on Again" (1980) by Genesis was a UK top-ten hit despite being in 13/8.

I had always believed that those tricksy Genesis tempos had

come from their drummer. I imagined Phil Collins smirking during a rehearsal and shouting: "Right, mates! This one's in 27/8, ha ha ha!" But when I spoke to Collins, I learned that the truth was more complex. "We never really thought, Let's do this in this time signature or that time signature," he said. "The 'Apocalypse in 9/8' section of 'Supper's Ready' was written when I was absent," he said. "Mike Rutherford had this guitar riff in 9/8, and I'm sure he didn't realize it was in nine: he just played it, and it ended up being in nine. Then Tony Banks's keyboard solo was improvised along to the guitar riff, and I came in after it was all written. When I played on it, I actually slipped between the two of them, because some of what Tony did was in four and some of what Mike was doing was in nine, so I would just go from one to the other and pick up on the 'greatest hits' of the solo, if you like. It was improvised, and that version of 'Apocalypse' on the record would've been the first take of that piece, and it just worked. They knew what they were doing, and I didn't!" Similarly, the end of "The Cinema Show" just ended up being in 7/8, he said. "We never really discussed it. Again, that was a guitar riff, and then when I played along, I discovered, 'Hey! It's seven.'" I asked Collins if, when he played those 7/8 and 9/8 sections, he was actually counting up to seven or nine in his head as he played. "No, I wasn't. But they were easy to play. I found that most of the time, if I could sing it in my head, I would be able to play it. I was never like a Cobham: Billy Cobham, it seemed, could play anything in any time signature."

Collins agreed that he may have tried to show off as a drummer in the early days of Genesis, but that there were always exceptions. "When they start playing in bands, a lot of drummers want to show what they can do, especially if they're just a player and not a writer. So you tend to be a little bit inappropriate on certain pieces of music, because you want to make it interesting for yourself. But there would also be certain songs where the playing side would take a backseat. In loose terms, I used to think, 'Okay, this is my John Bonham hat,' or I'd think, 'This is my Ringo hat,' and I'd play what was right for the piece. You'd have to make that kind of choice. I remember having a feeling that the song 'Harold the Barrel' [from the *Nursery Cryme* album] would be a Ringo-type song: you would play what would make the song sound good. I do see a lot of the wrong choices in some of the early Genesis stuff, in terms of what I would do now." There is certainly some messy overplaying by Collins, in my opinion, on parts of "The Fountain of Salmacis" on *Nursery Cryme*. But as the band's music became more streamlined and more commercial after he took on the role of lead singer, the Ringo hat was worn more and more often. "As time went on, we were all working at home in our little studio environments," said Collins, "and we inevitably worked with drum machines, which were normally in 4/4."

Chad Smith is widely revered for his irresistible funky grooves for the Red Hot Chili Peppers. Drumming experts have pointed out that one of the big secrets behind Smith's grooves is his use of "ghost notes," subtle but flashy little touches here and there, sometimes nearly inaudible, that help to drive the songs and keep the rhythm exciting. The effect of these ghost notes is hard to describe, but Smith had a try. "First of all, as a rock drummer, my role is to provide accompaniment," he told me. "It's a supportive role, and therefore I'm playing what the music calls for, and often that's simple. But within that, there are ways of putting nuances in your playing that will first of all make it unique—so it will have personality, it will sound like you—and that will also make the music feel better. I mean, to me, that's the most important thing if you're playing dance-rock music—can people dance or tap their feet or nod their head? So those little ghost notes, or grace notes, help. They don't make the drumming sound too busy, but there's something about them that makes it funky or rounder or not so stiff; they make the music sound good.

"I think a lot of those ghost notes come from the English players I listened to when I was growing up, who had a lot of jazz influences in their playing. My older brother, two years older than me, had a record collection that was a big influence on me: he had records by all these rock bands that came out of England from the late sixties, like Led Zeppelin and Deep Purple. And I started listening to all these drummers, like John Bonham, Ian Paice, Mitch Mitchell, Ginger Baker, Bill Ward, Roger Taylor from Queen, Simon Kirke from Free and Bad Company, Jerry Shirley from Humble Pie, and Keith Moon."

Like Phil Collins, Smith denied being an expert on difficult tempos: "I can't really think in time signatures that much: I just kinda hold onto the riff, or whatever. We've been writing music for a new record, and Flea comes up with lots of interesting bass lines, some of which is in odd times. I don't think he thinks of it as being in odd time—it's very natural for him—but for me, to make it sound natural and not too proggy, I have to come up with beats that don't make you fall down if you're trying to dance! No, my odd-time stuff is not so good—and I'm terrible at playing reggae."

Do people really become drummers because they are self-obsessed exhibitionists? I was beginning to wonder. There was a modesty about Chad Smith and Phil Collins that belied my impression of them both as flashy and exciting drummers, and other talented drummers I spoke to were similarly self-effacing. Also, drummers often do extremely skillful things onstage without anybody noticing. Omar Hakim played drums behind Madonna on her Girlie Show world tour of 1993, which kicked off in London and played twenty other cities including New York, Philadelphia, and Toronto. This elaborate stage spectacle was electronically sequenced, and Hakim played the entire show to a click track, a strict metronomic pulse that was inaudible to the crowd. "One of the challenges," said Hakim, "was to make sure that the show doesn't become stale because of the metronomic element—to make sure that the grooves sounded free and natural, as if there was no click track there at all. And Madonna could have got many fantastic drummers to play that concert tour, but she wasn't just looking for a player. To play with an artist of that stature in a show that huge, you want a veteran of the road, somebody with experience—for the moments when there's a problem onstage and a veteran would know what to do. The sequencing systems failed a couple of times on that tour. Suddenly the sequence went down, the click track went away, I had the band playing and eighteen dancers in front of me, and I had to keep this thing moving. If we were playing at a hundred and eighteen beats per minute, I had to keep it right there so that when the guy eventually turns that system back on, that I'm not playing the slightest bit faster or slower, that we're still on track, still playing a hundred and eighteen bpm."

Laying down a fantastic groove, said Hakim, is not about ego at all. "When you're looking for a really good groove, you need to surrender yourself to the moment. It isn't about you. It's about surrendering yourself to what the music is asking of you. I had a producer come up to me after a session one day, and he said to me, 'Omar, I just want to thank you for playing that beat like a fourteen-year-old.' And I understand what he meant—it wasn't an insult at all. He was saying that I'd abandoned everything to get to what that groove needed. It's all about that crazy moment: we have to lose ourselves—lose who we think we are, maybe—and serve the music."

There are plenty of great "song drummers" who do just that—surrender to the moment, drop their egos, and serve the music. For every Carl Palmer and Terry Bozzio, there are many drummers who don't draw attention to themselves, who "wear the Ringo hat" and play exactly what a given song needs and no more. They sit happily at the back like Charlie Watts, keeping the groove going and letting the lead singer hog most of the attention. I spoke to several famous drummers who said they would never play drum solos—and even Keith Moon used to say that he hated playing them.

"I'm not a flashy drummer," said Paul Thompson of Roxy Music. "I do know how to twirl drumsticks, but I've never, ever, done it onstage. It's superficial to what I am. It's a showmanship thing, and I don't consider myself a showman as such. I just want to be laying the groove or the beat down. I don't like drum solos. I've only seen a couple of drum solos that I thought were good: 'Moby Dick' by John Bonham, and one by Billy Cobham. I don't ever want to play a drum solo: to me, I'm part of a unit, I'm not an individual onstage."

"I never wanted to play drum solos," said Nick Mason. "I always thought it was a sort of gymnastic exercise, and frequently I still do. I do have a very low opinion of my own technical ability, as well. I'm very self-taught, never had lessons, never really learned all the rudiments, so maybe that's part of it: I think, What would I do in a solo that would make it really original?"

As another theory tumbled to the ground, it was time to take a closer look at drummers. Had I missed something? Had I, for example, overlooked an entire section of the drumming community?

4

SHE PLAYS
THE DRUMS

As I proceeded with my research into drummers and what made them tick, I kept getting this nagging feeling that I was missing something. And after I'd largely dismissed the idea that all drummers were flashy, working-class lunatics, one of my nagging feelings jumped up and bit me hard.

Up to this point, all of the drummers I've mentioned have had two fundamental things in common. Firstly, they have all played the drums at some point, obviously. Secondly, they all belong to the heterogametic sex; that is to say, they have both X and Y chromosomes. They're all men.

But the world of drumming isn't like the Vatican, or any of those stuck-up golf clubs who insist that your loud checked trousers have one specific variety of genitalia in them. There is no law, at least in the USA and the UK and the rest of the free world, that says you have to be male to be a drummer.

There have been many periods of history when such a law seemed to be in force. Female drummers were rare during the jazz age of the early twentieth century, but that's not to say that they didn't exist. There were female drummers in the occasional all-woman band, such as Viola Smith in the Coquettes, Pauline Brady in the Vi Burnside Combo, and Elaine Leighton in the Beryl Booker Trio.

In the testosterone-charged 1960s and '70s, the vast majority of pop and rock drummers were men, but again there were some shining exceptions. The Honeycombs, the British pop group who scored a hit in 1964 with "Have I the Right," decided that they had the right to employ a female drummer, Honey Lantree. This resulted in accusations from the stiff and starchy UK press that their choice of drummer was merely a "gimmick" designed to attract attention to the band, and that the group were keeping a big secret from the public: that Honey couldn't really play her drums. In 1965 the music newspaper *Record Mirror* quoted a peeved statement from the Honeycombs that read: "How can it be a gimmick just because we have a girl, Honey, on drums? Honey plays with us purely and simply because she is the right drummer for the job. If she wasn't any good, she wouldn't hold down the job." They also denied that having a woman in their midst created sexual complications when they went on the road: "On tour, we don't have any troubles by having a girl with us. We just operate as a group."

We might be able to look back and laugh at the fuss that Lantree generated in the British media—such comical, misogynous sixties attitudes!—if we were all so much more enlightened today. But are we? The 2013 London Drum Show featured live performances from fifteen top drummers—all of them men. Women make only occasional appearances in mainstream drum magazines. And there are whole books on drumming that entirely ignore the existence of female drummers.

I recently visited Foote's, the venerable old London drum shop (which has been serving the needs of percussionists ever since they were obliged to wear formal evening dress onstage), to listen to a discussion on the subject of female drummers. It was led by Mindy Abovitz, a thirty-three-year-old woman from Brooklyn, who is not only a drummer and a self-proclaimed feminist but also the editor of *Tom Tom*, a magazine for women drummers. A small crowd of people listened intently—mostly young women who knew their way around a drum kit—while Abovitz bemoaned the confusion, scorn, resistance, and prejudice that women still face when they dare to play the instrument. If you were casting an actress to play Abovitz in a movie, you might choose someone who resembles Jane Fonda circa 1970.

"I'm the editor of a drum magazine," said Abovitz, "and I still feel sheepish when I walk into a drum shop. I actually worked at the largest independent drum shop in New York City for two years, and I still go [nervous, girly voice] 'Hi! Actually, I'm a drummer . . .' It's like, what is happening when I walk into a drum shop? I'm not even sure. And, oh shit, do I have to play to show these people that I can play? It's super awkward."

She had been drumming for a while, she explained. "But I'd never consumed a drum magazine, because it didn't appeal to me, didn't speak to me, and I didn't see anything in it that seemed relevant . . . And I remember typing into Google 'woman drummer' or 'female drummer' or 'girl drummer,' and every search result brought up something like 'Can girls play the drums?' Like a Yahoo question: 'Can girls play?' 'How many women play?' And then it'd be a bunch of sexy pictures of women next to drum sets. And I was thinking, 'This is fucked! This isn't real! This doesn't match my world.'

"So in 2009 I set out to change the Google keyword-search

result, and I started a blog. And I also thought for sure there was a magazine for female drummers, and they would contact me and be like, 'Hey!' And I'd be like, 'Okay, cool, let's do this together!' So I started *Tom Tom* magazine as a blog, and I interviewed myself. You know, '*Tom Tom*: How did you get started on the drums? Mindy: Thanks for asking! . . .' I really did that. And then, six months in, I was getting all this feedback."

The "magazine for female drummers" never contacted her, because such a thing didn't exist—not yet. But people told her how much they liked her blog and said things like "I wish you were in print." Eventually she sorted some finance and hooked up with a photographer, some other writers, and a magazine designer, and suddenly *Tom Tom* was a going concern. "So we started the first issue, and I called it a quarterly, because I felt that that was the least possible commitment that I could make. It's actually an enormous commitment," she laughed. "And then I decided that this thing was gonna be really big. And I'm still in the same place: I want it to be bigger and bigger, and as big as it can possibly be.

"What I'm trying to do with the magazine," Abovitz told her rapt audience, "and I don't know if I'm doing it yet, is to normalize the girl/woman-drummer experience." A dozen well-coiffured heads nodded in the Foote's crowd, in perfect time. "If I have my way, in 2025 a woman or a girl will be able to walk into a drum shop and no one will bat an eyelid, and she'll buy her shit and walk out. And she'll go into her practice space and she'll play . . ." Following some clapping and restrained cheering, Abovitz continued: "And she'll go on tour, and no one will be like, 'Hey, you're such a good chick drummer'—it will just be normal." More applause. "There's no reason in my mind why it's not. I love the drums; I love playing drums. It's not about having a pair of tits or a penis when you're playing the drums: it's about making music. So whatever else is happening, I'm not really sure what that is, but it's unnecessary for certain, and it's some part of our socialization that I'm really working on undoing."

Abovitz explained how, on many occasions, she has found herself at odds with drum manufacturers. "The drum industry does not think we're there," she said. "There are five female drummers: there's Sheila E., Jess Bowen, Hannah Ford, Cindy Blackman, and Cora Dunham, and there's no one else. I know that's not true. One thing I set out to do with the magazine was to cover the average drummer . . . When I'm asking for advertising money from manufacturers like DW or Gretsch, Zildjian or Sabian, my challenge is to convince them that there are a lot more women drummers than they know . . . I've had to carve out a space for myself, and I got a reputation early on for being a hardass in terms of ad art. I did not want their typical ad in *Tom Tom*: I wanted an ad that was either product-based or showed a woman drumming in it . . . That's part of my politics with the magazine: not only to ask them to invest monetarily, but to ask them to think about the imagery they're putting out in the world . . . And if they can't find a woman drummer—often they can't—I will help them find a woman drummer. I will create ad art for them. I will introduce them to someone via e-mail. And I do this and it works . . . but the process is not easy, and oftentimes they're pissed until it happens and then they're happy, because they just widened their audience."

Women in Abovitz's crowd joined in with the discussion, telling their own stories. One of them, Michèle Drees, a regular at Ronnie Scott's jazz club, struck a chord when she talked about the phenomenon of "the before and after face." Often, she

said, when she was about to play the drums, she would see facial
expressions registering shock or incredulity: this was a woman?
Playing the drums? But after she had performed, demonstrating her proficiency on the instrument, these expressions would
be replaced by looks of pleasant surprise and appreciation: this
woman really can play! I had seen this expression metamorphosis
firsthand when I watched Drees give an impromptu performance
at the 2012 London Drum Show. Dozens of men were aghast as
she sat behind a kit and laid down some cool jazz grooves, before
switching to another kit and pounding out rock beats.

Mindy Abovitz had her own before-and-after-face story,
demonstrating the assumptions that are sometimes made about
female drummers before they have even struck a note. "I was
going to play a show, opening up for another band," she said,
"and a guy walked up to me before I'd started playing and said,
'You know, I give drum lessons.' I was like, 'Do you?' And then
I sat down on the kit and I played my set—probably harder than
normal—and when I got off he was like, 'Oh, you don't need
drum lessons.' "

Before the Foote's event, I had heard some entertaining,
if thought-provoking, stories from other female drummers.
"There are still people who have these prejudices in their
head," said Cherisse Osei, a diminutive Londoner who has
played many gigs behind the kit with the singers Bryan Ferry,
Paloma Faith, and Mika. "They look at me and go, 'Oh, you're
the drummer . . . but you're a girl.' I say, 'Yeah? And . . . ? Nothing wrong with that, is there?' You just learn to ignore those
kinds of people. Actually, I find it quite fun when I see their
faces drop. When I was sixteen, I was in a metal band and we
played the Earthshaker Fest in Germany. I was the only female
musician playing in the whole festival. And at one point I tried

to go onstage to sound-check, but there were these big tattooed guys saying, 'No, no!' I said, 'I'm sound-checking!' And this guy said, 'No, no! I'm sorry, little girl, you can't come onstage.' I said, 'Look. I need to get onstage. I'm sound-checking.' 'No, no, no.' In the end I had to call my guitarist, and he came down and said, 'Mate, she's in the band!' And the guy said, 'Her?' 'Yeah, she's our drummer.' So I played and then I came offstage, and the huge tattooed guy said, 'Can I have your autograph?'"

Jess Bowen is the Arizona-born female drummer in the Summer Set, whose other members are all male. "I hate it when guys put me down, or they don't believe that I'm a drummer, and they doubt my ability to play the drums," said Bowen. "I get very offended by it. I realize it's a male-dominated instrument, so people don't see as many female drummers—and maybe they don't see as many good female drummers. I feel like, unfortunately, in our generation, it's a stereotype I'm going to have to face for a little while, until there are a lot of other girl drummers that start coming up and playing at a professional level."

The British drummer Anna Prior is the only female member of the electronic band Metronomy, which has been praised as "Britain's most-loved, quintessentially English, modern pop act." "I'm usually the only woman in the touring party when we go on tour," said Prior, "and I do occasionally get men assuming that I'm a production assistant, or the tour manager, or a lighting person. When I say, 'No, I'm the drummer,' they're like, 'Oh! Oh, God, sorry.' I find that the reaction varies according to the age of the man that I'm talking to. If I'm talking to someone of my own age, in their twenties, they don't even mention the fact that I'm a woman and I'm a drummer: it's all cool. But whenever I talk to men that are my dad's age, in their sixties, that's when you get, 'Oh! A female drummer! Oh, you never see that!' And I'm like, 'Well, you kind of do. There are a hell of a lot more than there used to be, for sure.' And they'll start talking about all the old bands they knew with female drummers in them."

Certain drummers crop up frequently in such conversations. These might include the late Sandy West of the Runaways; Cindy Blackman, who played with Lenny Kravitz and later married Carlos Santana; and Samantha Maloney, who has played with hard-rock bands like Mötley Crüe and Eagles of Death Metal. Somebody is also bound to mention Maureen "Moe" Tucker, who created her own, highly distinctive drumming for the Velvet Underground from the mid-1960s. Tucker was an androgynous figure who stood up instead of sitting down, played with mallets, and used a drum kit that even some of the earliest New Orleans jazz players would have called primitive. She had a snare drum, a floor tom, and a bass drum without a pedal, which she turned over and played like an oversized tom. She contributed basic, repetitive beats, but these worked brilliantly within the band's austere East Coast sound. Listen to "Venus in Furs" on the album *The Velvet Underground and Nico*: would you prefer to hear Carl Palmer, Terry Bozzio, or Keith Moon going nuts all over that song?

Moe Tucker disliked the frequent drum rolls of flashy drummers, and she wasn't keen on cymbals: she had one, which she once described as resembling "a garbage-can lid that had been run over six times." As she explained when she was interviewed in 1997 by Claudia Gonson (who has herself played drums in the Magnetic Fields), "I always hated songs where if you rolled at every opportunity, there would be a constant roll throughout the song. Or crashed a cymbal at every opportunity, or every place where you felt like you should do that. So I consciously avoided it. While you're crashing, you can't hear the vocal and you can't hear the guitar part, you know? I just always felt like the drums shouldn't take over the song. They should always be under there, obvious, but not taking over the song so that suddenly you realize all you hear is drums."

Lou Reed once honored Tucker by saying that "There is only one human being who can play that way." But Tucker herself has said that she never thought of herself as a musician, and when she started playing the drums—beating along to records by the Beatles, the Stones, and Bo Diddley on a secondhand kit in 1963—she wasn't thinking of taking up drumming seriously. One of her earliest inspirations, she told an interviewer in 1998, came all the way from Africa: "You remember Murray the K? He was the biggest DJ in New York. He used to open and close his show with this African music and it was always the same song. Every time I'd catch it, I'd say 'Oh man, this is great!' But he never said who it was. It was really frustrating. One night he mentioned it, for some reason: 'That was Olatunji, "Drums of Passion."' So I ran out and got it the next day. I love that stuff.

"It's funny, because in '62, I was in the high school library when an announcement came over: 'Anyone who would like to sell candy to help pay for an African drummer named Olatunji to come to assembly to play, please go to the office.' So I ran to the office for that! So, in our silly little Levittown [Long Island] school, we got Olatunji and his full troop with 10 or 12 musicians and 10 or 12 dancers. It was just stunning . . . I asked the teacher for the next class after the assembly if I could get a pass, so I could find him and get his autograph. She did let me go, and I got an autographed picture . . ."

A few million stylistic miles from the Velvet Underground were the Carpenters, whose slushy MOR music was elevated by the mellifluous vocals of Karen Carpenter. According to her brother and musical partner, Richard, she was happier behind a kit than behind a microphone. As he once recalled, "I never thought twice about her being a 'girl drummer.' 'How quaint,' they said. Oh, really? She was a reluctant singer, though—she considered herself a drummer who sings."

Interviewed in 1973, Karen revealed that her drumming career began with a ploy to avoid athletic activities at school. "When I was in high school, I joined the band so that I could get out of gym classes," she said. "The marching band was considered a substitute for physical education, and I wasn't for running around a track at eight o'clock in the morning." Initially she was given a glockenspiel to play, which she didn't like, and that's when she moved on to the drums. "I had this friend who had been playing them since he was three, and he was fantastic, so I copied him. And the rest came naturally."

As teenagers in the 1960s, Karen and Richard teamed up with a bass player named Wes Jacobs and formed the Carpenter Trio, which featured Karen on drums. Later, when they started recording as the Carpenters, she was still behind the kit, but that wasn't always practical when she became the singer. "At one stage, we realized that somebody had to go out front, and everyone was looking at me, so we hired another drummer to play when I'm doing the lead vocal." In that early interview, she already sounded weary of the reactions she was provoking as a female drummer: "They've been telling me for five years that it's unusual for a girl to be playing drums, but that doesn't matter. The drums were the only thing I could play."

Thirty years ago, I met an extraordinary young woman whose career seemed to have become distorted by negative attitudes toward female drummers. It was 1984, and I was interviewing Sheila E., who was then twenty-six years old, in the London offices of her record company. A woman of Mexican, African-American, and Creole heritage, she was dressed to the nines in smart 1980s designer gear, including a stylish broad-brimmed hat. Though she was already a phenomenal percussionist, the people around her seemed to be trying to mold her into a singing superstar. After playing with a galaxy of musicians including Prince, Marvin Gaye, and Billy Cobham, she had just released a solo album, *The Glamorous Life*, on which she sang as well as playing percussion. But for a solo star who was supposed to be promoting her new album, she was remarkably frank when I asked her about her role as a vocalist. How long, I asked her, had she been singing? "Just this year," she replied. "I don't like to sing. The last band I was in was Lionel Richie's, and he had me singing live background vocals, so I got comfortable doing that. I didn't want to sing any lead parts, though. They wanted me to sing Diana Ross's part in 'Endless Love,' but I didn't want to. And earlier this year, Prince asked me to come in the studio and do a lot of singing, so I went in the studio and sang with him, and did some other things. And he thought I should have a solo career and sing. So I tried it. I'm getting used to it. It's a challenge. I do a lot of playing and singing at the same time." I asked Sheila if she wanted to be a big star, and she said: "No. I just want to be a musician, a person that everybody likes and says, 'Yeah, she's good!' I just want to make people happy. I don't like being quoted as a star."

I asked her if the idea of a female percussionist had provoked any reactions among anybody, and she replied: "Just a lot of negative things when I first started playing, from male drummers, I guess who were kinda jealous in a way. They used to put me down. A lot of bad things were said about me: that

I couldn't play because I'm a woman, 'You've only got this gig because you are a girl,' that kind of thing. But it never really bothered me, because I was confident in my playing—I knew that I could play. I had to prove myself, which took me a while. It's okay now."

With all the carping coming from the sidelines, many female drummers may benefit from extra support of some kind, and it was clear that Sheila E. was supported by a very musical family. Born Sheila Escovedo in 1957, she started playing music with her father, Pete Escovedo, and his brother Coke in their band the Escovedo Brothers when she was as young as five. Her brothers, Juan and Peter Michael, were also percussionists. "I stopped playing for a while," Sheila told me, "and then started playing again when I was about fourteen, drums and percussion, and I played another show with my father, and the response was so good that I decided I wanted to be a professional musician. So I quit school and went out on the road with my father, and started touring with George Duke and people like that. And that's all I've been doing since."

Like many male drummers, Sheila E. came from an underprivileged, working-class background. And in the early days, she didn't see her musicianship as having monetary value. "I grew up in a real poor environment," she said, "a bad part of Oakland, California. It's been real rough all my life. Even when I started playing, I thought it was an insult to take money from people. So I would play for free, and my father would get mad at me, tell me, 'You have to take the money. You have to eat, you have to help support the family.' I was fifteen years old. And after a while, when I saw that there wasn't any food in the refrigerator, I said, 'Okay!' It's been hard all our lives . . . but we've still been happy. That's what counts."

Like many male drummers, too, Sheila had a passion for sports, and she recalled that as a young girl "I was running a lot of track and playing soccer, and I kind of wanted to probably be in the Olympics or something."

Jess Bowen, too, was drawn to sports as well as music, and played soccer as a girl. "But music was always my passion, and I had to pick one or the other, and I did end up picking music." Like Sheila E., Bowen was born into a musical family, in 1989. Her father and brother were both drummers, and there was pressure for her to become a drummer as well. When she decided she would play guitar instead, her father said he would buy her a guitar on one condition: that she try playing drums in the school band for at least a year. The experience gave her a passion for the drums. "I'd always wanted to play guitar, and we always had drums round the house and I wanted to be different," she said. "I didn't want to be another drummer in the family. But I'm glad now that my dad did encourage me to do it. There's not a lot of female drummers out there, and I guess I appreciate being able to maybe help and encourage other girls to do it. I've had a lot of people coming up to me and telling me their parents don't let them play the drums because they don't think it's a very feminine instrument."

Bowen has recently been encouraging more girls to drum in an official capacity: as the spokesperson for the 2014 Hit Like a Girl contest. This awareness-raising competition, launched in 2012, invites female drummers around the world to send in video clips of their performances, which are judged by hundreds of thousands of online voters and a panel of experts. Drummers from forty-two countries entered the 2012 contest, and the entrants received votes from more than four hundred thousand people around the globe. The winner in the over-eighteen category in 2013 was the twenty-five-year-old Chilean drummer Valerie Sepulveda, who won with a flashy, jazzy piece of music in 7/8 time. Alexey Poblete from Las Vegas, just ten years old, triumphed in the under-eighteen category of the competition with her performance of a tune by the LA metal band Five Finger Death Punch.

For many of the female drummers playing today, there was nothing like Hit Like a Girl to help them when they began. The stories of how they started playing are so often marked by vague yearnings and chance events. Anna Prior was fourteen years old and attending a school in Doncaster, South Yorkshire, when she had her eureka moment. "There was this girl at school who was always a bit of an underdog," said Prior. "She was a tomboy with really short hair, and I was always intrigued by the fact that she would disappear at lunchtime. One day I asked her where she went, and she said, 'I go to the music block, and sit and play drums.' And I thought, 'Wow, excellent.' I'd tried to play lots of instruments before, like flute and piano, and as much as I wanted to be musical, those kind of instruments didn't scream out to me; I found them boring. So I asked if I could go with her one lunchtime, and we went in and she taught me a few little beats.

"Then, I remember, this guy from the sixth form poked his head round the door, wondering what all this commotion was. And he was like, 'Two lasses, playing the drums! You can't be doin' that!' I think that was my first proper experience of feminism—you know, 'I'm not having a man tell me that I can't play drums!' I went home that evening and spoke to my dad about it, and he was brilliant: he said, 'Okay, well, let's get you some lessons.' And I started taking lessons and got into it very quickly, and my parents got me a drum kit."

Debbi Peterson of the Bangles wanted to be in a band when she was young, but she was seriously considering playing bass or guitar. "I never really thought about being a drummer," she said. "In fact, I thought, 'I don't want to be stuck at the back, playing the drums.' When I was fifteen years old, my sister Vicki had a bunch of high school friends who were playing in a band together, and they were looking for another female drummer—they'd just got rid of one. And the bass player, our friend Amanda, suggested me to my sister, who thought, 'Hmm, that's kinda strange.' So I went to a rehearsal, and I sat down on the drum set and started playing, like I'd been doing it before, and everybody was amazed. They said, 'Okay, you're our drummer! You got the job!'"

"I was always drawn to rhythm, and drums always resonated with me," said Cherisse Osei. When she was just five years old, Osei received a drum kit of sorts as a gift from her uncle. "It was a tiny little thing," she recalled, "a pink Mickey Mouse drum kit, with three drums and a little crash cymbal. Then, years later, when I finally saw a real drum kit, I went, 'Oh! Hello . . . okay, I remember . . .' I was actually a dancer before I was a drummer; I was always dancing. But when I listened to music I'd always be finding the drum parts." There was an impressive music department at her school in the Southgate area of north London, and Osei discovered that she could count on the support of her parents and her best friend. "They had a few drum kits there at school, and when I was eleven I started playing there. My best friend Emily Dolan Davis and I started drumming on the same day, and we used to practice together at seven o'clock in the morning before school, at break time, lunchtime, and after school, for six years solid. My parents bought me my first drum kit when I was thirteen. They said if I was serious about playing drums, it was actually a good thing, because there weren't many female drummers around; it was quite rare. They said if I worked hard at it and became really good, I could probably get a lot of work out of it."

Patty Schemel, who used to play with Courtney Love in Hole, discovered the drums at the age of eleven in Seattle. "Drumming was such a physical thing to do, and I enjoyed that part of it, and I enjoyed the fact that I didn't see a lot of women doing it. Also, it was really powerful and made a big sound. I got a snare drum first, and shortly afterward I got more drums because I wanted to audition for the jazz band at school."

A great many drummers start playing as children or teenagers, but there are exceptions. Julie Edwards of the American female duo Deap Vally told me she was a late starter who began more or less by accident. "I was twenty-five when I took up the drums—I'd already lived a few lifetimes," she laughed. "I was starting my first band, the Pity Party, with my best friend, Mark. We'd been hatching the plan theoretically, just talking about what we were going to do, and then finally we rented some rehearsal space. But we had no clue what he was going to play or what I was going to play: we were approaching it from a very DIY, craft standpoint. Before then, I'd done a lot of singing and taken piano lessons, and I'd done a lot of very private guitar songs. But when we showed up to rehearsals, I ran behind the drum kit first. I'm not really sure why. And Mark strapped on a guitar and plugged into an amp, and we wrote a song."

However, she wasn't fully satisfied playing the drums. "We did some more writing, and after a little while I was really missing a melodic instrument. So I cooked up the idea that if I put a keyboard on my left-hand side, I could play melodically from time to time. Once that keyboard was there, my left hand almost never played drums again for seven years. I would play really simple beats—almost like drum-machine or hip-hop beats—and with my left hand I would play bass lines on this Yamaha DX7 keyboard wired through a distortion pedal."

Most drummers derive a certain pleasure from playing the drums. They're doing something they enjoy, creating a powerful sound, and the physical act of drumming sends endorphins whizzing around the body. But again, Julie Edwards is the exception. "Sometimes I feel fine after a show," she said. "Occasionally I'm elated—but that is rare. Usually I'm angry after a show. I think it's my personality: I'm a little bit uptight and impatient. I'm kind of like a fighter and an activist, and I've always been that way. And when you feel an emotion, you can attach it to a reason, but I don't think they necessarily go together. Like I could just say I was angry because I didn't like my monitor sound, or because the kick drum was traveling away from me, or something, but I think at the end of the day those things can still be fucked up and I can still enjoy the show. It's just the way I am: even when I was six years old, I remember being in a state of indignation about something."

Edwards's fiery personality is all over Deap Vally's 2013 debut album, *Sistrionix*—especially in the monster beats on the songs "Gonna Make My Own Money" and "Woman of Intention." I asked Edwards if she had been indignant about a particular review of the album, which had mentioned her "cavewoman beats." "Oh, I get that a lot," she said. "Well, maybe I am a cavewoman. I hit hard all the time—that's how I play right now. What I didn't like was when one reviewer said I had a 'fundamental' grasp of the drums. That made me so mad. By that time, I'd been playing for nine years. I've played for a long time, and I have my own style and a level of competence, and I really don't think it's fair to say I have a fundamental grasp. I think the reviewer saw a woman playing the drums and decided that's how a woman is with an instrument."

The word *cavewoman* has been used before, of course, to describe the drumming style of another famous American woman. When Meg White played in the White Stripes, her primal, apparently untutored style was castigated by many critics. However, there are many people who take a different view. Dave Grohl has called her "one of my favorite fucking drummers of all time. Like, nobody fucking plays the drums like that."

Her ex-husband and former bandmate Jack White has said that "when she started to play drums with me, just on a lark, it felt liberating and refreshing. There was something in it that opened me up." Answering her critics on another occasion, he commented: "Her femininity and extreme minimalism are too much to take for some metalheads and reverse-contrarian hipsters. She can do what those with 'technical prowess' can't. She inspires people to bash on pots and pans. For that, they repay her with gossip and judgment."

Clem Burke is another fan. "I think Meg White's great," he told me. "She was perfect for what the White Stripes were doing."

"I always thought Meg White was kinda sexy, you know," said Steven Drozd. "I liked her caveman style of drumming."

"I love Meg's drumming," said Butch Vig. "Her drumming is loose, but when she played with Jack, they had a thing that worked—a push-and-pull thing."

"I really like what Meg White does and the simplicity of it," said Patty Schemel, "and I love that she exists, because it's proof that you don't have to be technical to be an amazing drummer. I believe she's super talented." Schemel teaches young drummers at the Rock 'n' Roll Camp for Girls in Los Angeles in the summer, and uses the White Stripes song "Seven Nation Army" as a valuable teaching aid. The song features Meg beginning with a simple beat on the bass drum and floor tom before she introduces the snare drum, crash cymbal, and hi-hat. "It's such a great song for teaching dynamics, and for demonstrating a basic beat that builds into something," said Schemel. "It's something that they can get right away, and they can feel that they've accomplished something. All the kids know the White Stripes, and it was such a cool band."

There is another stereotype that people like to slap on female drummers, besides the image of the barely competent cave dweller with a fundamental grasp of her instrument. I heard it expressed by a customer standing in a queue at the London Drum Show when he saw a well-built, short-haired woman sit behind a kit on one of the manufacturers' stands and start playing. "You know what I think?" he said to the men around him. "Female drummers are lesbians, aren't they?" I heard evidence of it again during the Foote's discussion, when Bex Wade, a British photographer who works for *Tom Tom*, said that her mother had been telling people that Bex worked for a lesbian drum magazine.

It certainly isn't true that all female drummers are gay; it isn't true of many of the women I interviewed. Debbi Peterson and Julie Edwards have husbands, and others talked about their boyfriends. But Patty Schemel is openly gay (her film, *Hit So Hard*, includes the touching story of the day she came out to her mother in dramatic circumstances), and Jess Bowen has mentioned her girlfriend in interviews. "Well, maybe drums *make* you gay," joked Mindy Abovitz. "No, I don't think it's uncommon for women drummers to be gay. I think it's to do with the fact that whenever you find women defying the norm or breaking down barriers, like female drummers, you find women who are already trailblazing in some way, already defying something."

Julie Edwards echoed Abovitz's thoughts. "Homosexuals forge the pathways," she said, "because they're used to being at odds with everything anyway. They're social pioneers."

I asked Jess Bowen if people had tried to stereotype her as a butch tomboy. "Yeah, sometimes," she said. "I've always been a tomboy, and I grew up being athletic. But I don't consider myself to look like a butchy drummer: I have kept my feminine image. I still have long hair. I've always had this long hair whipping around while I'm playing—it's a kind of trademark."

Other drummers succeed in retaining their femininity behind the kit, despite the fact that they are doing a hot, sweaty job. Anna Prior was featured in British *Vogue* magazine in 2012 as a stylish role model for female drummers. The article, "Percussion Power," featured a full-length photograph of the immaculately styled "flame-haired percussionist" wearing an elegant Yves Saint Laurent jumpsuit, and revealed that she had worn a "sparkling emerald gown" when Metronomy had headlined at London's Royal Albert Hall.

Prior told me that it was not only possible to dress glamorously as a drummer, but it could bring surprising advantages. "My mother, who's a really good seamstress, made some sequined jumpsuits for me, and I was wearing one when we played the Coachella festival recently. We were playing at three P.M., and it's basically in the desert in California, so the sun was incredibly hot—it was about forty degrees [Celsius; 104 degrees Fahrenheit]—but I found the sequins reflected a lot of the sunlight, so I didn't get that hot."

Having discovered that many male drummers are keen

collectors of all kinds of things, including drums, I wondered if that applied to female drummers as well. "Well, I collect empty jam jars," revealed Prior. "I don't know why, but I find them quite beautiful."

Julie Edwards said she collected My Little Pony toys as a child, and she now has a series of collections, including stock-piles of mugs and fridge magnets. "And I've kept every pass we've ever had from each show, and every wristband."

"I used to collect spoons from different states of America," revealed Patty Schemel. "You know—they have the name of the state on them. I had that collection for a long time. I've collected a lot of albums and singles over the years. And I have three drum kits. One of them is a '67 Ludwig that looks just like Ringo Starr's drum kit."

"I can't seem to get rid of any of my drum kits," confessed Jess Bowen. "I have four kits, and I have a fifth one coming. I have this great connection with a drum company, SJC Custom Drums, and I can design kits any way I want, and that has become a passion of mine. That's why I have so many kits, and that's why it's so hard for me to let them go: because I designed them all myself."

I was also looking for evidence among female drummers of tattoo culture, so prevalent among male percussionists. "Well, you're not gonna find any here!" laughed Debbi Peterson. "I don't know what it is with guy drummers and tattoos. I have known younger girl drummers who have tattoos, but it's usually not that many—one on the ankle or one on the shoulder, maybe."

"I do have one, on my right shoulder," said Jess Bowen. "It's a lyric from Jimmy Eat World, a band from Arizona that I'm a big fan of. It says 'Sing while you can,' and it's a metaphor for living my life the way I want to, and to the fullest extent."

"I got one of my first tattoos when I was in Hole and we finished our first tour of the States," said Patty Schemel. "And I just started decorating my arms. I don't know why; I guess it's just part of being a drummer. I have John Bonham's runes—the three circles—and an Asian design on my left arm."

But tattoos might not be a great idea for many other female drummers, according to Mindy Abovitz. "Women sometimes have a hard time getting the opportunity to play the drums, and they don't want to rock the boat," she said. "Tattoos might be just another reason to write a woman off."

Abovitz's mission to raise the profile of female drummers has taken several forms. She has organized museum events that turn drumming into performance art, where she and other women play their drums in spaces that are usually reserved for quiet contemplation. When she took over the MoMA PS1 building in New York City in 2013, she had a woman playing a drum kit in the lobby, another playing in the boiler room, one in a conference room, and two on the stairways. "And I had a woman beatboxer traveling between all the drummers. She would beatbox at us, and we would drum back at her."

When the CMJ Music Marathon was running in New York, Abovitz asked female drummers to meet her in Union Square. "I knew that women were coming from all over the world to play in that festival, and I asked them to bring buckets and any other kind of percussion that they had, and I brought buckets. We had about a hundred drummers there, and we played real fucking loud!"

During the discussion at Foote's drum shop, Abovitz told her audience that she had considered another, less ethical means of raising the profile of women drummers. "I think about lying, be-cause the media oftentimes lie, to persuade us that something is true. I could simply print a report and say, 'Women are fifty per-cent of drummers now! It's very normal to play drums if you're a girl'—just to see, if I keep saying that, if I start convincing everybody that that's true, if it actually becomes true.'

Julie Edwards said she expects a rise in that percentage before long, thanks to Meg White. "Meg created a situation where there are so many killer female drummers now," she said, "because they were like nine years old when the White Stripes were huge, so they were like, 'Oh . . . I could be a drummer.' I know of so many young women drummers in LA who are nineteen, twenty, twenty-one, and so good—way past me. So this whole notion that there aren't as many women as men on the drums—it's going to go right out of the window."

Michèle Drees argued that female drum teachers are also making a difference. "I've been teaching for a long time, and half my students are girls. But, more importantly, half are boys, and I think that's going to have more of an impact—because the boys will become fine drummers, and when they see sexist behavior around them, they'll say, 'What's that about? I was taught by a great woman drummer!'"

Raising the profile of women drummers in 2013 was an anonymous white-haired old lady who became an Internet sen-sation. An online film clip showed her playing a version of the Surfaris' 1963 hit "Wipe Out," complete with stick twirling, on a kit at the Coalition Drum Shop in La Crosse, Wisconsin. Within two days, the film had a million people staring slack-jawed at their desktops, laptops, tablets, and smartphones. "We don't know anything about her," shrugged the manager of the shop, Dustin Hackworth, "except that her name is Mary; she comes in, plays 'Wipe Out' for about ten minutes, and leaves. She's awesome."

The search was on for the "mystery grandma drummer," though nobody could confirm that this was actually a woman with grandchildren. She turned out to be sixty-three-year-old Mary Hvizda, who had drummed in many bands in her youth, including the Chantells, the first all-female rock band in La Crosse. She had sold her drum kit back in 1990, she said. Touchingly, the drum shop celebrated her sudden fame—and the amount of publicity she had brought to the business—by giving her a new electronic drum kit. And no, Hvizda had never had any children, so she wasn't even a mother, let alone a grandmother.

A talented drummer—male or female—can impress a lot of people by walking into a drum shop, sitting behind a kit, and laying down a great groove. But there's a much tougher arena for drummers—a place in which every single beat and cymbal strike is analyzed and picked over, a place where drummers either succeed or fail. I was becoming aware that I needed to consider how drummers behaved in that highly demanding arena. It was time to enter the recording studio, and to look at the skills that some of the best studio drummers use to survive.

5

STUDIO MADNESS

No matter how sparkling and sophisticated the manufacturers make them, no matter how many nifty bells and whistles they stick on them, there is no escaping the fact that drums are the most primitive musical instrument devised by mankind. But "primitive" certainly does not mean "simple," and all kinds of problems emerge when this ancient, complex instrument comes into direct contact with the latest recording technology. It has been happening for the best part of a century, and it looks as if it will continue for a very long time to come. Musicians, producers, and engineers have spent billions of studio hours and squillions of record-company dollars trying to record drums to their satisfaction, fiddling and adjusting and tinkering until they find something approaching the sound they want. Sometimes, nipping off to find the Holy Grail might be a piece of cake by comparison.

For this reason, drummers usually need to possess a quality that we don't usually associate with snare whackers, tom pounders, and cymbal smashers. Very often, in the recording studio, they need to have the patience of a saint. And not just any old saint, but Saint Monica herself—the patron saint of patience and perseverance.

At least two of the main problems with recording drums stem from the fact that the drum kit is really a collection of instruments, rather than a single instrument. One problem turns out to be one of the qualities that makes a kit so appealing: its broad tonal range, from the biggest, deepest bass drum to the tiniest, tinniest cymbal. Another difficulty is the sheer number of different ways the drums can be recorded. For example, you can use just one or two microphones to pick up the sound of the kit, or you can use a microphone for every single component of the kit: one for the snare drum, one for the bass drum, one for the crash cymbal, one for the cowbell, and so on and so forth. If you really fancy, you can use two or more mikes for some components. Then you have all the nerdy, techy business of which types of microphone to use. Studios over the years have advocated hundreds of "right ways" to record a kit, some of which are laughable now. For instance, in the early days at Decca Studios in London, engineers refused to mike up the bass drum because they believed it was just there to keep the band in time, and not to be heard on recordings.

In addition to all those miking decisions, you need to decide which drums you're going to use. Does this kit sound better for the song or album you plan to record than this one? Thousands of different kits have been made over the years, and thousands of them have been customized and personalized by drummers, and you don't have a long enough life to try them all. And where is the best part of the studio to record that particular drum kit? The proliferating permutations of kit choice and recording setup are potentially mind-boggling.

In the early days of Motown, drummers didn't have the luxury of choosing exactly the right drums for the track. They played the drums that happened to be in the studio, and the first in-house sets for Motown's Detroit studio were mixtures of secondhand drums of different brands. There may have been some reluctance to purchase shiny new sets for the studio because the first Motown drummer, William "Benny" Benjamin, was notorious for sneaking into the studio to grab bits of kit and take them to the pawn shop for cash. Another Motown drummer, Uriel Jones, once recounted that Benjamin was late for a session one day, and a fellow musician—a vibraphone player—offered to sit in on drums in his place. There was a sound baffle placed in front of the kit, and when he went behind it, he discovered a big empty space where the kit had been. "Benny had come in the night before," said Jones, "and convinced the night watchman that the set was his, and he pawned them."

It is still possible to spend days in the studio to find the "right" drum sound before the drummer has even recorded a single thwack or bonk. The producer Phil Spector, famous for his Wall of Sound, once suggested that the quest for drum sounds contributed to his unstable mental condition, admitting that in the 1960s, "if I couldn't get a drum sound I'd go crazy. I'd go out of my mind, spend five or six hours trying to get a drum sound. And it's really hard on the musicians, because they're playing the same thing over and over." But when Spector got it right, as on the gorgeous "Be My Baby" by the Ronettes, it was probably worth it.

There was considerable drum-sound tinkering at Motown, too, where songs were often recorded with two drummers rather than one. Richard "Pistol" Allen, who played on such classics as "I Heard It through the Grapevine" by Marvin Gaye and "Baby Love" by the Supremes, once explained: "We experimented all kinds of ways. We played with the front bass drum head off, with some blankets stuffed in it. They'd stick the mike right in there. For the snare, we'd place the microphone right on the head or sometimes on the side near the air hole. For the floor tom, I'd tune it to a G, and then they'd mike it from underneath with a boom stand." And to achieve a nice, crisp sound, Allen said he would use electrical tape to keep the snare as tight and as close to the drum head as possible.

Drum sounds are a matter of endless debate and disagreement. However, all the important people in the studio, the people who are truly in charge, need to agree on what the "right" drum sound is. And if you're the drummer in a young band that hasn't yet shifted a lot of units for the record company, you might not get a say in what your instrument sounds like on the final recording. Woody Woodmansey was the drummer on the album *Hunky Dory* by David Bowie, who was a quirky, little-known British singer-songwriter when this set of songs was recorded in 1971 at Trident Studios in London. After Woodmansey heard the finished album, he complained that it sounded as if he were hitting cornflake boxes, cardboard packs of cereal, rather than proper drums. (The drum sounds on the tracks "Kooks" and "Queen Bitch" are especially boxy.) Several months later, the band reconvened to record the next Bowie album, which would be the career-launching 1972 work *The Rise and Fall of Ziggy Stardust and the Spiders from Mars*. Knowing how Woodmansey felt about that drum sound, the producer of both *Hunky Dory* and *Ziggy*, Ken Scott, played a little prank on him. Scott recalled years later that on the first day of recording at Trident for the new album, "I sent the tea boy at the studio out to get as many different sizes of Kellogg's Corn

Flakes that he could find, and then I had the roadie set up the drum kit out of purely different-sized Kellogg's Corn Flakes packets. So that's what confronted Woody when he walked in, and he just fell about on the floor laughing."

After everyone calmed down and the drummer's kit was set up for real, Scott and Woodmansey worked hard to ensure that *Ziggy* had an overall stronger drum sound. "That same sound on *Ziggy* wouldn't have worked," said Scott, "because *Ziggy* is edgier and it is a bit livelier . . . We wanted it more rock 'n' roll."

Roger Taylor wanted some rock 'n' roll, too, when Queen entered Trident to record their self-titled debut album in the early 1970s. But he was to be disappointed. "Trident Studios were famous then for this dry, hi-fi-type, dead drum sound, which was very Americanized," he told me. "In those days that was the thing, to have this dry sound, and that's exactly what I didn't want. So it was hard for me to get over that on the first album, and I never got the sound I wanted. I had a better sound on the demo tapes we did before the album, which was much more open and natural sounding. I just started to get the sound I wanted with the second album, *Queen II*."

Taylor achieved one of his favorite drum sounds in Queen's oeuvre with the song "Crazy Little Thing Called Love," which was No. 1 on the Billboard Hot 100 for four weeks in 1980. The number, Freddie Mercury's tribute to Elvis Presley, was recorded at Musicland Studios in Munich and had a suitably 1950s rockabilly feel. "It was recorded in a nice room which was just right, with four very simple mikes, and nothing too closely miked, so it had a very natural ambience," said Taylor. "We were working for the first time with a producer called Mack, a very talented guy who had worked with Giorgio Moroder. He seemed to know the sound we wanted, and he got it very quickly. I think ambient mikes are the most important mikes for the drums. You don't need fifteen mikes to mike a drum kit, but a lot of people do use them."

In 2014, Elbow's sixth studio album, *The Take Off and Landing of Everything*, became the band's first album to top the UK album charts. Their drummer, Richard Jupp, told me how they had been recording part of it at Peter Gabriel's Real World Studios in Box, Wiltshire, when he had embarked on a lengthy quest with a studio engineer for the perfect bass-drum sound. "I was trying all these different kick drums—a Yamaha, a Premier, a Gretsch—just trying to find this particular kick-drum sound. We even bought a little shit one from a local music store, hoping it would have the sound we wanted." Eventually they brought out a very special bass drum—one used by Manu Katché, who had contributed some skillful drumming to Gabriel's breakthrough 1986 album *So*. "And straight away we said, 'Yes! That's the sound!' So I used Manu Katché's kick drum. I was very, very careful with it."

Of course, not all artists are looking for a lovely, pristine sound for the drums. When the Flaming Lips recorded their 1993 album *Transmissions from the Satellite Heart*, they deliberately created a heavily distorted sound on the final track, "Slow•Nerve•Action." "That was the first Lips record I played drums on," said Steven Drozd. "I was really wanting to do some over-the-top distorted drums, and on that song the drums are just utterly distorted to the point where it's obviously some kind of effect. And after we did that track, we liked the distorted drums so much, we would go back to that from time to time." Six years later, the Lips' ninth album, *The Soft Bulletin*, kicked off with a glorious clattering drum sound, introducing the song "Race for the Prize." "The song has these 1970s soft-rock elements, with strings and a harp and stuff like that," explained Drozd, "and I wanted to mix all that with some heavy, John Bonham–sounding drums. I was pleased with how that came out."

Drums like that would have been frowned on by many recording personnel in the 1960s and '70s. In fact, it was fashionable then for studio killjoys to ask drummers to damp down some of their drums, to prevent them from ringing out too loudly. For Pink Floyd's debut album, *Piper at the Gates of Dawn*, recorded in EMI's Abbey Road Studios, the producer Norman Smith placed some special dampers over Nick Mason's drum heads: tea towels, rectangles of fabric that are more commonly used to dry dishes. "I personally like the damping of drums," Mason told me. "What I like to do is damp them right down, and then put some reverb on them."

Ringo Starr enthusiastically adopted the Abbey Road tea-towel policy for his later work with the Beatles. Film footage of the band in the studio from 1968, such as a clip of them recording "Hey Bulldog," clearly shows some cloth action. Before he started using tea towels, Starr would modify his snare drum by attaching a cigarette pack to it. As he explained in a 2007 interview, "It was too bright. I've always liked a deep sound, and so I put my pack of cigarettes on it, to take it down a notch. Then I started putting tea towels on top of everything. Then I put towels on every drum. It gave it that deeper quality."

Finding the right drum sound is one thing, but reaching agreement on exactly what the drummer plays is another. This can also be a protracted business, as various ideas may be tried out and rejected, accepted, or adapted. In 1975, Paul Simon was working in a small recording studio on Broadway in New York, laying down tracks for his album *Still Crazy after All These Years*. He was working on the song "50 Ways to

Leave Your Lover," but the drums weren't quite right, particularly at the beginning of the song.

Fortunately, the drummer was the session genius Steve Gadd, who started working on some interesting patterns between takes, using his left-hand stick on the hi-hat, his feet on the hi-hat pedal and bass drum, and an almost military-style snare-drum part. Paul Simon and his coproducer, Phil Ramone, liked what they heard, and Gadd tried his new pattern in the intro. The unusual feel of this drum part lends the song an atmosphere and a gravitas it may not otherwise have had, balancing the triteness of lyrics like "Hop on the bus, Gus" and "Make a new plan, Stan." Asked years later if he was amazed that he had created such a classic drum part, admired by thousands of drummers, the modest Gadd replied: "I'm grateful, of course. Amazed? I don't know if I'm amazed . . . Actually, yeah, I am amazed. You know, I just went in as a sideman, and came out with this piece of music that everybody talks about. You never think that's going to happen. When you go in to do a session, you just want to make the songs work for the artist. You don't think about anything other than that."

Finding the right drum part is often more of a collaborative process. A few years ago, the prolific British session player Ash Soan received a call from the producer Fraser T Smith, asking him to play on the new album by Adele—the record that became the British singer's multiplatinum smash hit, *21*, which topped the album charts in both the UK and the USA in 2011 and became Amazon's best-selling album ever. Soan went along to Smith's studio in Fulham, west London, where he was surprised to find Adele herself. "That's unusual, because for most of the drum sessions I do, the artist isn't there," he explained. "But I walked in, and there she was, sitting on a stool and having a cup of tea. She asked me what other artists I'd played for, and I mentioned Will Young, and she told me how much she loved Will Young." Soan listened to the track "Set Fire to the Rain," which had some very rough drums on it as a guide. "And she said, 'I hear this sort of military snare drum,' and she sang to me the kind of thing she wanted. So I was working on a few little ideas, and suddenly I saw her through the glass, standing up and sticking both thumbs up. I listen to that song now and I can hear her drum part very clearly; it was very much her idea."

Roger Taylor recalled the process of trial and error that often led to the drum part for a Queen song. "We would run through a song," he said, "and if the drum part wasn't working, it was almost always because I was playing too much. The thing to do was just to simplify it, so I would come to the part by a process of elimination, really." Now and then, he recalled, he would act on suggestions from his bandmates, including Freddie Mercury and guitarist Brian May. "Brian would sometimes ask me to play things that don't really work on drums, and we'd have to compromise somewhere."

In the experimental hotbed of the recording studio, drummers occasionally go beyond the conventional drum kit in search of the perfect sound. The Queen song "Seaside Rendezvous" required a "tap-dancing" effect, explained Taylor. "So I did a tap-dance routine with Freddie, just using a couple of thimbles on the metal bit of the recording desk." Although many listeners imagine that the almighty beat of Queen's classic anthem "We Will Rock You" was created on record using drums, it was in fact achieved by members of the band vigorously bashing their feet onto a drum riser at Wessex Sound Studios in London. "We were sitting on the back of the grand piano and just stomping and clapping," explained Taylor.

However, Taylor had to interpret the stomps using ordinary drums when they played the song live.

"On our album *A Saucerful of Secrets*," said Nick Mason of Pink Floyd, "we tried hitting a cymbal and then lowering it on a string into a bucket of water. You get some weird sounds off that." The Floyd were serial sonic adventurers: following the enormous global success of their 1973 masterwork, *The Dark Side of the Moon*, the band frittered away untold amounts of studio time on a project involving everyday objects instead of proper musical instruments. The resulting album, which never even came close to completion, was provisionally titled *Household Objects*. "We did a lot of hitting and banging things around that time," said Mason. "I remember we used an ax against a lump of wood, thinking it might be a good bass-drum effect. It was a waste of time."

But found objects can sometimes work well for discerning drummers. In the 1970s, Bill Bruford found a strange cymbal in a rehearsal-room trash can, presumably abandoned by the unknown drummer of another band, and he adopted it for his kit. It had been bent so that it would fit in the trash can, and, as Bruford later wrote, "Its maltreatment had bequeathed it this fabulous trashy sound with a very short, fast decay. It looked so sad; I took pity on it and we fell in love." The cymbal can be heard clattering away in the song "One More Red Nightmare" on King Crimson's extraordinary 1974 album *Red*. Not long after that, the cymbal split and was consigned to the trash again.

Glenn Kotche, drummer with the Chicago-based band Wilco, was browsing one day in a specialist hubcap-and-wheel store in Libertyville, Illinois, and striking the merchandise to see what sounds he could produce. Like Goldilocks, he eventually found something that was just right: an inexpensive

Chrysler hubcap. Kotche put it to good use on Wilco's 2002 album *Yankee Hotel Foxtrot*, and it features among the drums, cymbals, and other bashed objects on the atmospheric opening track, "I Am Trying to Break Your Heart."

During the recording of Blur's 2003 album *Think Tank*, the producer Ben Hillier assembled a unique set of percussion for the band's drummer, Dave Rowntree. "At one point during the recording of that album," recalled Hillier, "Dave said to me, 'I'm really bored with playing a drum kit. I've played a drum kit on every bloody album that we've done. I'm quite happy to play drums, but not a drum kit.' And for the first single, 'Out of Time,' I wanted a simple drum part, and I didn't want it to be rocky. Dave found a djembe drum and suggested using it as a snare drum for that track. But he had to hit the djembe with a stick in a very specific way, with just the right velocity at the right point, to get the right sound. So because the djembe put him under this pressure, he had to concentrate on this very simple beat. For the bass drum on that track, Damon Albarn had a big old calfskin bass drum, like a Salvation Army marching drum, and we managed to wedge a bass-drum pedal on it. When you hit it, the sound went on for ages. We had that really loud in Dave's headphones: he didn't hit it a lot, because it almost deafened him when he did! And the only other thing we gave him was a ride cymbal made out of a thirty-inch gong." Sure enough, this peculiar drum setup gives "Out of Time," which reached No. 5 on the UK singles chart, its own special charm.

The days of percussive adventurousness in the studio are far from over. In 2013, while recording their third album, *Holy Fire*, the British band Foals decided they needed some fresh animal bones to use as percussion, so they acquired some bits of cow and sheep from a nearby butcher. "That was an idea we had early on," confirmed their drummer, Jack Bevan. "We were recording the album in London, but we wanted to do everything we could to make us feel like we weren't in London. So we covered up all the windows so that there was no natural light coming in, and we got a lot of plants into the studio, so we felt we were in the jungle or something. And the thing with the bones was semi-tongue-in-cheek, but we were trying to make ourselves feel as if we were working on something magical. But first we had to boil these bones over and over again to get all the decaying meat off them. And then, when we eventually put a microphone in front of them and hit them together, it sounded pathetic—like a couple of pencils being hit together. I think, just to make it all worthwhile, we left the odd bone-click on the record somewhere. But for future reference, I'd say to any drummers out there: don't bother with bones. Percussively, they're awful."

You don't necessarily have to play pretend like Foals: you could actually travel to an exotic location to record, but this can bring its own special problems. When the Police arrived to record their fifth album, *Synchronicity*, in George Martin's AIR Studios on the island of Montserrat in 1982, they found that Stewart Copeland's drums had an unappealing, rather dead sound when he played in the main studio area. The producer, Hugh Padgham, decided to put the drummer in the dining room instead, using a camera to monitor him from the control room. It was also a useful means of keeping Copeland physically away from Sting, as the two of them weren't getting on. But recording at night proved to be a bad idea: there was no glass in the dining-room windows, and the tree frogs outside made a god-awful noise that was picked up by the microphones. And during the heat of the day in this non-air-conditioned room, Copeland would perspire heavily, causing his drumsticks to shoot out of his hands and his headphones to slip off. Padgham took drastic action, taping the sticks to the poor man's hands and the headphones to his head.

Of course, you don't have to record in a studio at all: you can find a more sonically unpredictable building and install all your gear there instead. In 1977, Aerosmith recorded their fifth album, *Draw the Line*, at a former convent—the Cenacle in Westchester, New York—and Joey Kramer had his drums set up on the altar of the building's echoey, high-ceilinged chapel. Six years earlier, Led Zeppelin had obtained unforgettable results at an old English manor house when they moved in to Headley Grange in Hampshire to record *Led Zeppelin IV* with the Rolling Stones' mobile studio. This three-story stone building, with its steeply pitched roof, had been built in 1795 as a workhouse to accommodate and occupy local poor people, and had later become a private residence. Jimmy Page later remembered it as "a pretty austere place": the heating wasn't working, and while he loved the atmosphere of the house, his bandmates "got a bit spooked out" by it. "There was a bit of toing and froing over who was having what bedroom," he recalled.

Initially working in the main drawing room, Jimmy Page, Robert Plant, John Bonham, and John Paul Jones recorded tracks such as "Rock and Roll" and "The Battle of Evermore." During the band's stay at the Georgian workhouse, they took a fateful delivery: a fresh new Ludwig drum kit for Bonham. He was eager to try it out, but the recording room was in use at the time, so a drum technician set the kit up in the building's impressive entrance hall, beneath the grand staircase. When Bonham started playing the kit, the band and the engineer Andy Johns were taken aback by the sound. Hanging two microphones from the second floor, they captured an awesome new drum sound for the album's closing song, "When the Levee Breaks." They didn't even need to mike the bass drum.

When I interviewed him thirty-nine years later, Page was still proud of that drum sound. "You can hear the ambience of the rooms on that album," he said, explaining that the idea had its roots in the music he grew up with. "On the early records that I used to listen to, Chicago blues records and rockabilly records that were recorded with minimal microphones, you could really hear the sound bouncing off the walls in the room, and you could almost imagine the size of the room. What we did at Headley Grange was chart new ground in recording techniques. I'm absolutely convinced that we pushed the boundaries, with this extension of ambience into this cavernous space. After that, everyone was trying to replicate what we'd done."

But who would have expected Simon & Garfunkel to get the jump on Led Zeppelin? In late 1968, more than two years before *Led Zeppelin IV* was recorded, the American folk duo were doing some intensive recording in New York City. For the classic song "The Boxer," Paul Simon, Art Garfunkel, and the producer Roy Halee fancied a big drum sound for the song's wordless "lie-la-lie" chorus. They didn't have a big old Georgian manor house to play with, but they found what they were looking for on an upper floor of the Columbia Records building—and scared the living daylights out of an old man who was working there. The prolific session drummer Hal Blaine, who played on the track, later told the story. "Roy Halee would walk around clapping his hands, looking for kind of an echo effect," he said. "And we were at Columbia in New York—on the sixth floor, I believe it was—and from the studio you kind of walked out and down, and it went around almost like a ramp to the elevator. And he found a spot right in front of the elevator that had a tremendous echo, and he loved it. This was a Sunday, and we were doing 'The Boxer,' and they had me set up . . . I set up two giant tom-toms right in front of the elevator where Ray had found the great echo. And, of course, there was a line coming out for my headset, so I was obviously the only one who could hear the music . . . 'Lie-la-lie, POW! Lie-la-lie-la-lie-la-lie, lie-la-lie, POW! . . .' And at one point my hands came down to hit that smack, and the elevator door opened, and there was an elderly gentleman in a security-guard uniform. And I guess he thought that he just got shot! It was like a shotgun, POW!"

Thirty years later, the rock band Garbage alarmed several more innocent Americans. Desiring some special acoustics for their second album, *Version 2.0*, the band hauled their drums and some other equipment out of their studio in Madison, Wisconsin, into an old industrial building elsewhere in the city. "A guy we know found this old deserted building about six or seven blocks away from the studio," explained Garbage drummer and coproducer Butch Vig. "It was the old Madison Candy Company. We went by to check it out, and it was huge, with brick walls and wood floors. We spent all day setting up, and we started recording at night."

Unfortunately, the building was on a street that was largely residential, it wasn't soundproofed—in fact, some of the windows were broken, allowing the loud music to leak out into the street—and some of the neighbors started kicking up a fuss. "Within about two minutes the cops showed up, and said we were making too much noise and we had to stop right away," said Vig. "But then one of the cops recognized me and realized we were in Garbage, and asked what we were doing. I said we were recording some new songs, and asked if he could just let us carry on for a while. He said, 'Okay, man, I'll give you a couple of hours. We'll look the other way if you can just get it done.' But he said we couldn't go past ten P.M. or something. So I ended up doing three takes of each song and then going straight on to the next song, and we decided we'd just edit it later.

"We used a lot of stuff from the Madison Candy Company on the album: those drums went on five or six songs. Not only that, but when we went on tour for *Version 2.0*, almost all the samples that I triggered onstage were taken from that place. They later gutted that whole building and put offices in there. So what was a cool warehouse, with this gigantic, intense-sounding room, is now all corporate offices." Sadly, there isn't even a tiny plaque on the building to commemorate it as the site of a great 1990s recording adventure.

It wasn't the first time that Butch Vig had shown creative flair in the business of recording drums. Wearing his producer hat in the late 1980s, he recorded a succession of punk bands at Smart Studios in Madison, including Tar Babies, Killdozer, and Laughing Hyenas. "The songs they played were really fast," he recalled, "and it always really annoyed me that these drummers would play the hi-hat really loud, but they would just tap on the snare. So I would take an empty pizza box and cut a little triangle out of one corner, and I would put the box over the hi-hat, leaving just this little triangle where they could hit the hi-hat. It worked!"

In 1991, when Vig came to produce Nirvana's classic album *Nevermind* at Sound City studios in Los Angeles, he modified Dave Grohl's kit to get a special drum sound. "I wanted that record to sound like a band playing together in a room—a real band and a real performance," explained Vig. To beef up the sound of the bass drum, he added a couple of extra bass-drum shells to the front of it. "I wanted to get an extension on the low end of the sound of the kick drum—more of a *whooomph*. So we built this kind of tunnel. It brought the kick drum out by another four or five feet, so we were able to put an ambient mike pretty far away from the kick, and then isolate it so it didn't pick up the sound of the cymbals. When you turned that up, you got this big *whooomph* that worked really great. It wasn't a fancy thing: it was totally rigged up. I think it was all wrapped with blankets and duct tape." Vig refuses to take full credit for that almighty sound. "At Sound City there was incredible drum room, which sounded great. And then, of course, you had Dave Grohl's impeccable playing. He's just a monster on the drum kit."

There have been plenty of other occasions when recording studios have become drum workshops, with technicians reinventing the wheel and rebuilding drum kits to get the perfect sound. When they worked together on the Michael Jackson song "Billie Jean" in 1982, the producer Quincy Jones asked the engineer Bruce Swedien to bring some "sonic personality" to the track. "What I ended up doing," Swedien said later, "was building a drum platform and designing some special little things, like a bass-drum cover and a flat piece of wood that goes between the snare and the hi-hat. The bottom line is that there aren't many pieces of music where you can hear the first three or four notes of the drums and immediately tell what the piece of music is. But I think that is the case with 'Billie Jean'—and that I attribute to sonic personality."

The drummer who played those famous beats was the highly experienced American jazz and funk player Ndugu Chancler, who recalled the session more than thirty years later. "Oh, yes, I remember that one like it was yesterday," Chancler told me. "It was my wife's birthday on the day we recorded it. We were having a party at our house, and I had arranged everything for it, but I came late to the party because I was recording 'Billie Jean.' We took the toms off the drum set for that song, so the ambience of the toms was gone and you could zero in on the sound of the kick drum, the snare, and the hi-hat. We got that old R&B sound. It didn't need anything but that groove."

Despite his phenomenal solo career and his longtime membership in the band Genesis, Phil Collins has found the time to play a wide variety of drum sessions. One of the most important and memorable of them was for the multimillion-selling Band Aid charity single "Do They Know It's Christmas?" in November 1984. The musician Bob Geldof had been spurred into action by news coverage of famine in Ethiopia, and had teamed up with Midge Ure to write the song. Geldof then persuaded many famous British singers and musicians to assemble for its recording at SARM West Studios in London's Notting Hill.

"I was finishing my album *No Jacket Required* at the Townhouse in London," recalled Collins, "and one night I got a call from Bob Geldof, asking if I'd seen the news about Ethiopia. I said I hadn't, because I'd been working, and he said he wanted to do something about it, and he wanted a famous drummer. It wasn't like 'I want you because you're good'—he wanted someone who was going to bring some publicity and newsworthiness to it. So I said, 'Well, yeah, okay. Who else is doing it?' And he mentioned Sting and George Michael and Midge Ure. So I said yes, and I went to the session not knowing really what to expect, and not knowing the track. And by that point, everybody and their aunt was there! There was great excitement.

"I set the drums up in the studio, and I remember Jon Moss, the drummer in Culture Club, sitting quite anxiously, waiting for the master to play," laughed Collins. "Everybody sat round and watched everybody else do their bit. We were all in the control room when Bono sang, and Sting and Paul Young and Boy George sang. I heard the song in the control room once or twice, and then I went out to play it. And I was a bit nervous, because all these people were watching. It was other musicians watching, which isn't the same as a normal audience. And Midge said, 'Well, that's it, that's great, that's all we need.' I said, 'Oh, I'll just do it one more time.' They didn't have a lot of time, but I persuaded them to let me do it again. And I still have no idea whether they used the first take or the second one. I just played what I felt was right for the song—you know, you just make it up as you go along."

But drumming can turn into a nightmare if you can't deliver exactly what the people in charge require. On Montserrat in 1982, the sweaty, frog-plagued Stewart Copeland reportedly struggled for weeks to give Sting the beat he wanted for "Every Breath You Take," that smash-hit anthem for stalkers everywhere. Copeland's adherence to the band's usual reggae feel was met with disapproval from Sting, who wanted a more conventional rock beat for the song. And when David Bowie came to record his 1980 hit "Ashes to Ashes," with its distinctive tricksy, bouncy rhythm, he was so unhappy with the performance of the drummer Dennis Davis that the singer demonstrated exactly what he wanted using a chair and a cardboard box, and Davis went home to learn the part for the following day.

In the 1970s, producers and engineers found another stick to beat drummers with: the click track, an electronic pulse played in the studio to keep the drummer in time. Bill Bruford has written scathingly about the use of click tracks in the late 1970s and early 1980s: "In an era when producers were increasingly uncertain about what was or was not 'right' in drumming, here was scientific proof, measurable, visible on a screen, with which the poor drummer could be berated as his hapless bass drum flammed with the click from the machine, an unforgivable seven milliseconds late (or early). Recording sessions in the 80s were peopled with drummers terrified of being humiliated in front of their colleagues because they couldn't play 'in time.' The producer's lip would curl into a sneer as he stopped the take after about two measures, pointed to the drummer, and suggested he 'tighten it up with the click.' Take 2, of course, only got worse."

Interviewed in 2001, Dave Grohl said he was "heartbroken" when he was asked to play to a click track for the first time in Nirvana. The band had played a few takes of the song "Lithium," but the producer wasn't happy: "Butch Vig brought us in and said to me, 'You might want to think about using a click track,' and I immediately felt worthless and horrible. But I learned that as long as you can play within the click track you can still achieve a natural feel. I'm convinced, and I used to be a purist and think, 'John Bonham never used a click track!' But I think it depends on what you are trying to achieve. If there's something that you want to sound completely chaotic, and has not only a dynamic but a tempo dynamic that moves up and down—okay. If there's something that you want to be completely solid—okay. I'm not opposed to trying new things."

Debbi Peterson, drummer with the Bangles since the all-woman band was formed in 1980, told me about her early aversion to the click. "What used to really drive me crazy in the eighties," she said, "was you had to be perfectly in time with the click track, because the producer wanted to make sure the drumming was completely spot-on. There was no flow allowed, no inaccurate humanness. That was driving me crazy, because to me that just took the organicness out of the song and out of the band, and made it very stiff." Nevertheless, after many years of playing with a click track, she confessed that she had now mastered the technique: "I'll sit down with a click track now, and I'll just get into this zone where I don't even hear the click track, because I'm spot-on. I'm kinda freakishly good!"

The click track is just a tool to help drummers, and it doesn't have to be strictly obeyed, according to the top American session drummer Russ Miller. "On an instrument like a saxophone or guitar, you can sustain the notes you play," said Miller. "But a drumbeat is a drumbeat, and drummers have to create note sustain mentally. If I want to lengthen the sustain, I'll lay back a little bit and play after the click. If I want to shorten the sustain, I'll play right on top of the click." Drum sustain is an illusion in the minds of the audience, he explains: hearing a piece of music, people will notice the difference between the strict timing of the piece and the playing of the drummer; if he is slightly behind the natural rhythm, that creates the effect of "long" drumbeats.

Miller has been known to vary the sustain of his beats within the same song, as when he played on Nelly Furtado's international smash hit "I'm Like a Bird." "They brought me a demo where a drum machine was basically playing the same thing through the whole song. But they wanted the verses to feel nervous and small, and the chorus to explode and be big. They had no way of saying, 'Do this' or 'Do that,' so I had to interpret all of that. So I decided to use the ability to control the feel of the music. In the verse, I played on top of the click to shorten the notes, to create a sense of urgency. Then, coming into the chorus, I left a hole in the fill, so that during that rest I could adjust the note sustain, lay my playing back a bit, to make the chorus really open up and feel big."

When drummers talk about click tracks, they will often mention another, even more fiendish innovation in the same breath. It was around the late 1960s that drummers began looking nervously over their shoulders, suddenly aware of a new threat to their livelihoods. This was the drum machine, or "rhythm box," which used synthesized sounds to emulate real drum and cymbal sounds and could be programmed to produce a variety of rhythms and speeds. Unlike human drummers, this innovation didn't require food, praise, or session fees—just small quantities of electric power.

Drum machines sneaked into the singles charts on "Saved by the Bell," the 1969 solo hit by Robin Gibb of the Bee Gees; "Somebody's Watching You" by Little Sister in 1970; and the 1972 integrationist hit "Why Can't We Live Together" by Timmy Thomas. Little Sister were backup vocalists for Sly and the Family Stone, and it was Sly Stone who had given their hit song the percussive backing of a Maestro Rhythm King (MRK-1) machine. Stone and his studio engineers loved the MRK-1 so much, they nicknamed it the Funk Box, and the machine enjoyed an extensive outing on Sly and the Family Stone's 1971 album *There's a Riot Goin' On*. On this landmark soul recording—a musical reply to Marvin Gaye's earlier question, *What's Going On*—the beats of the Funk Box sometimes combine with real drums to create an intriguing new texture. The Germans also cottoned on to drum machines around this time, though with less soulful results: the avant-garde band Can used one on their 1971 album *Tago Mago*, and the electronic group Kraftwerk featured one on *Kraftwerk 2*, released the following year.

Phil Collins said he had changed his mind about the merits of drum machines at an important juncture of his career. "When Genesis played in Japan in 1978 for the first time," he recalled, "the Roland company gave us each a drum machine, which was the CR-78, fresh off the conveyor belt. It was more flexible than most drum machines then, because you could record little bits of drumming yourself and use them. Originally I said, 'I don't need one, because I'm a drummer.' But that was before I started writing my first solo album, *Face Value*. My divorce coincided with me coming back from Japan, and I was inspired and started to write a lot of songs on my own at that point—much more than I'd done in Genesis until then. And it was useful to have something to keep time to when I was writing, so I said, 'I don't know where that drum machine is, but I wouldn't mind using it.' So I got the CR-78 back and started fooling around with it, and I used that on all the demos I recorded, which became the basis for the album. The drum machine was crucial to tracks like 'In the Air Tonight.'" The CR-78 has a brooding presence right from the beginning of "In the Air Tonight," but of course the song is more famous for its real drums—specifically the monster Collins drum explosion that arrives more than three minutes in.

The CR-78 attracted the attention of other contemporary musicians. Chris Stein and Jimmy Destri of Blondie bought one in New York. Lead singer Debbie Harry later recalled: "Chris and Jimmy were always going over to 47th Street, where all the music stores were, and one day they came back with this little rhythm box, which went 'tikka tikka tikka.'" Blondie took the gadget into the studio when they started recording their classic album *Parallel Lines* with the British producer Mike Chapman, and they were playing with it when Chapman remarked on how much he liked the sound. At the time, they were trying to make one of their older songs work—a number they had messed around with unsuccessfully many times. The dusty old song and the shiny new toy were eventually combined to create the smash "Heart of Glass," which would top the charts in both the US and the UK.

I discussed the making of that record with Clem Burke. "We had already recorded that song in the early seventies," he said, "and I think the idea was that it was supposed to be a reggae song, though I had no idea how to play reggae. When we met with Mike Chapman, after we'd gone through the songs that the various members of the band had written, he asked if we had anything else, and we gave him this song."

It was decided that the track should feature a combination of the CR-78 and real drums. The drum machine was linked up to a synthesizer, but these were the days before MIDI (Musical Instrument Digital Interface), the studio system that automatically synchronizes instruments and saves countless studio headaches. "You couldn't MIDI the kick drum to the synthesizer program then," said Burke, "so we laid down the synthesizer track, and then in order to synchronize the drums we had to do it piecemeal—measure by measure, more or less. We were manually triggering the synthesizer and I was playing the bass drum in sync, but after a bar or two the triggering would go out of phase, so then you'd have to begin again. But I always hear about 'the terrible, arduous process' we went through to record 'Heart of Glass,' and that's not how I recollect it. I enjoyed it all: I was never inhibited by the studio." For drumming inspiration on that song, Burke turned to another recent example of white disco. "I recall trying to do that song and thinking of 'Night Fever' by the Bee Gees. I really liked organic dance music, and if you listen to the drums and the hi-hat on 'Heart of Glass,' they're very reminiscent of 'Night Fever.'"

I told Burke I was always fascinated by the instrumental breaks in the song, which mix standard four-beat bars with three-beat bars; it sounds as if it has several beats missing. "Right," he said, "which is not what you would normally do for a dance song. You know, I think it might have been the tape editing that was responsible for that. But I'll take the credit for it!"

Drum machines became much more sophisticated and useful when they were able to use sampled versions of real recorded beats, rather than approximate synthesized versions. A 1982 interview with the late British producer Mickie Most, who produced the Animals' classic version of "The House of the Rising Sun" and many hits for the folk singer Donovan and the pop band Hot Chocolate, found him reveling in the possibilities these machines provided. "It's not going to be long before we won't actually need a musician in the studio," he announced, chillingly but inaccurately. "The errors come from musicians, and with electronic equipment that's available now, we're using machines for drums which no drummer could ever equal either in sound or technique. And they don't sound sterile, because they have as much movement in them as in an actual player—they're on a pulse, and if you feel the song needs to slightly speed up, or get more dramatic in the chorus, you can include that information and it'll do it. I really like that idea, because it means I don't have to spend two or three hours searching for a bass-drum sound, because I know it's already on my chip—I've got every drum sound I want, from Led Zeppelin's to Steve Gadd's to Pink Floyd's. And to me it seems that's the way records must go."

Debbi Peterson recalled how drum machines became fashionable in the decade that followed. "In the eighties there was a lot of 'Bring the drum machines in.' A lot of drummers I know were being replaced by machines, and the producers were very keen on it," she told me. When the band came to record their quirky hit "Walk Like an Egyptian," Peterson was unhappy that the beat was to be provided by a machine instead of her drum kit. "That wasn't how I was seeing the band," she explained. "I was seeing the band as 'We're all musicians; we all play.' Now I see it in a different light, but at the time I felt like I was going to be replaced. It was like, 'This can't happen! We're organic—we don't need this mechanical interference.' But I went, 'Okay, I'll work with this, I'm gonna try this.' So I worked with the producer, David Kahne, on the drum-machine part."

The Bangles' megahit "Eternal Flame" had "a little tick-tock drum-machine thing" on it too, said Peterson. "But I played a little bit of snare drum at the end of the song too, because our manager, Miles Copeland, came into the studio when we were recording it and said, 'Okay, girls, it's a really good song, but y'know, if you really want it to be a big smash hit, you gotta have drums at the end of the song.'"

Other drummers have expressed their disapproval of drum machines and the tyranny of click tracks. Topper Headon of the Clash once complained: "I hate electronics, because it's not what music is about. People like to dance because the rhythm is connected to the beat of their heart. Drumming is like a heartbeat. When you get excited, your heartbeat speeds up, so why shouldn't a drummer? It's all part of dynamics to be able to speed up, especially when you're playing live. On the other hand, if you tie yourself down to a machine, you can't be that loose."

In 1989, Cozy Powell noted: "There's such an overflow of 'machine records' right now; it's just so dreadful, and it seems to me that people these days have forgotten what it's like for a drummer to sit down behind a kit and play a track from start to finish with highs and lows and all the feel that it involves."

Powell continued: "It seems that everybody's trying to get it machine-perfect and the whole idea of the feel of the track has gone out of the window. People have got so used to hearing machines on records that they've forgotten what it's like to hear a drummer in full flow, as it were. There was a survey recently in one of the papers where, out of all the records in the Top 40, only THREE had real drummers playing on them—the rest were all machines, which is a bit of a sad state of affairs."

Sometimes drum machines have been treated in studios like real drum kits—that is to say, they were messed about with, pulled apart, and tinkered with by producers and musicians in search of the right sound. Paul McCartney once told an alarming story about recording the hit "Ebony and Ivory" on Montserrat with Stevie Wonder—whose long list of talents includes drumming. Wonder ended up playing real drums on the song, said McCartney. "But we started off with a rhythm box, one of the first Linn drum machines. He brought it to Montserrat, and, as you know, he's blind. He kept opening the top and fiddling in it, sticking his hand in it. The guys would say, 'Stevie, watch out, man, it's switched on; it's live.' And he'd say, 'Yeah, I know.' Bloody hell! I'd never stick my fingers in there—I'm not mechanical, you know. Stevie just knows what he's doing. So while he's sticking his fingers in there and adjusting stuff, I'm saying, 'I hope he doesn't hit a live wire in there.'"

Since those early days of drum machines, sampled drumbeats have been looped to create drum tracks for countless artists. An early pioneer was the studio engineer Roger Nichols, who worked with Steely Dan and created a beat-looping machine called Wendel, which the band used on their 1980 album *Gaucho*.

"Airbag," the first track of Radiohead's much-garlanded album *OK Computer*, uses an unusual collage of drumbeats. Generally unhappy with the part played on that track by the drummer, Phil Selway, band members manipulated some of his beats using an Apple Mac computer and a sampling machine. As Selway explained, "I went in and drummed for a quarter of an hour, and we took the three seconds' worth of any value out of it, and then put it back together to form this angular track that you don't generally get from programming or loops."

In 2011, the Flaming Lips pushed the envelope by recording a six-hour song, "I Found a Star on the Ground." While it doesn't feature drums for its full duration—it has periodic chilled-out and drumless passages—its long sections of relentless drumming give the impression that one (or both) of the band's two drummers, Steven Drozd and Kliph Scurlock, may have approached the point of exhaustion in the studio. Scurlock left the band in 2014, but not before I asked him about that track.

He explained that the band had had very little time to record it after the Lips' singer, Wayne Coyne, announced it to the press before they had recorded a note. "I think Wayne just gets excited about ideas, and whoever he's talking to he blurts them out, and then it gets printed and we're like, 'Oh, I guess we're doing this, aren't we?' But we had just three or four days between tours to do it. I had to come home and take care of some stuff around the house, so it ended up being Steven. And he had to put it together quickly, so the drums on the track are a less-than-one-minute-long loop of Steven playing."

Sampling your own drumming is one thing; sampling another drummer's playing is another. The most frequently sampled passage of drumming has had such an extensive afterlife that it may now have been heard, in some recycled form, by millions of people several times over. On a cold day in November 1969, James Brown was recording in King Studios, on Brewster Avenue in the Evanston neighborhood of Cincinnati, Ohio, and led his band through an improvised funk workout. At one point he announced that the band should "give the drummer some," and the drummer Clyde Stubblefield enjoyed a drum break of about twenty seconds, basically emphasizing the extremely tasty, infectious beat he had been playing throughout the number. When he played that pattern of beats, Stubblefield would have had no idea that he wasn't just playing for Brown: he was laying down a rhythm for countless artists to come.

After the drum break, Brown paid tribute by declaring over the music that "the name of this tune is 'The Funky Drummer,'" and he repeated the title to hammer it home. The track, which lost its definite article and became "Funky Drummer," was released as a single the following year. But it seemed to attract more attention after it appeared on a compilation album in 1986. Other performers, especially hip-hop artists, loved that drum break so much that they started sampling it for their own records. Public Enemy grabbed it in 1987 for "Bring the Noise" and then came back for more, using it again on "Rebel Without a Pause" and "Fight the Power." Meanwhile, N.W.A put it in their attractively named protest number "Fuck Tha Police," and Run-DMC sampled it for "Run's House." Other artists who have been drawn irresistibly to Stubblefield's 1969 beats include LL Cool J ("Mama Said Knock You Out"), the Beastie Boys ("Three MC's and one DJ"), the Roots ("The Next Movement"), and Doctor Dre ("Let Me Ride"). Some more unlikely uses of "Funky Drummer" have been made by Sinéad O'Connor, My Bloody Valentine, and even the Simpsons.

Stubblefield's drumbeats have been borrowed countless

times, but in many cases he has failed to receive a credit for them, and payment hasn't always been forthcoming either. When artists have paid to use the "Funky Drummer" beat, the royalties have often gone to James Brown or his estate, as he was credited as the writer of the song. Stubblefield's plight was highlighted in 2010 when he appeared in a documentary about the sampling phenomenon, *Copyright Criminals*.

But Stubblefield received some serious respect in 1995 when some musicians who shared his home city of Madison, Wisconsin, came calling. Garbage booked him to actually play drums on the songs "Queer" and "Not My Idea" on their self-titled debut album. "What happened was that we'd bought a couple of CDs with samples on them," said Butch Vig, "and some of them had Clyde Stubblefield's playing taken from James Brown recordings. Some of them sounded cool and some didn't, and I was like, 'Well, the Funky Drummer lives here in Madison. Let's actually get Clyde in to play some real drums.' So he did, and it was amazing to watch him play. It's these little grace notes that he plays on the hi-hat and the snare that give his playing this amazing feel. You don't use a sample when the genius who played the sample lives down the street from you."

Another ubiquitous drum break, sampled over and over again by gangsta rappers and TV commercials, is labeled "the Amen break." It was originally recorded on the B-side of a 1969 single by an R&B band called the Winstons. That B-side was called "Amen, Brother"—hence the name of the break. The original drummer was Gregory C. Coleman, and the way he played, coupled with the pitch of the snare drum, has made it an appealing snatch of percussion for countless artists to borrow, loop, and generally mess around with. Coleman died in Atlanta in 2006 without ever having earned a rusty dime in royalties for the widespread sampling of his legendary snatch of drumming.

But if creating drum tracks by electronic means—using drum machines or sampled beats—is so wonderful, why haven't human drummers become completely redundant in the music business? Why are young people still falling head over heels in love with the idea of whacking drumsticks on snares, toms, bass drums, and cymbals? And why are drum kits still coming off the production line in their thousands?

"It's easy to get an electronic beat going," said Ash Soan, "but what isn't easy is getting a dynamic drum performance that's all joined up, and that works fantastically with the singer and the song. That's why I still get asked to play sessions."

"There's no substitute for real drumming," said Ross Mc-Farlane. "There's something about real drums, about the air moving, about the microphone and the human element that makes a huge difference to the sound. Imagine a great record like 'When the Levee Breaks' by Led Zeppelin, but with a drum machine instead of John Bonham and that big sound. It would be horrible. I was recording recently with the engineer Dom Morley, who won a Grammy for his work on Amy Winehouse's *Back to Black* album. I was playing drums, and I said to Dom, 'You're a great programmer—you could just program all this, couldn't you?' And he said, 'Yeah, but why? It's got to be a real drummer playing a real drum kit. You could program it within an inch of its life, but I could still tell it was a program.'"

"There's something that human beings can do that a machine can't do," said Omar Hakim. "I call it spontaneous imperfection. There's human emotion, and also a drummer brings so many other things to the table—years of influences and experience that come together to create this subtle blend of things that make you unique. Like the fact that I grew up with a father who played swing and bebop, I studied with drummers who taught me all these interesting concepts, and then I had these musical adventures with all these different artists—that's the kind of thing a machine can never replicate." The "subtle blend of things" that makes Hakim unique can be heard especially well on the title track of Weather Report's 1983 album, *Procession*, and on their supercool instrumental cover of Marvin Gaye's "What's Going On" on the 1985 album *Sportin' Life*.

Even Daft Punk, the French duo famous for their electronic music, understand the value of real drums as opposed to programmed beats. The band's hugely successful 2013 album *Random Access Memories* features not one but two great drummers: Omar Hakim and John "JR" Robinson. And unlike the duo's previous albums, it won them five Grammy awards and topped album charts across the world—in the US, the UK, Canada, Mexico, Russia, Spain, Switzerland, Norway, Portugal, Hungary, Finland, Australia, and New Zealand.

Hakim said he found it "very interesting" when this famous electronic outfit contacted him out of the blue. He remembered being called by the producer, composer, and Daft Punk collaborator Chris Caswell. "I thought, Why are they calling me? I initially thought, Okay, maybe they'd like me to help them program some drums, or maybe they want to use electronic drums, because I play Roland V-Drums. But Chris said, 'No, Omar, they want you to play acoustic drums.' They made a very deliberate decision, I think, to have some sessions with a West Coast rhythm section, with John, and then separate sessions with an East Coast rhythm section, with me. John and I both have a signature sound; we have different approaches to the groove. When I got to the studio, I discovered that instead of a typical recording session, it was more of a sampling session, where I helped to create grooves that would be used in the construction of the songs for the album. They had some specific ideas for riffs and bass lines, and we'd learn those and play and develop them."

While real drummers are still appreciated, the business of making records has changed in other ways. Thanks to modern technology and the tight economies of today's world, the recording experience is often very different today from the old band-in-a-studio setup. "When I started out, there were a lot of studios," said Russ Miller, "but a lot of those are gone now. I used to be in a commercial studio three, four, or five days a week, but now I'm in a commercial studio maybe two or three times a month. For the rest of the time, I'm recording in my own room at home." Miller has often provided drum tracks for Hollywood movies, but much of that is now "remote recorded" in the comfort of his own California studio. "It may be a hundred-million-dollar movie, and I'm doing the drums at home. A lot of the composers I work with are just used to that now, and they're comfortable with it. The music goes up on a server and I download it, get it into my system, and I do the drums and put it back up there, and they take it back."

Miller said he often missed the feedback he would receive from producers and engineers in a commercial studio; however, the opportunities to search for audio perfection are greater while working at home. "There is a loss of interaction. But I can experiment sonically a lot more in my room, because I have the freedom of time. So in a commercial studio it might be,

'Let's try another snare drum . . . Okay, that's enough, let's go.' But what happens more now is, 'Let's pull up one other drum set and try it.' I think there are more interesting things going on sonically."

No matter how clever the mechanics of recording become, it looks as if studio drummers will continue to face a barrage of bizarre sonic challenges for the foreseeable future. For that reason, drummers need to be open-minded, cooperative, resourceful, inspired, and, perhaps above all, almost superhumanly patient. These, then, are the true qualities of the classic, ideal drummer—not flashiness, craziness, stupidity, or tattoos.

But they need even more than that. They need to tolerate pain, in all its hundreds of varieties. I was finally getting close, I believed, to the absolute truth about drummers.

6

THE WORST JOB IN THE WORLD

Listen to "Helter Skelter" on the Beatles' *White Album*, and at the end you'll hear Ringo Starr scream that playing the song has given him "blisters on me fingers!" The drummer was complaining about the wear and tear on his hands after he had bashed away at the hard-rocking track at Abbey Road studios for so long, after it had basically turned into a jam session. Fast-forward forty-four years to March 2012, and fifty-six-year-old Butch Vig is behind the kit as Garbage rehearse before relaunching themselves into the world following a seven-year hiatus. Vig endures about fourteen days of nagging muscular pain before posting this message online: "After 2 weeks of rehearsal, my hands have finally stopped aching!"

What's that loud noise? It's the sound of drummers roaring with laughter at these trivial complaints. Big deal! Blisters and aches are nothing compared with the accidents, agonies, traumas, and misadventures that so many drummers have suffered over the years, and continue to suffer.

Just because you're sitting down on a cozy drum stool while the rest of the band are on their feet most of the time, don't think for a moment that this is going to be an easy ride. The drums are usually the most kinetic instrument in the band: in order to play your parts, you have to move a whole lot more than the other musicians do. The singer and guitarist might be running all over the place, contorting their bodies and throwing all kinds of shapes as they sing and play, but those are theatrics: they don't need to do that to perform their musical parts. You, on the other hand, have to navigate the distances between your sticks and your drums and cymbals every time you need to hit something. Your shoulders, arms, and hands are going backwards and forwards, backwards and forwards, for long periods of time. Meanwhile, your legs and feet are pounding at the bass-drum pedal and the hi-hat pedal and whatever other pedals you have. If your name is Terry Bozzio, you have an almighty amount of pedaling to do.

With thousands of drum and cymbal strikes to accomplish during a gig or a recording session, are you going to make all of them, or are you going to miss a few? There are many ways to miss, and many consequences of missing. "A couple times," Steven Drozd told me, "I've hit my left hand with my right hand, really hard."

"I've caught my knuckles on the edges of my cymbals now and then," said Richard Jupp of Elbow. "You get a nice little spray of blood."

"It's horrible when you misjudge something and you smack yourself really hard in the face with a drumstick," said Cherisse Osei. "Or you go to choke a cymbal and it catches your nail. Ouch! I've had loads of cuts. A few times, I've been playing and suddenly I've seen blood on my snare drum—'Oh! I'm bleeding!' And I look at my hands and they're covered in blood."

I've slammed my finger onto my snare drum," said Jess Bowen, "and my finger has swelled up like a golf ball. I've smacked myself in the face with a drumstick and almost given myself a black eye. And one time, the drum riser was too small for my drum set, and when I went to play, my stool fell backwards off the riser, and I fell off with it."

Nicko McBrain of Iron Maiden gave me a little summary of his behind-the-kit injuries. "I've busted my nose, given myself a few black eyes, and I've hurt my hand a few times and buggered my thumb up," he said matter-of-factly.

In May 2013, Eloy Casagrande, the man behind the kit in the Brazilian/American thrash-metal band Sepultura, was keeping the beat nicely at a concert in Bourg-en-Bresse, France, when he made one mistake. He accidentally hit one of his fingers exceptionally hard on his snare drum. "He smashed his finger on the snare and blood was everywhere," said Andreas Kisser afterward. "He managed to finish the set but his finger was in bad shape. He went to the hospital, had some stitches and the doctor demanded total rest." Casagrande was a young drummer, just twenty-two at the time, but he was certainly not inexperienced: he had been drumming since he was seven.

Note that innocuous little phrase "He managed to finish the set." It seems that for many drummers, the show has to go on: even if they are hurt, they are often expected to keep thrashing away until the end of the final number. As Phil Collins has noted, "There's never that moment when you say, 'God, I'm a bit tired' . . . You work through the blood and the pain and the broken blisters. There's no alternative but to keep going."

"You have to carry on," said Cherisse Osei. "It's like an unwritten law."

"I remember doing gigs with the flu," said Roger Taylor of Queen, "and absolutely being at death's door. But you somehow get your aching body up there, and after a few songs you almost forget about it."

Pain and suffering are such commonplaces in drumming that you really do have to wonder: are they part of the attraction? Are many of the people who sign up to a life behind the kit essentially masochists? Is drumming just a fancy way of self-harming? Before we reach a conclusion about this, let's look closely at some other nasty and unfortunate things that have happened to drummers over the years.

In 2006, while playing a gig in Bologna, Italy, with the American band Interpol, the drummer Sam Fogarino suddenly realized he had lost the feeling in one of his arms. Off he went to the hospital—eventually—where he was diagnosed as having a stressed nerve. Later the same year, Matt Tong of the British "post-punk-revival" band Bloc Party became unwell while drumming at a gig in Atlanta, Georgia. In hospital, it was found that the twenty-seven-year-old had a collapsed lung, and he was ordered to remain there for three days. In a statement, a spokeswoman for the band dared to use that three-letter adjective that haunts percussionists: "Matt is known for his energetic drumming style. He can be quite mad. Everyone is very worried about him and it's not clear at this stage when he will be fit to resume performing."

Given the intense physical demands of drumming, it's not surprising that many players succumb to exhaustion, plain and simple. In 1994, Neil Peart talked about arriving home after completing a Rush tour "in the usual wrung-out state of exhaustion." In 2009 the band Dirty Little Rabbits had to cancel tour dates when the drummer Shawn Crahan became exhausted after a long spell of touring—with his better-known band, Slipknot—and recording. Crahan explained that "after weeks of going all over the world and playing some of the biggest shows of my career, and now being in the home stretch on completing the Dirty Little Rabbits debut album, I'm just mentally and physically drained." In 2005, Nine Inch Nails at least had the decency to cut their set short in San Diego when their drummer, Jerome Dillon, suffered what he later called "fatigue and exhaustion." Fans wished him well as he was stretchered off to an ambulance, and he spent the night in hospital "for observation." Despite receiving a clean bill of health, Dillon was hospitalized again nearly two weeks later after playing a show in Sacramento, California.

Science has now confirmed that drumming is an almost unreasonably exhausting business. The British scientist Dr. Marcus Smith, based at the University of Chichester in Sussex, has made extensive studies of the physical challenges of a wide range of demanding sports including boxing, football, weightlifting, wrestling, and judo. By the late 1990s he realized that there were certain professional musicians who were also pushing their bodies to the limits. A Blondie fan, Dr. Smith asked the band's drummer, Clem Burke, to be the first guinea pig for a series of physical tests conducted under controlled conditions. Dr. Smith teamed up with another expert, Dr. Steve Draper at the University of Gloucestershire, where a "unique dedicated drumming laboratory" was built on the campus. Burke was also wired up to a heart-rate monitor while he played live with Blondie, bashing out classics like "Heart of Glass" and "Atomic."

In the first decade of the twenty-first century, the Clem Burke Drumming Project (CBDP) began yielding some mind-blowing results. I first spoke to Dr. Smith in 2011, when the project was still developing. "As a physiologist, what I'm interested in is how the body reacts to different stresses and challenges," he said. "And we've been testing Clem, and other drummers, in the same way as we've done Olympic athletes. I've sat alongside Clem when he's been playing, and it's really strenuous: his heart rate has gone up into the 180s and 190s." Burke's average heart rate during an eighty-two-minute gig was recorded as 145 beats per minute, considerably higher than the normal resting heart rate of sixty to one hundred beats per minute, and his energy expenditure was about 2.7 times greater than normal.

When you factor in the demands of a world tour, said Dr. Smith, the expectations placed on the shoulders of drummers become almost ridiculous: "People don't fully appreciate how demanding touring is. They'll play ninety to a hundred dates around the world, and you'd never get professional footballers doing that, for example. Footballers can normally expect to play forty to fifty games a year. But in one twelve-month period, Clem played ninety-minute sets at about a hundred Blondie concerts. When you consider the implications of touring on top of the performance requirements for drummers, it becomes clear that their fitness levels need to be outstanding.

"We're looking at the effects of jet lag on a performance as well. I've done some video analysis of Clem when he's jet-lagged and playing the same songs, and to the ear you wouldn't be able to tell the difference, but when you watch him you can see the fatigue, and the limitations of his enjoyment of playing. But there is still this expectation that drummers will keep on performing, and it's when the wheels come off big-style that all of a sudden people think, 'Well, they are human, after all.'"

Other drumming guinea pigs have followed Burke's example and stepped forward for analysis in Gloucestershire, including the highly regarded Mark Richardson of the British band Skunk Anansie, and Matt Tong of Bloc Party—he of the collapsed lung in 2006. Smith emphasized that the point of the CBDP is not to say "Look! Drummers are working way too hard!" but to find a way to make their workload more manageable.

"When we launched the project, we had a number of solicitors contact us, who were representing drummers who felt they'd been overworked. They were after data to use as evidence, but we're not into that. We're trying to promote the incredible talent these people have, and to see if we can cut down the fatigue that they suffer. Fatigue suppresses a drummer's creativity, and we're trying to see how science can help with that—how it can enable the creativity to continue, allow the performer to stay in that creative bubble for longer. We're trying to provide information that will help drummers play and enjoy playing even more."

After Blondie played a triumphant ninety-minute gig at the Roundhouse in London on July 7, 2013, I followed Clem Burke as he left his kit, slipped backstage, and headed for his dressing room. The fifty-seven-year-old had just finished playing the demanding, hyperactive beats of the band's song "Dreaming." Dr. Marcus Smith was also in hot pursuit; when he caught up with Burke, the drummer lifted his shirt up to reveal a belt-like apparatus around his torso, which he had been wearing throughout the show. Attached to the belt, pressed against the middle of his back, was some digital equipment with flickering numbers on it. Smith removed the belt and the digital para-phernalia, which had recorded the Blondie drummer's chang-ing heart rate. It transpired that Burke's heart rate had peaked at 154 beats per minute during the gig.

Stuck on Burke's dressing-room door were the words DR. CLEM BURKE, reminding all backstage visitors that he has now received a doctorate for his contribution to the science of drumming. "It's a source of pride," said Burke. "Getting the doctorate was an amazing achievement for me. It was a great reward."

Lately, Dr. Marcus Smith has been looking at how drum-mers suffer when they play in exceptionally hot and humid venues. He collected some alarming data from a gig by the UK Subs at the 100 Club in London: the heart rate of Jamie Oliver, the drummer in the British punk band, had soared into the 190s and reached a peak of 208 beats per minute. The air tem-perature in the club exceeded 93 degrees Fahrenheit at times, the relative humidity reached 84 percent, and Oliver sweated so much that his body mass decreased by 2.6 percent.

At least the guy got through the gig. Another British drum-mer, Malcolm Holmes of OMD, recently collapsed during a sweltering gig in Toronto, where temperatures soared above 113 degrees Fahrenheit. Holmes suffered cardiac arrest and was hospitalized, and strongly advised to stop drumming for a few months.

Despite the fact that drummers cry out in pain and keel over with exhaustion all the time, the mantra of many drumming

teachers remains "practice, practice, practice." If these musicians want to master their trade and improve their abilities,
they have to spend hours and hours hitting those drums and
cymbals over and over again. It is no wonder that this repetitive activity often leads to RSI—repetitive strain injury. RSI is
now an unfashionable term among many health practitioners,
who prefer the description "overuse injuries." These injuries
are nothing new—they were documented in Italian industrial
workers in 1700—and they affect all kinds of people, including production-line workers, employees who spend long periods using computers, and tennis players and golfers—"tennis
elbow" and "golfer's elbow" being classic forms of old-fashioned
RSI.

The trouble is, the muscles of the arms do not cope well
with short and fast motions over sustained periods of time.
To keep working, these muscles demand a lot of energy from
stored glycogen in the body, and if the glycogen runs out, serious fatigue will set in. If a drummer simply carries on hitting
the drums and the cymbals when he is fatigued, the muscle
fibers can be torn, and the drummer may experience nasty
symptoms such as tingling, numbness, weakness, soreness, and
agonizing pain. Carpal-tunnel syndrome (CTS), another medical phrase known to countless drummers, is a specific type of
overuse injury. In CTS, the median nerve that runs through
the wrist is squashed and stops functioning properly, leading to
more of that numbness, weakness, and sheer pain. Wrist tendinitis is another horror, with the tendons of the wrist becoming
painfully inflamed.

Online drumming forums are full of the grim symptoms
of overuse injuries. But these aren't conditions that only affect
low-profile musicians. Paul Thompson has had a long career

behind the kit, most notably laying down rock-solid beats for Roxy Music since the early 1970s. "I have a few more aches and pains now," he told me, shortly after reaching the age of sixty. "I've had problems with my wrists—tendinitis. I've got arthritis in my metacarpals, and carpal-tunnel syndrome, and a cartilage that's starting to pull out. I just had a little operation and sorted it out—I had some surgery on my wrists."

"I've developed some problems on my left side," said Joey Waronker. "When I was playing with Atoms for Peace, I was playing a very quick motion that repeated for a couple of minutes, and I was moving my left arm for its full range, all the way from one side to the other. At the time I thought, 'Oh, that'll be cool,' but there's a reason why you don't do that."

Injured sportspeople are usually taken off the field. However, for drummers, overuse injuries combine with that unwritten law of musical performance—that drummers must continue to play, even if they are injured—which only leads to more physical damage.

Flashy drummers who enhance their performances with pyrotechnics have even more hazards to consider. In 2005, Tommy Lee was showing off during a Mötley Crüe gig in Casper, Wyoming, when he came a cropper. He was strapped into a harness and "flying" about thirty feet above the stage, between one suspended drum kit and another, when a firework stunt went wrong and he was scorched by sparks. Lee soldiered on for one more song before being taken to a hospital.

Most of those injuries and ailments suffered by drummers behind the kit are understandable: just as there are specific occupational hazards for roofing contractors, lion tamers, and people who defuse unexploded bombs, there are specific dangers for drummers, too. But drummers have suffered an astonishing catalog of mishaps and serious accidents even when they are not drumming—when they are miles away from the nearest drum kit. It may be that an unusually high number of people who are attracted to the occupation of drumming fall into a category of personality characterized by an unusual lack of fear and caution, or by a faulty instinct for self-preservation. Perhaps the very act of drumming—and the feeling of power that drummers derive from whacking things over and over again, day after day, night after night—engenders an illusory feeling of superhuman invulnerability, or at least an overconfidence in their abilities.

Why else would Shawn Crahan—also known to Slipknot fans as the Clown—almost kill himself by diving into a dustbin during an Ozzfest tour in 1999? "I jumped into a garbage can headfirst," he recounted later, "and I didn't realize it was half-full of water. I got stuck in that thing for about thirty-five seconds, and I remember thinking, 'You've done it! You fucking went somewhere you shouldn't have gone, and now it's going to get you!' It was serious."

In December 2012, Brian Tichy was mountain-biking when he fell and broke his collarbone. Tichy had drummed for Foreigner, Billy Idol, and Ozzy Osbourne but was then a member of Whitesnake. He later announced online: "I am now going to be more METAL than ever before. I am going to have a metal plate and screws on my right collarbone . . ."

Ash Soan remembered falling on some stairs and spraining his ankle in his twenties, when he was on an American tour with the Scottish band Del Amitri in the 1990s. "We had about three gigs left of this tour," he said. "It was my bass-drum foot, and I didn't think anything of it, but it swelled up. We were in Sacramento, and eventually they got me to the doctor's and gave me an injection to take the swelling down, which really hurt. The band got a two-thousand-dollar bill and I had to buy some crutches." Soan soldiered on, receiving scant sympathy when he arrived at the next gig hobbling on his new crutches. Members of the band's Scottish road crew started laughing, apparently believing this was some kind of drummer's prank. "I played the gig, and straight after I was in the tour bus with my foot in the air and some ice on it. And I did the remaining gigs like that."

As a young man, Ginger Baker seemed to throw himself from one chaotic episode to another, displaying a rock 'n' roll recklessness that led to an assortment of injuries. His eldest daughter, Ginette, told me: "We grew up with traumas all the time, because Dad seems to attract disaster. Once, when I was about nine years old, he was carving a wooden totem pole in the loft in the early hours of the morning, and he put the chisel through his finger and severed the tendon and the nerve. He was running round the house at three in the morning, going, 'Get a tourniquet! Get a tourniquet!'

"When we went to Jamaica in the early 1970s, he went diving. He went to the loo on the boat, and then as he jumped off the boat to get back on the quay, the boat moved and he hit his jaw hard on the quayside and his teeth fell out. He came back with this bandage round his head, looking like Marley's ghost. And on the way back, his taxi had been involved in a terrible accident and three people died."

Tré Cool of Green Day has form here, too. In 2002 he managed to dance so enthusiastically that he dislocated one of his knees, which required surgery. On *The Late Show with David Letterman*, he capriciously decided to toss some cymbals up in the air and catch them; the result was a nasty gash on his hand.

And it's apparently no joke that he lost one of his testicles in a unicycling accident when he was young.

The horrific history of drummers' accidents includes one notorious case of self-defenestration. On Friday, June 1, 1973, the British drummer Robert Wyatt was enjoying a party in Maida Vale, north London. The former Soft Machine player was about to make a record with his latest band, Matching Mole, and was very drunk, having adopted the habit of alternating glasses of sticky Southern Comfort with shots of numbing tequila. That Friday evening, he might have added some whiskey to the mix as well. At one point, he exited from an upstairs window (he may have fallen, but he has also used the word "jumped" in recollections since), hit the ground, and was paralyzed from the waist down. He later revealed that the traumatic injury, as awful as it was, resolved a musical dilemma that had been bothering him. Being a drummer meant that he always had to be in a band, but he had a hankering to be a solo artist: he wanted to sing more, play other instruments, and develop more of his own compositions—"to do actual notes," as he has put it. Now that he could no longer be a drummer, his solo career was suddenly able to blossom. Wyatt soon became a unique voice in music, recording highly original, jazz-tinged albums such as *Rock Bottom* and *Ruth Is Stranger Than Richard*.

Alcohol and other drugs have had a powerful effect on the lives and careers of a great many drummers. Of course, stimulants and rock 'n' roll are old friends, and there are plenty of guitarists and singers and keyboard players who have had misadventures while "under the influence." But drummers seem to have done this more frequently and more spectacularly. Matt Helders of the Arctic Monkeys was forced to miss part of the recording sessions for the band's chart-topping album *AM* after he broke his hand. He said afterward that it had been the result of "a bizarre incident" one night when he had punched a wall that was "harder than I expected . . . I was just messing about, drunk." Pete Thomas, longtime drummer behind Elvis Costello, filled in for Helders in the studio.

Over the course of his brief life of thirty-two years, Keith Moon must have consumed a quantity of stimulants equivalent to the contents of dozens of breweries, distilleries, vineyards, drugstores, and narcotics factories. Such was the power of the manic energy that raged inside him—whether he had ADHD, bipolar disorder, ants in his pants, extreme fruitcake syndrome, or all of the above—that he would habitually self-medicate to calm himself down or bring bouts of insomnia to an end. For much of the time, he could do this and somehow remain vaguely coherent and hugely entertaining. It didn't work on November 20, 1973, when he consumed something before going onstage with the Who at the Cow Palace in San Francisco, at the start of the band's Quadrophenia tour. His drumming was even messier and more chaotic than usual that night, and in the middle of "Won't Get Fooled Again" he stopped playing altogether, having passed out. He was dragged and carried backstage and stayed there for about twenty minutes while Pete Townshend, Roger Daltrey, and John Entwistle tried to soldier on as a trio. Back came Moon eventually, with just enough energy to launch into their early hit "Magic Bus" before collapsing again. This time he was rushed to a hospital, where medics found the cause of his problem in his stomach: he had taken the notorious anesthetic PCP, also known as "angel dust." That night, an eager volunteer from the audience—Scot Halpin, nineteen, from Iowa— lived out the dreams of a million bedroom drummers when he walked onstage, sat on Moon's stool, and helped the Who finish the show.

This episode, and others like it, should have acted as a warning. Despite his larger-than-life cartoonish image, Keith Moon wasn't an invincible superman, and if he kept on self-medicating, one of these days it could finish him off. All he had to do was take too much of something, or the wrong cocktail of stimulants. On September 6, 1978, he left his flat in Curzon Place, London, to attend a star-studded party and a subsequent screening of the new movie *The Buddy Holly Story*, organized by Paul McCartney. Moon chatted with showbiz friends at the bash and was reported as seeming happy, genial, and relaxed. At this stage, he was trying to avoid the booze, but to counter the severe alcohol-withdrawal symptoms he had been suffering, he had been prescribed the drug Heminevrin, generically known as chlormethiazole. For reasons known only to Moon, or perhaps unknown even to him, he started popping those pills like candy. Early in the morning after the screening, Moon's Swedish girlfriend, Annette Walter-Lax, found him dead in his bed. A postmortem revealed that he had consumed a moderate amount of alcohol, and an enormous dose of thirty-two Heminevrin tablets, one for every year of his life. The cause of death recorded by the coroner on Moon's death certificate was "Chlormethiazole (heminevrin) overdosage self administered but no evidence of intention. Open Verdict."

John Bonham's capacity for alcohol was as legendary as his superhuman bass-drum triplets. This was a man who could sink Brandy Alexanders—brandy mixed with cream and crème de cacao—by the dozen in a single sitting. Long drinking sessions would often inspire his most outrageous antics. One day he joined a guitarist friend, Stan Webb, for a session at a pub in Soho, London, where they each ordered a large concoction that combined many liqueurs from various bottles behind the bar. Later, after Bonham and Webb were joined by Led Zeppelin's tour manager Richard Cole, they hatched a scheme to hire some costumes, dress as Arabs, and have some fun. Reports of the subsequent events vary, but it seems that after driving round for a while in a rented Rolls-Royce, the "Arabs" entered the May Fair Hotel, outraged some American tourists in the lift by raising their robes and exposing themselves, and then ordered a ridiculously large number of steaks and lobbed them around the hotel room.

Drink was ultimately Bonzo's undoing. On September 24, 1980, he was driven to Bray Studios, near Maidenhead, Berkshire, for band rehearsals before Led Zeppelin embarked on another tour of North America. On the way, he stopped for breakfast, which included four quadruple vodkas—sixteen measures in all. He carried on drinking heavily later that day; you can only imagine how well he was playing during those rehearsals, which ended late in the evening. The band went back to Jimmy Page's house, the Old Mill House in Clewer, Windsor, where Bonham fell asleep and was taken to bed. The next morning, the band's bass player, John Paul Jones, accompanied by their road manager, found the drummer dead. An inquest found that he had had inhaled his own vomit while asleep and suffered pulmonary edema (fluid accumulation in the lungs). It was concluded that he had somehow managed to consume about forty measures of vodka in total the day before. Like Keith Moon, he had managed to reach the age of thirty-two.

Ginger Baker has expressed an alternative theory about Bonham's death. Apparently, forty vodkas might not have been enough. In his autobiography, *Hellraiser*, Baker calls Bonham "a dabbler in heroin," and says that a well-known drug dealer in London "had got hold of some extremely strong smack." When Baker himself took it, he recounts, "I was so stoned that I left my car in Chelsea, walked all the way to Acton and back to Chelsea again until I was able to drive. That same night, Led Zep had the party when John died. I had a habit and could handle the extra-potent gear, but, being only an occasional user, he could not."

For decades, people in the music business have been aware of the dangers presented by certain drummers. Joey Kramer, who has documented his former appetite for drugs and drink in his own autobiography, told me that there were forces at work in the 1970s to keep him and his hero John Bonham from ever meeting one another. "We were purposely kept apart by the people surrounding us," he said, "because we were too much alike—we had way too much going on in the early days, as far as the cars and the drugs and the women were concerned. Though, of course, I would never in a million years consider myself his equal."

Kramer finally got to visit Bonham during a trip to England in 1989. Robert Plant had given him the location of Bonzo's grave, in a churchyard in Rushock, Worcestershire, and Kramer went to pay his respects on a drizzly winter's day.

In 1983, Dennis Wilson of the Beach Boys reached the end of his roller-coaster life after a day of heavy drinking. His mounting debts had recently forced him to sell two of the things he cared most about: the Santa Monica recording facility Brother Studios, which he had set up with his brother and bandmate Carl Wilson; and his beloved sixty-two-foot boat, the *Harmony*. Three days after Christmas Day in 1983, when he was just thirty-nine, he decided to dive repeatedly into the ocean at Marina Del Rey and retrieve some souvenirs—pieces of junk he had once thrown overboard from the *Harmony*—despite the fact that, as usual, he had been consuming heroic quantities of alcohol. He was later found, drowned.

Richard Manuel was a highly talented member of the Band from the late 1960s, and played occasional drums and percussion in addition to singing and playing a series of other instruments, including keyboards and harmonica. By the mid-1970s, he was said to be getting through eight bottles of Grand Marnier liqueur a day—in addition to an unquantifiable amount of cocaine. In 1986, he hanged himself after a Band gig in Florida, but not before downing one last bottle of Grand Marnier.

Jimmy "the Rev" Sullivan, superfast drummer and founding member of the American goth-punk band Avenged Sevenfold, was only twenty-eight when he was found dead at his home in Huntingdon Beach, California, just after Christmas in 2009. After toxicology tests, a coroner determined that Sullivan had taken a lethal cocktail of alcohol and strong painkillers. His death was the result, he said, of "acute polydrug intoxication due to combined effects of oxycodone, oxymorphone, diazepam/nordiazepam, and ethanol."

Back in the early 1960s, Ginger Baker became a resourceful dope cultivator, growing big cannabis plants together with lettuce, carrots, runner beans, and radishes in the little back garden of his flat in London's Ladbroke Grove. "He's always advocated smoking dope," his eldest daughter, Ginette, told me. "When my brother and sister and I were kids, he'd say, 'Have a couple of joints, and don't let anyone tell you it's bad for you.'"

Ginger Baker's introduction to hard drugs came in May 1960, when he was just twenty years old and playing in jazz bands. It was a sunny day, with blossoms brightening many of the trees, when he and his wife Liz walked to the apartment of a fellow jazz drummer he had just met, Dickie Devere, in Fordwych Road, near Kilburn Underground station in north London. Devere brought out some heroin in the form of tiny white pills, which they crushed up and snorted from a pound note. Soon afterward, according to Baker, he was suddenly able to do something he had never accomplished before: finish the crossword puzzles in his newspaper.

Soon after that first experience with smack, Baker had a gig with the Johnny Scott Band in the seaside town of Brighton, where he made a discovery. "As a result of the smack, I was feeling really super-good when Johnny came to pick me up," he later recounted. "They all said I played fantastically well that night and I thought, I've found the answer here. All the barriers were down and I was just playing."

Heroin seemed to improve his drumming, he said—it made him "fearless"—and so began an addiction that dogged him for decades. As his eldest daughter, Ginette, remarked to me, "Heroin addiction is more of a lifetime commitment than a marriage. If you have a heroin addiction, you've got it for the rest of your life." I asked Ginette if she thought her father would have been a cheerier soul if he hadn't touched heroin. "It's hypothetical. My mother says he was a nice, quiet, shy person before he started taking it. But then her mother said he was the most miserable person she'd ever met!"

Baker tried to shake off his smack addiction and "get straight" by escaping from the suppliers and relocating to exotic places. At one stage he took his family to live in Hawaii, which was a mistake: he found that there was abundant heroin there too. In 1982 he took a more drastic step: he decided that getting straight meant escaping "from anybody I know," so he left his first wife and shacked up with his daughter's boyfriend's teenage sister in the Tuscan hills. The girlfriend became wife number two before she abandoned him.

When I met Baker in 2010, he was seventy, and although he was off the smack, he still needed to be comforted by a daily dose of morphine. This highly experienced user had some strong opinions to vent about two of the world's most widely available stimulants: "I think alcohol and tobacco are two of the most dangerous drugs on this planet. I haven't drunk for nearly twenty years now. That's why I don't socialize: people start drinking and you see the change in their character. I don't like that."

When Topper Headon joined the Clash in 1977, it seemed for a while that Britain's most successful political punk band had found its perfect drummer. "Train in Vain," from the sensational album *London Calling*, demonstrates Headon's ability to develop an economic but highly effective drum pattern and then to play it faultlessly, almost metronomically, but with plenty of feel. That drum part is so good, it was sampled by Garbage almost two decades later for their stomping hit song "Stupid Girl." Headon wasn't limited to one style, either: he could lay down nifty reggae beats as well, and the whole musical idea of the band's 1982 classic "Rock the Casbah" was his. Sandy Pearlman, producer of the Clash's second album, *Give 'Em Enough Rope*, was so impressed with Headon's percussive reliability that he called him the Human Drum Machine.

But Headon began to change when the Clash went out on tour: this previously clean-living fitness enthusiast started partying hard and hitting the bottle. Opening up years later about that period, he made a simple connection between drumming and alcohol that might ring a few little bells for other drummers. "I've got an addictive personality," he said. "All I ever did was drum, drum, drum. Then I went on the road and discovered booze. All I did was drink, drink, drink." If he saw the slippery slope looming before him, he just carried on regardless: he discovered cocaine and threw himself at it with the same impetuosity. What had started as an offstage habit then became an onstage problem. He later claimed that he would stop playing after every three songs to snort a line of coke. It wasn't long before he had a serious heroin problem as well, and the rest of the band couldn't fail to notice that he was frequently vomiting and turning up late for rehearsals. In May 1982, Headon was sacked from the band before an American tour, the official reason being "a difference of political direction." Desperately trying to cling to the band he loved, the drummer offered— unsuccessfully—to play the whole tour without wages. He was replaced by the band's former drummer, Terry Chimes. The singer and band spokesman Joe Strummer later let slip in an interview that Headon had really been sacked for being a junkie.

Though a multi-instrumentalist, Steven Drozd joined the Flaming Lips in 1991 as the drummer and continued to man the kit in concert with America's most successful modern psychedelic rock band until 2002, when Kliph Scurlock relieved him and freed Drozd to play guitar and keyboards onstage. Drozd confessed to me that this "live drumming" period of his life was marked by stereotypical but dangerous rock 'n' roll behavior. "When I joined in October 1991, at that point in my life, my focus, my whole thing, was I just wanted to be a crazy, intense rock drummer. I wanted to become Keith Moon meets

John Bonham meets Dale Crover from the Melvins or something. And it's almost like, from the time I joined the Lips to the time I stopped playing drums live, I did live this life of wild excess. I definitely existed in the cliché of the wild drummer for a few years. I think I wanted to live life to the fullest, and one of the things that to me indicated that I was living life to the fullest was partying and then hitting the drums as hard as I could. That, to me, all seemed very rock 'n' roll, and it seemed like what I wanted to be. And then, luckily, I got into my late twenties and I discovered other dark avenues, which didn't involve staying up for three or four days at a time and boozing for two weeks straight."

What dark avenues were these? "Well, then I got into heavier drugs—I got into opiates, I got into heroin and those kinds of drugs. I think people think that junkies are living this wild, crazy life, but really all you want to do is not be sick, and to stare at your big toe for days on end. So it's one thing to be up drinking and partying and doing cocaine for two weeks, and it's another thing to be shooting heroin, sitting in your room by yourself, without anybody around. It was a different kind of rock-star excess, you know: I went from one rock 'n' roll cliché straight to another one. And now I'm trying to pull out of all of it, which I mostly have. I'm on the straight and narrow! I still have cigarettes and coffee in my life, but really nothing else."

Had heroin affected his drumming? "Well, there is this notion that heroin improves your creativity and stuff like that, and I think what it does, at least in the beginning, is it frees your mind of anxiety, and I've always been a very highly anxious person; it's just part of my personality. I would do heroin and my anxieties would melt away, and therefore my brain was free to be more creative. And that actually worked for me for a little while, until I got really addicted to it—and then you've just always got to have it or you're sick."

Sometimes drummers succeed in kicking one addiction only to have to kick another. In 2013, Steven Adler, former drummer with Guns N' Roses, made a similar sensible decision when he postponed a tour by his new band, Adler, to battle his alcohol problem. The forty-eight-year-old drummer explained to fans in a blog: "I picked up a bottle and drank. This occurred a few times and that is a few times too many. I knew that this had to permanently stop. That is the moment I picked up the phone, before it got out of hand, to get help. I had kicked hard drugs several years ago and now it is time to get rid of the urges of drinking alcohol. I am at a great facility and will stay here until I am comfortable to be home to work the program on my own."

At some point in the noughties, Travis Barker of Blink-182 became dependent on the painkiller Vicodin. It took years, Barker has revealed, for him to shake off the addiction.

Of all the drummers I interviewed, none had reached the depths to which Patty Schemel sank after she quit Hole in 1998. This was when Schemel, who had previously had problems with alcohol and other drugs, lost contact with her family and friends and began living on the streets of Los Angeles, addicted to crack cocaine. For more than a year, her prime motivation was to get another fix, and she lost so much of her self-image that she almost completely forgot that she had once been a musician. One day she found herself in a church, where she noticed a "crappy drum set" and had a brief awakening, remembering for a lucid moment that she had played an instrument like that in her former life.

"I lost everything," said Schemel. "I had nothing. And then finally I reached out and went into rehab. I spent a lot of time in rehab and began living sober and started my life over again. But I didn't play drums for a long time. I didn't get back on the drums at least for a couple of years into sobriety. I didn't want to; I was fearful of doing it." Was she afraid that if she started playing drums again, she would resume her old lifestyle as a drug addict? "Yeah, exactly."

For Schemel, the enjoyment she derives from drumming seems closely related to the narcotic highs she has experienced. This was especially evident when she described the relief and tranquility that drumming had given her. "When I was a kid, I was pretty wound up a lot," she recalled. "Drumming was such a relief, and I would feel at my most peaceful then. The closest I've ever felt to the feeling of being on drugs was after playing: that peace and endorphin rush from playing."

Schemel said she deeply regretted her years of drug abuse. "I think back on my life as a drummer. I achieved so much, and I'm so grateful, but also I wish . . ." She fell silent, apparently finding this subject difficult to discuss. Did she wish she had stayed sober for longer? "Yeah. But it is what it is, and I am who I am, and who knows what I would've been? I put myself at such a disadvantage at times."

When I spoke to her, Schemel had been sober for many years and was playing in a variety of bands, including a garage-punk band called Death Valley Girls and a pop band called Upset. "I'm the busiest drummer I've ever been in my life. I play a lot of different styles of music, and it's like how it was when I first started playing: I feel excited again about drums and what they sound like. Nowadays I make sure that I'm in good shape and that I'm eating properly—all these corny things, but it helps me to have the stamina I need and to play a good show."

If there are social pressures on rock stars to take drugs—because parts of the media, other musicians, rock tradition, and even elements of their audience expect it—then there may be extra pressures on drummers, who are frequently seen as "characters." This factor was highlighted by the former Oasis guitarist and singer Noel Gallagher, who attended the 2013 BRIT awards in London and was disgusted by the squeaky-clean behavior of some of his peers. "I saw the drummer from Muse smoking an electronic cigarette," he complained afterward. "A cigarette with a battery in. I had to say to him, 'Really? Really? Is that where you're at? Do me a favor, mate: either have a proper one outside, or don't have one.'" Gallagher introduced his whinge about the BRITs with a telling statement: "There are no characters left in the music business," he spat. Come back, Keith Moon! Wake up, John Bonham! Rise from the dead and bash those skins for us again, come to the party, and we'll line up all the hard stuff like back in the good old days.

Substance abuse is one thing; automobile abuse is another. You might think that with their superior coordination and mastery of foot pedals, drummers would be skillful drivers, but in many cases their love of cars has had unpleasant consequences.

On July 4, 1973, the British band Slade were riding high in the UK charts with their latest single, "Skweeze Me, Pleeze Me," when their twenty-six-year-old drummer, Don Powell, left a nightclub in Wolverhampton in the early hours of the morning with his girlfriend, Angela, and set off for the drummer's home in his brand-new white Bentley. Around one A.M., for reasons that are still mysterious, the car collided with a wall, and the impact threw them both out of the vehicle and into the road. Angela was killed. Powell suffered injuries to his head, limbs, and ribs; he was in a coma in hospital for nearly a week, and on two occasions his heart stopped beating, but then started again. Forty years after the crash, sixty-six-year-old Powell said he still didn't know exactly what had happened. He had a fragmentary memory of opening a bottle of champagne at a girl's birthday party, but no memories of the events leading up to the accident. Other memories were gone too—when he was finally fit enough to sit behind the kit again, he had to relearn the drum parts to all the Slade songs. Shortly after the tragedy, he turned to drink for a while, notching up two bottles of vodka a day.

In 1977, Joey Kramer of Aerosmith was driving his red Ferrari on the Massachusetts Turnpike early in the morning when he suddenly noticed a truck motoring along in front of him. His car was so low-slung that it slid under the truck, which crushed his windshield and left him with shards of glass embedded in his forehead. "We had been filming a commercial," explained Kramer, "and I'd been under the hot lights all day and I was really tired. I shouldn't have been driving to begin with, but I was so anxious to get home, I just went and did the trip anyway, and I fell asleep behind the wheel."

Twenty-one years later, Kramer was sitting in another Ferrari at a gas station near Boston when it was suddenly engulfed in flames, after an inattentive pump attendant had caused a major gasoline spillage. "The guy put the hose in the car, walked away, and it fell out," recalled the drummer. "And it didn't click off, so it filled the ground up with, like, fourteen gallons of gas. And, it being the middle of July, it combusted.

Flames suddenly surrounded the car, and I had to get out. The convertible top was down, so I had to get out by going through this wall of flames."

One of the most serious and notorious injuries in the world of drumming happened to Rick Allen of Def Leppard down a road near Sheffield in South Yorkshire. Allen later gave journalist Mel Bradman a detailed account of what happened. "It was New Year's Eve, 1984, and it started like any other day," he said. "I'd already started to lose interest in playing the drums. The underbelly of rock 'n' roll—drink and drugs—had more appeal. We were partway through recording our new album, *Hysteria*, and that was dragging on and on. I was twenty-one, still a kid, and going out and driving my car was one way to get my frustration out. We'd done incredibly well, sold millions of albums, but the old saying that money doesn't buy you happiness, that's really true. You have to be at peace with yourself. I'd just come back to England for the Christmas break—we'd been recording our fourth album in Holland. I took my girlfriend, a Dutch girl called Miriam, home to meet my parents. I was having problems at home—couldn't see eye to eye with anybody, and headed out for a drive."

Allen started motoring through the beautiful Yorkshire countryside in his Chevrolet Corvette, showing Miriam the sights. "We headed out to Ladybower Dam, parked, walked around, then got back in the car. I was in a really good mood, simply because I was out and had changed the energy; wasn't hanging around the house. I was frustrated for many reasons: not only the music, but personal life and a bunch of other things. So me and my girlfriend decided to take the roof off the car. The Corvette was beautiful and I loved it, but not very practical in England, because it was a left-hand drive. We put our seat belts on, and headed off down this dirt road, and turned left onto the A57, driving at an easy pace.

"Two or three minutes after I pulled out, this red Alfa Romeo went flying past and took off in the distance. Then I saw him up ahead, slowing down, slowing down. So I tried to pass him, but he speeded up. We played this stupid game for about four miles down the road, where he was going too slow for me and I couldn't pass him. Finally, I really lost my temper and put my foot down. I guess because I was in this left-hand-drive car, I'm going round this corner and I didn't get to see the ground properly and ended up rolling over the car and—from what they tell me—destroying a football-field length of stone wall. Really did a number. But I blacked out before I went round the corner, and don't actually remember anything about it. I remember standing up in the field, saying something bizarre like 'I'm a drummer and I've lost my arm.' From what I can gather, because of how my arm was damaged, the seat belt took my left arm off. But if the seat belt hadn't done that, I may have ended up with a different kind of injury. I'm just blessed to be alive."

The accident had broken Allen's right arm as well. He was eventually noticed by a district nurse as he wandered around the field. "She had ice and all her medical supplies. She said it was an awful scene, and what she had to do was restrain me, because I was wandering around in this field, not knowing what was going on. So she grabbed me and started to bind me with bandages, almost like a mummy. She wanted me to relax, calm down. But I think the thing that kept me alive was the fact that, yeah, I went into shock, but I stayed conscious, and that stopped me losing blood."

The drummer was rushed to the Royal Hallamshire

Hospital. "It wasn't until I got to the hospital, and they put me under the anesthetic, that I started to lose blood at an alarming rate. Apparently, I used the hospital's entire blood supply! Initially I got through twenty-odd pints of blood. Later, one nurse told me that as quick as we put the blood in one end, it was coming out the other.

"My girlfriend escaped with just a couple of cuts and scratches. I'm just so glad that, for her, the seat belt did what it was supposed to do. We hadn't known each other for that long, only about a month, and it threw her into a situation that was horrific, but that strengthened our relationship.

"A few people have told me that I actually died, and that I'm a different person from who I was before the accident. But there's a part in all of us that is such a strong survival mechanism that you make a choice right there and then. At the scene of the accident, the only thing I remember was no pain, but making the choice to be here or go. I knew I wasn't here—I was halfway between here and there—and that's where you're given that choice to stay or go."

At the hospital, surgeons worked to reattach Allen's arm while he was anesthetized. "But a few days later my arm was starting to get infected. And because it was so close to my heart, they had to take the arm off in case the infection killed me. The good thing was, I didn't know anything about it, because I was out for the count."

Many drummers would have accepted at this point, however reluctantly, that their career had ended. But Rick Allen proved to be an ultra-determined character and refused to throw in the towel. "Ten days after I came round, I realized I could still play the drums. I was listening to music, piped through the hospital system or on the radio, and I realized I could play all the basic rhythms using my feet. So when the guys in the band visited me, I showed them how I could use my feet to play, on this piece of foam at the bottom of the bed. One night, a junior doctor came in and said, 'You know, you're never going to play drums again.' That really fucking blew it. I said to my brother, 'Don't let that guy anywhere near me.'"

After convalescing, Allen collaborated with engineers to design a custom-built electronic drum kit that he could play with his three limbs. The acid test for this gutsy musician was his reappearance with Def Leppard in 1986, in front of tens of thousands of people, at the Monsters of Rock festival at Castle Donington, Derbyshire. As the world's most success-ful one-armed drummer said later, "I was so overwhelmed by how behind me the crowd were. I felt so much love coming off them; everyone was rooting for me. Then I started crying, thinking, 'I'm gonna cry over the electronics and be electro-cuted. But it won't matter.'"

"I have an incredible respect for Rick Allen," Joey Kramer told me. "So many other people would've just sat it out and let somebody take his place, but he didn't do that. What he does is so amazing to me, so unbelievable, that I think he should be given some kind of special award, and I would be honored to be the one to present it to him."

Such is the power of the Rick Allen legend that a Def Lep-pard tribute band, based in Dallas, Texas, and calling them-selves Pyromania after one of the original band's albums, once advertised for a one-armed drummer to complete their lineup. The ad stipulated that applicants must have no prosthetics, and their own professional drum kit "& stick" (note the singular there). Surprisingly, it seems that Pyromania found their man: not long after the ad was placed, I called the listed telephone number and heard a voice message saying: "If you're calling about the Dallas-based Def Leppard tribute band Pyromania, we found our one-armed drummer, and I want to thank everyone who auditioned, but the position is filled."

Cozy Powell once confessed to an interviewer that "I drive like I drum—madly." The fifty-year-old British drummer wasn't wearing his seat belt when he drove his black turbocharged Saab 9000 at more than one hundred miles per hour along the M4 motorway near Bristol, England, in April 1998. He was also talking on his cellphone—an act that didn't become a punishable offense in the UK until five years later. He was talking to his girlfriend, who heard a loud bang followed by silence. He had been drinking alcohol, the Saab had a puncture, and he lost control and crashed into the central reservation, dying of his injuries later in hospital.

Joey Covington played the drums for Jefferson Airplane in the early 1970s; a cheerful and capable musician, he was also a founding member of the blues-rock band Hot Tuna, and later rejoined some of his old Airplane chums when they became Jefferson Starship. Early one Tuesday evening in June 2013, sixty-seven-year-old Covington was driving his Honda Civic not far from his home in Palm Springs, California, when the car slammed into a retaining wall at the side of the road. The drummer died at the scene of the accident.

In the 1984 mock-rockumentary film *This Is Spinal Tap*, it becomes clear that the most accident-prone and least fortunate member of the band is whoever happens to be sitting on the drum stool at the time. One of these fictional characters, Peter "James" Bond, succumbs during a gig to spontaneous combustion—the paranormal phenomenon in which the body appears to be suddenly and inexplicably consumed by fire.

Another drummer, Eric "Stumpy Joe" Childs, chokes to death on "someone else's vomit." And their original sticksman, John "Stumpy" Pepys, dies in a "bizarre gardening accident."

In August 1992, it seemed that life had cruelly imitated art in the case of Jeff Porcaro, a prolific and highly rated session drummer who had played with Steely Dan, Aretha Franklin, Michael Jackson, Diana Ross, and Eric Clapton and had been a founding member of the band Toto. Porcaro became ill at the age of thirty-eight after spraying his garden in Hidden Hills, Los Angeles, with pesticide, and died later that day at Humana Hospital–West Hills. One story in circulation was that he had inhaled the pesticide and experienced an extreme reaction to the substance, and because of a weak heart or "undiagnosed heart condition," this reaction had been enough to kill him. However, a report in the *Los Angeles Times* contradicts this version of events, saying that the LA coroner determined the cause of death as atherosclerosis—a thickening of the artery walls—brought on by the consumption of cocaine.

In 2008, rumors of a "bizarre gardening accident" circulated again when a successful drummer was found dead, with cuts to his neck, in his garden on the Spanish island of Mallorca. Sixty-one-year-old Ola Brunkert had been the drummer with Abba, performing on many stages around the world with the mega-successful Swedish pop band, as well as drumming on all their albums. An autopsy quickly confirmed that Brunkert's death had indeed been an accident, but no horticulture had been involved: he had stumbled against a glass door in his dining room, breaking the glass and injuring his neck. He had wrapped a towel round his neck to stem the flow of blood and had left the house, apparently to find help, but had collapsed in the garden and died.

The dangers of drumming, and even of manufacturing drums, are sometimes entirely invisible. In the summer of 2007, the director of an African drumming program in the city of Danbury, Connecticut, was making a djembe drum, an African-style hand drum, in a shed in his backyard—something he did quite often. He had just bought some goat hides from a dealer on a street in New York City, and after soaking one of the hides in water and stretching it over a drum, he was smoothing the hide by sanding it. Suddenly he felt a stinging sensation on his right forearm, and he went to the bathroom to wash his arm. Two days later, he noticed a peculiar lesion on his arm, and on seeking medical help, the drum maker was prescribed treatment for a suspected spider bite. But instead of healing, the patch on his arm became inflamed, and a specimen was eventually sent to the Connecticut State Laboratory. He was found to have been infected with *Bacillus anthracis*—deadly anthrax.

The drum maker's eight-year-old child was also found to be infected with anthrax, and a scientific investigation was conducted at the house, where several drum heads—including the one he had been sanding—were found to carry the disease. The FBI became involved, since anthrax had been used in the past by terrorists. It became clear that the goat hides, which were from the West African state of Guinea, had been contaminated. The house was fumigated and the drum maker and his son were given appropriate treatment and survived. But the following year, a musician and drum maker in Britain was not so lucky. Fernando Gomez, thirty-five, originally from Spain, died in Hackney, east London, after he was believed to have inhaled anthrax spores from the animal hides he was using to make drums.

While young drummers certainly run the gauntlet of

occupational hazards, drummers who are fortunate enough to survive into their fifties, sixties, seventies, and beyond face a whole new world of challenges. When I met Ginger Baker in 2010, the septuagenarian drummer was complaining about persistent dorsal pain: "I've got degenerative osteoarthritis. My back's killing me!" We were in his room at the K West hotel, a favorite haunt of rock stars in Shepherds Bush, west London, and I was supposed to be interviewing him for the British newspaper the *Sunday Times*. Ever since the 1960s he had been notorious for being grumpy and difficult in interviews, and immediately I started getting some worrying reactions to my questions. I would ask him something reasonably innocent, enunciating the words clearly, and he would give me a puzzled or exasperated look, knitting his gray brows above his spectacles, or shake his head. However, it turned out that he didn't dislike the questions: he just hadn't heard them properly. He was seriously deaf.

Baker's back was hurting so much, he asked if he could lie down on his hotel bed while I conducted the interview. I agreed and stood at the foot of the bed, calling out my questions in a loud voice, some of which I had to repeat. His deafness wasn't the result of hitting his drums too hard, he said, though that might have been a factor. It was from playing onstage in Cream, when his bandmates, Eric Clapton and Jack Bruce, were known to "turn up their amplifiers to 11." Baker's autobiography elaborates on these claims: "The constant gigging meant our performances weren't always that good, though we'd get on stage to a standing ovation before we'd even played a note. It was also a terrible strain on my hearing. Jack always turned the volume up as loud as he could and then Eric would have to turn up to hear himself and I was sitting in the middle of this. Eric stopped playing once and stood in front of me and then I stopped playing and we both stood there with our arms folded while Jack was in front of these huge speakers, playing away. He was totally unaware for two choruses that we'd stopped.

"That was where all that smash, bash drumming came about. I was hitting my drums that hard because I was trying to hear what I was playing. It was totally insane. I'd get into the hotel after a gig and my ears would be making terrible noises." Cream's famous farewell gig at London's Royal Albert Hall was certainly not Baker's favorite moment: "I didn't enjoy it at all. I just couldn't stand the volume and the last year of Cream damaged my ears permanently."

But in a moment of humor during my interview (I'm convinced that he was never "the comedian in the band" in Cream, Blind Faith, Ginger Baker's Air Force, or any other of his many short-lived ensembles), Baker told me a comical story relating to his deafness. He recounted that during a drumming demonstration he had given once, someone had asked: "How did you start on drums?" Mishearing the last word, he had replied with a stern lesson about why "drugs are a bad idea."

Deafness plagues many other drummers. "I'm losing my hearing," Paul Thompson of Roxy Music told me. "I'm losing certain frequencies. If I'm in a crowd of people and somebody's talking away, I can't hear what they're saying, can't pick it out. It's only happened over the last ten years. I use in-ear monitors now, and I have to have them cranked right up, because I've got to be able to hear what the rest of the band's playing, as well as what I'm playing."

It's not just the senior citizens who are struggling to hear things properly. Ash Soan told me he suspected his hearing had been damaged in the 1990s, when he was in his twenties and playing in Del Amitri. "I've lost a considerable amount of hearing in my left ear," he said. "When I'm in a pub, I'm the one that's always going, 'What's that? Sorry?' When I played originally in Del Amitri, I had the biggest possible submonitor behind me so I could hear the music. They put all the sound through it, including the drums, and it was fairly loud. I was so young then, I just trusted the monitor guy to do my sound. These days I use in-ear monitors, which are much, much better. The next generation of drummers, all these guys using in-ear monitors, they're hopefully going to be the ones with much better hearing."

Phil Collins lost much of his hearing in his left ear abruptly in 2000. "I went to a doctor," he explained later, "and he told me I had sudden deafness syndrome, which the medical world knows very little about . . . They told me it's just random bad luck." The deafness turned out to be temporary, but he expressed fears that it would return. Nevertheless, Collins agreed to a Genesis reunion tour in 2007. During that tour, he performed his customary drum duet with Chester Thompson night after night. "Chester and I always used to write the drum duets in a hotel room towards the end of rehearsals," Collins told me. "We'd start playing on a hotel-room stool or chair, and we'd record it and listen back to it, and we'd put the best bits together. We might spend the whole night doing this, and then the next day we'd apply it all to the drums. I thought the sound of sticks on a leather stool always sounded great, so I thought, for the reunion tour—the last time we were going to do this, probably—why don't we actually start off on the stools on-stage and then take it to the drums, like we would do during a rehearsal? So we did, and we called it 'A Conversation with Two Stools.'

"It worked fantastically well, and over a couple of weeks the duet got a little bit faster and a little bit more intricate, and I started to do some African chanting at the climax of it. And I think, one night, my neck gave out. Something happened to my neck and/or my left arm, and from that point, slowly, the nerves started to do funny things. And during the last part of that tour, I could only just hold on to the drumsticks by the end of the show. I've since had operations, and I have physiotherapy now, but I can't grip a stick like I used to. So basically my playing career, in terms of how I used to play, is over. And that applies to playing the piano, as well: a couple of my fingers are numb, so they don't do what they're supposed to."

"I get more aches and pains now," said Nicko McBrain, who turned sixty in 2012. "It's the fact that I've abused my hands, my arms, and my knees for thirty or forty years. I don't hit the kit as hard as I used to: I've learned to expend less energy and still get a good result. I hit the drums smarter rather than harder now. And I've got a lot of trouble with my knees. When I walk up the stairs, they squeak. They hurt as well: sometimes I'm in excruciating pain for a few seconds."

Around 2012, there was a plan for the original members of Black Sabbath—Ozzy Osbourne, Tony Iommi, Geezer Butler, and the drummer Bill Ward—to reunite for an album and a tour. But according to Osbourne, rehearsals did not go as well as expected. "When Bill came along," explained the singer, "we all had to ask, 'Can he do an hour-and-a-half/two-hour gig? Can he cope?' My suggestion was that we run through a set and see how he got on, because he was so out of condition, and the drummer is the most demanding job in the whole band.

We looked at Bill, and he couldn't remember what the fuck we were doing." Osbourne said he was displeased that Ward had stuck little Post-it notes on parts of his kit, apparently as aides-memoire to help him play the songs. Later, Brad Wilk of Rage Against the Machine stepped in to play drums on the new album, *13*.

However, Ward maintained that the real problem was that he had not received a contract that was acceptable to him. "Since Spring of 2011, I've waited patiently and hopefully for a signable contract," he explained on his website. He said that his criteria for that contract were "based in mindful principles, respectability, and acknowledgement of my history within the band."

But there is no doubt that a minority of drummers are affected by extremely serious memory problems. Max Roach, for example, spent the final years of his life in assisted living. He developed Alzheimer's disease, the commonest form of dementia, and died in a New York hospice in 2007 at the age of eighty-three. At the end of his life, this phenomenal drummer, a virtuoso of bebop who changed the rules of jazz percussion, probably had very little memory of his tremendous musical achievements. One obituary went as far to say that Roach "was the first jazz musician to treat the drum set both functionally and as an autonomous instrument of limitless possibility." Dementia seems a cruel fate for somebody so talented and groundbreaking, but for a small number of drummers it's par for the course: it was recently estimated that thirty-five million people across the world were living with dementia, including more than five million Americans and nearly one million Britons. Some of those people will be musicians, and a proportion of those musicians, of course, will be drummers.

When I started researching this book and requesting interviews, I hoped that I would get to meet one of my favorite rock drummers from the 1970s. This was Dale Griffin, alias Buffin of Mott the Hoople, one half of the mighty rhythm section that made this band so enjoyable to listen to. It wasn't just me: David Bowie was a fan of Mott, too, and wrote their biggest hit, "All the Young Dudes," after he heard they were about to split. Years before he played guitar in the Clash, Mick Jones traveled around Britain just to hear them play. "I followed Mott the Hoople up and down the country," he later recalled. "I'd go to Liverpool or Newcastle or somewhere—sleep on the Town Hall steps, and bunk the fares on the trains, hide in the toilet when the ticket inspector came around. I'd jump off just before the train got to the station and climb over the fence. It was great times, and I always knew I wanted to be in a band and play guitar. That was it for me."

I tried to contact Buffin in 2013 and discovered the sad news. He had Alzheimer's disease and was living in a care home in Wales, so there was no possibility of an interview. But I spoke to his partner, Jean Smith, who not only told me Buffin's story but put me in touch with his lifelong friend Overend Watts, the other half of that mighty Mott rhythm section.

Buffin had met both Watts and Jean when he went to Ross-on-Wye Grammar School in Herefordshire, England, around the time that the 1950s turned into the '60s. Jean remembered him as an intelligent, erudite, thoughtful, and kind young man. "When we were at school he used to follow me round all the time," she told me. "But I was only twelve and I didn't know why he was following me!" she laughs. "After we'd left school, we met up one night at a club in Hereford. He walked me home that night and it was raining, so he let me wear his shoes so that my feet didn't get wet." Jean and Buffin lost touch shortly after that, as Buffin set off to make his name as a drummer.

"He was quite a shy bloke," said Overend Watts, "but he would do crazy things at school. I thought he was so eccentric for a thirteen-year-old. He'd fall into a puddle of water in the playground, and then he'd roll around in the puddle. I'd pick him up and ask if he was all right, and he'd say, 'Yeah, fine!'" Watts and Buffin started playing music together after the young drummer acquired a beautiful Premier blue sparkle drum kit. "I invited him to my house one afternoon with his drum kit," said Watts. "I was about fifteen and Buffin would've been thirteen. He sat at the kit and he was instantly amazing." The two friends played in a local band, the Soulents, before they became part of Mott the Hoople in the late 1960s.

Buffin never played long drum solos or flew through the air on his drum kit, but this baby-faced drummer propelled Mott's songs expertly, dramatically, and with subtle little flourishes and offbeats that the casual listener might miss. Some of his best work can be heard on "All the Way from Memphis," from the *Mott* album, and on the band's earlier recording of the Velvet Underground song "Sweet Jane."

After years of silence, Jean Smith said she had a chance meeting with Buffin in Ross-on-Wye in 1979, by which time Mott the Hoople was history. "I was with my mother, and I was heavily pregnant with my first daughter. I think Dale was in the throes of divorce at the time. We had a little chat in the street, and then went our separate ways." Twenty-one years later, Smith registered on the Friends Reunited website, which helps old school friends become reacquainted. "And the only person who contacted me was Dale. He was living in London, but he was broke and was a bit worried about how he was going to keep his flat there. Eventually, he left London and came to live with me in Usk, in Wales."

Buffin was losing his memory by the time Mott reconvened to play some reunion shows in 2009, so there were doubts about whether he could take part. "We had some rehearsals in Usk," said Watts, "and Buffin hadn't been too well, and in the first rehearsal I didn't think he was going to be able to do anything at all. But we rehearsed there for four or five weeks, and gradually he got better and better. He started remembering what he used to play, and getting confident. He couldn't do anything new, but he remembered those old drum parts." However, he wasn't deemed well enough to play whole gigs, and Martin Chambers of the Pretenders was brought in to play in his place—though when the band played London's Hammersmith Apollo, Buffin came onstage to play encores. "And then it was like the old days, almost," said Watts. "The power was there, he was really good, and the only problem we had was stopping him when he was playing, because he tended to look at the kit; he wasn't looking up as much as he used to."

Buffin's brief but triumphant return to the kit lingered in the drummer's memory for a while. "For some time afterwards," said Jean Smith, "I'd talk about Hammersmith and he would remember it. Not very clearly, but he certainly was aware that he'd done something. And we'd walk past the British Legion club in Usk, where the band had rehearsed, and he'd say, 'Oh, that's where I used to go to work!'"

The band reunited again four years later, by which time Buffin was clearly less able to participate. "It's a progressive illness," said Watts, "and it wouldn't be fair to try and put him through it. I don't think it would be the right thing to do."

Jean Smith talked poignantly about visiting Buffin at his care home. "I think he still knows I'm someone that he knows and likes," she said, "but he doesn't remember my name anymore. I walk around with him—that's all he does all day, walks around the home, which is quite exhausting." Buffin's fate seems particularly cruel, given that he had previously had an excellent memory. "His memory was phenomenal," said Smith. "He remembered everything. Before 'Mr. Alka Seltzer'—as he used to call it—took its awful toll on his memory, he did tell me lots of stories about his time with the band."

Of course, there is no evidence that drummers such as Buffin and Max Roach contracted Alzheimer's as a direct result of their percussive occupation. But it is clear that drumming can be a damaging business, leading to a variety of nasty physical conditions from broken bones and carpal-tunnel syndrome to serious disability in some cases. Nevertheless, I am not convinced by the idea that most drummers are masochists, reveling in the physical problems that their chosen instrument brings. Some highly experienced drummers claim that they are so careful when they play that they have never been hurt or damaged in any way. Indeed, they give the impression of believing that injuries are actually unprofessional. If session drummers admit to being physically injured five times a week, that might even make them less employable by top producers. And when drummers have described their long lists of ailments to me, it has often been with a regretful air, a world-weary sigh, or a shudder of horror. The injuries are occupational hazards, that's all they are, and they are prepared to suffer these hazards because they love what they do.

Perhaps, in our quest to discover what turns people into drummers, we have been looking too closely at the present day. Could the answer lie in the past—somewhere in the long history of drumming, or in the stories of how famous drummers started out on their individual percussive journeys?

7

THE BEGINNING
OF TIME

People will complain about this book—you can bet your rare 1964 Ludwig Black Oyster Pearl drum kit on that. The impossible-to-please whingers and trolls who lurk in the cold, damp crawlspaces of the Internet will moan that I have featured such practitioners of percussion as Ginger Baker, Ash Soan, and Debbi Peterson of the Bangles, but that I have inexcusably left out their Favorite Drummer of All Time. What was I thinking? They will take the omission personally before attacking me personally. "Call this a book about drummers? Where was Harry 'Nuts' McHenderson of Superhardcore Zombie Klan, globally recognized as the best living drummer from Saskatchewan and the surrounding area?" Every time *Rolling Stone* or *Spin* magazine runs a chart of the world's greatest drummers, the whingers and trolls are out in force, telling them they've got it all wrong, and why didn't they ask them to write the chart instead? The concept of subjectivity may be beyond their grasp.

Well, I have news for the trolls. I have actually left out hundreds of thousands, possibly millions, of drummers from this book. I had no choice: we simply don't know their names. These are the people who played the drums through the many millennia of prehistory—including our ancestors from the Stone Age, Bronze Age, and Iron Age—together with the drummers in other ancient civilizations, such as Incas, Minoans, ancient Greeks, and ancient Egyptians, whose names went unrecorded or have been lost over the centuries.

Just as innumerable individuals from distant millennia "invented" the wheel and discovered fire independently, so countless ancient people discovered the percussive properties of hollow logs and found that you could create a pleasing and powerful sound by stretching an animal skin over a log, a clay vessel, or a frame, and then beating it. The unearthed remains of some of these drums have proved to be up to seven or eight millennia old. Ancient artworks also testify to the practice of drumming. One stone carving found in Carchemish in Mesopotamia, dating back to about 800 B.C., shows three people standing in a row, with the central figure apparently holding a large circular object that is being beaten by his two compadres. They are all wearing hippyish-looking headgear that wouldn't look out of place on the head of Neil Peart or Chad Smith. Very early cymbals have also been found in China and across the Middle East. However, creating an actual drum kit—bringing various drums together to make a set for laying down a complex groove—appears to have been beyond the wit of primitive man.

Ancient drums were not only used to make music: they enabled people to communicate over long distances, and they had ceremonial and ritualistic functions that we may only partly understand today. They were also used to rally troops and terrify enemies. During my conversation with Nick Mason of Pink Floyd, he observed: "The drum is such a primitive instrument. And most instruments, be it the lute or the clavichord or whatever, are tied into the concept of love, whereas the drum is entirely designed for going to war, it seems to me. Drums started off as a tribal dance instrument, but they became this extraordinary marching, military thing."

During the Battle of Halidon Hill in 1333, the forces of King Edward III of England fought the Scots using musical instruments including drums as well as weapons. An account of the battle, written soon afterward, tells of "Englische mynstrelles" beating "tabers" and making "a great schowte upon the Skottes."

"Tabers," written elsewhere as "tabors" or "tabrets," were small portable drums that often had snares stretched across their heads to intensify their sound. Despite the fact that drums had already been played for many thousands of years, you won't find the word *drum* mentioned in any literature of this period. The word only came into use in English around the 1540s, and even then it didn't become widespread for a while. Even today, that curious lexicographical fact has occasional repercussions in Christian communities, when somebody objects to the playing of drums in a church, viewing the instrument as ungodly or even satanic. At times like these, the objectors will often use the line "You won't find drums in the Bible."

Well, it's true that you won't find the word *drum* in the earliest King James Version of the Bible, completed in 1611. However, you will find plenty of timbrels, tabrets, and panderetas in early Bibles, which are just drums by other names. There are several references to cymbals as well, *cymbal* being a much older word. The ancient Greeks and Romans both had a name for the cymbal—*kymbalon* and *cymbalum*, respectively—and it

was known as *cymbale* in Old French. And in one exciting bib-
lical example in the Second Book of Samuel, we have the early
makings of the drum kit, when drums (timbrels) and cymbals
are used together:

> And David and all the house of Israel played before the
> LORD on all manner of instruments made of fir wood,
> even on harps, and on psalteries, and on timbrels, and on
> cornets, and on cymbals. (2 Samuel 6:5)

In many parts of Africa, drums have long been used for
dancing, to accompany rituals, and for communication. Africa's association with drumming is so strong that African drums
have made their mark on racist language. In 2013, when the
politician Godfrey Bloom was a member of the UK Indepen-
dence Party (Ukip), he declared at a public meeting that he
thought Britain should not be giving so much money in foreign
aid to "Bongo Bongo Land."

The transatlantic slave trade, which prevailed from the sixteenth to the nineteenth centuries, brought many African drums
to America, though many slave owners banned their use when
they realized that slaves could use them for clandestine communication. The oldest African-American object in the British
Museum in London is a hand drum known as "the Akan drum,"
which was carried over the sea from West Africa in the eigh-
teenth century and ended up in the Colony of Virginia. A few
years ago, this drum became the focus of a special exhibition,
which suggested that during its sea journey it may have been
used in the practice of "dancing the slaves"—in which African
captives were forcibly exercised to music aboard the slave ships.

In a 1906 history book about the French Revolution, we find

ceremonial drumming adding drama to the execution of Louis XVI in 1793: "There was a surging among the crowd eager to catch a glimpse of the doomed man who had been their king. But the soldiers kept their ranks, and at the hoarse command of [General] Santerre the drummers beat out a roll of thunderous music which drowned the beast-like cries of the excited mob." Less than a century later came the American Civil War, in which drummers on both sides played a crucial part. One of the best-loved archetypes of that conflict was the brave drummer boy, not old enough to fight but prepared to risk injury and death while beating out rhythms to rally the troops and intimidate their enemies. Drummers usually carried a single drum that hung at an angle from a strap, freeing their hands to hold the drumsticks. They played when it was time for soldiers to rise in the morning, when it was time to assemble, and when it was time for breakfast or dinner. They played to instruct men to begin marching, with their rhythms helping to keep them in step. Their drumbeats carried coded instructions on the battlefield, telling soldiers to advance or retreat. There was also an important place for drummers in Civil War brass bands, and they would accompany stirring patriotic tunes on snare drums, bass drums, and cymbals.

The 1905 book *Drum Taps in Dixie: Memories of a Drummer Boy* details the life of a young Union drummer in the Civil War. This biographical volume was written by Delavan S. Miller, who was a twelve-year-old boy living in West Carthage, New York, when the conflict began in 1861. Drummer boys like Miller were required to learn many traditional drum rudiments, such as the "double drag" and the "long roll"—which is played using rapid alternate double strokes (left-left, right-right, left-left, right-right, et cetera)—and were often required to play for agonizingly long periods of time. According to Miller, "A boy would not 'pass muster' in those days unless he could do the double and single drag with variations, execute the 'long roll,' imitate the rattle of musketry, besides various other accomplishments with the sticks."

One of the drummer boy's many tasks was to beat the reveille. "In a camp there were always some heavy sleepers," writes Miller, "and it was the business of the drummers in beating the morning reveille to make noise enough to awake them. Many a time have I seen a fellow rush out of his tent attired in nothing but shirt, drawers and cap and take his place in the ranks hardly in time to answer 'here' when his name was called." Occasionally, transgressive soldiers would have to be drummed out of the ranks, as Miller once witnessed: "The only man I ever saw drummed out of camp was down in front of Petersburg. He was a coward, and large placards proclaiming the fact were suspended from his neck, one on his breast and the other on his back, his head was shaved and a fifer and drummer marched him all through the division to the tune of the 'Rogue's March,' and then he was given a dishonorable discharge and sent home."

When the Civil War ended in 1865, dramatically reducing the need for military percussion, thousands of drums ended up in junk shops and pawnshops, fueling a sudden peacetime craze for marching bands. Excitingly, it is at this point, sometime in the late nineteenth century in the USA, that we finally start to see groups of drums coming together under the control of a single drummer—the creation of the drum kit.

The much-asked question "Who invented the drum kit?" is unanswerable. Its creation is a perfect example of what the intellectual musician and producer Brian Eno has called "scenius." When we explore the history of a particular technology, the traditional human tendency is to find the solitary genius who created it; but often it has been created by a whole cultural "scene" involving any number of people. New Orleans has been cited more than any other place as the likely crucible for the drum kit. This lively port, a great multicultural crossroads where the rhythms of Africa mingled with European music, was the birthplace of jazz. The musicians in the city's marching bands would often settle down to play at night in riverboats and in the dance halls of Storyville, the red-light district. And as soon as drummers stopped marching and sat down to play, the potential for innovation suddenly increased. They could play a snare drum and a bass drum at the same time; they might hit the bass drum with sticks or they might actually kick it, giving it the name "kick drum," which it still enjoys today. Before the first drum stands were manufactured, drummers might position their drums on chairs or stools. They might start attaching other percussive odds and ends, like cymbals, to the bass drum.

The writer Jon Cohan has provided a colorful description of this great moment in musical history: "In New Orleans near the turn of the century, musicians found much of their work in the cathouses, saloons, vaudeville pits and riverboats of that great delta city. The traditional brass band had to be pared down to fewer players to fit in these smaller spaces. Just one drummer was now faced with the task of recreating the sounds of many drummers. Military beats and rolls were modified to fit into the new ragtime music. By necessity, all the percussion instruments had to be gathered together and, in some way, played by one musician."

The drummer's weird assortment of instruments became known as "traps," short for "contraptions," and soon it would typically include additions such as toms, a hi-hat, woodblocks, cowbells, a triangle, and a tambourine. The drum kit is one of the greatest marvels of multiculturalism, combining European percussion with Eastern cymbals, toms from the Native American and Chinese traditions, a big bass drum from Turkey, and all manner of exotic doodads from other parts of the globe. And there was a great leap forward when somebody rigged up an early version of a pedal for the bass drum, so it could be struck much more easily and the hands were liberated to play other drums and cymbals. The Ludwig drum company took notice and began manufacturing its own spring-driven bass-drum pedal in Chicago around 1910.

However, just because the drum kit had been invented, it didn't mean that its use became universal overnight. The jazz icon Dizzy Gillespie once recalled going to church in the 1930s and seeing the old-fashioned division of labor in operation:

"Johnny Burch played the snare drum, and his brother Willie beat the cymbal; another one of the Burch brothers played the bass drum and the other the tambourine. They used to keep at least four different rhythms going, and as the congregation joined in, the number of rhythms would increase with foot stomping, hand clapping, and people catching the spirit and jumping up and down on the wooden floor, which also resounded like a drum."

Around the same time, Gillespie played in a band with a drummer called Wes Buchanan, who worked wonders despite the fact that he had only one drum—a bass drum: "Wes Buchanan was terrific. Never since have I heard anyone beat a bass drum like him. He used to put his free hand and his knee up against the bass drum and make different tones, hambone sounds and other funky stuff. I've never heard that since and have come to realize that Wes Buchanan was actually great.

Drummers today get a similar effect by using their elbow on the snare drum or tom-tom; it's the same basic idea."

Gillespie remembered that Buchanan would occasionally step out from behind his drum and start dancing, following a long tradition among drummers. Early drummers were not only enormously influenced by the rhythms of tap dancers, but they often tap-danced themselves. As a young man, the American jazz drummer Papa Jo Jones worked as both a drummer and tap dancer in carnival shows during the early twentieth century. The great Buddy Rich could be seen performing in theaters as a tap dancer when he was a small boy, and another brilliant jazz player, Louie Bellson, was taught to tap-dance by his sister when he was growing up in Illinois. "Dancing is rhythm and timing and pacing," Bellson explained many years later. "Those two feet are very important to drummers; you want to reiterate with your feet what you do with your hands, and tap really helps."

In the 1937 film *A Damsel in Distress*, Fred Astaire managed to tap-dance and play a set of drums (with his feet as well as a pair of drumsticks) in the same routine as the band played Gershwin's "Nice Work If You Can Get It." And the connection between drumming and tap dancing isn't just an old-fashioned curiosity: in fact, the discipline of tap has helped some modern drummers develop their foot-pedal skills. Long before he became a legendary session drummer, Steve Gadd performed tap-dance routines with his brother Eddie, and Gadd tap-danced for TV viewers on a *Mickey Mouse Club* show in the 1950s. Ahmir "Questlove" Thompson was introduced to the magic of tap as late as the mid-1970s as a five-year-old boy learning the drums in Philadelphia. "Right away, I learned something interesting about drum lessons: they don't let you touch the drums," Questlove recalled recently. "Instead, they make you take tap-dancing lessons, because tap is a good way to coordinate your hands and feet. I was a latter-day Sammy Davis, Jr., a real Philly hoofer."

The British drummer Michèle Drees keeps the tap-dancing tradition alive in the twenty-first century. She has accompanied some extraordinary hoofers in exciting shows at Ronnie Scott's jazz club and at the London Jazz Festival. "I'm a drummer because of tap dancing," she said. "Tap dance was my first love when I was about five. I was growing up in a little village in Cornwall when I saw the Nicholas Brothers dancing in the film *Stormy Weather*, and it was mind-blowing, like seeing something from Mars." Drees has been researching the links between drumming and tap, and new discoveries keep emerging. "One of my biggest heroes, Max Roach, used to say how influenced he was by tap dancers when he was younger. And when I saw the drummer Roy Haynes play recently, he walked to the front of the stage and started tap-dancing. It thrilled me so much to see that."

That other big tradition from the history of drumming— the marching band—lingers on in the US today. Every American college worth its salt has an ensemble featuring drummers who can beat out rhythms, march through the streets and over football fields, and probably chew gum at the same time. There are the Harvard University Band and the Yale Precision Marching Band, as well as more colorful-sounding outfits such as the Arizona State University Sun Devil Marching Band, the University of Kansas Marching Jayhawks, and the University of South Florida Herd of Thunder. It is tempting to imagine that the Washington State University Cougar Marching Band is composed entirely of seductive older women. Other marching bands represent significant sectors of the population, such as the San Francisco Lesbian/Gay Freedom Band and the Leftist Marching Band.

Marching bands loom large in the early lives of many modern rock, pop, and jazz drummers. Steve Smith, who played on ten albums with the band Journey, was inspired by the drums played by marching bands parading around his home state of Massachusetts. Steve Gadd, Billy Cobham, Mike Portnoy, Glenn Kotche, and Travis Barker all spent part of their youth drumming in marching bands. Ndugu Chancler played the snare drum in his high school marching band in Louisiana. David Lovering of the Pixies had an uncomfortable memory of playing in a marching band in Massachusetts in 1976, when he was a fourteen-year-old freshman in high school. "I was marching along in the band, playing the bass drum, and my best friend Scott had the tri-toms—the three drums in front of him, which were what I really wanted to play. A local newspaper took a picture of the parade, and it was a shot of me and Scott. I was much shorter then and Scott was really tall, and you could really see the height difference in the picture. And they called it 'The Tall and Short of It.' That hurt. That hurt incredibly bad!"

John Densmore of the Doors was ambivalent about playing in his high school's marching band before the Swinging Sixties arrived. As he reflected many years afterward, "With our horrible plumed hats and gaudy, rigid uniforms, I felt like I had joined the army. In those days, playing in the marching band ranked next to having leprosy, but I loved the feeling of power one got when playing with forty other musicians." After he went to study at Santa Monica City College in 1963, the teenage Densmore opted again for marching duties, and the college ensemble triumphed in a citywide competition. This was a surprise result, as one of the rival bands—who ended up in second place—was an "ultra-cool black band from LA City College. I didn't think it was possible for a marching band to swing, but these dudes did it."

Clem Burke told me about his days in the St. Andrews Drum and Bugle Corps in New Jersey. "I was being mentored to take over from the guy who played a thing called rudimental bass drum, which involves playing all the rudiments as you would on a snare drum, and all the drum parts, but you have a bass drum strapped to you, and you have two huge mallets and you're playing the rudiments—you're not just going '*doong . . . doong . . . doong.*' And you're marching in front of a whole band. It was fun. But I can recall the day when I quit the marching band in order to continue with my high school rock band. There was a priest involved, and I had to go to him to tell him I was quitting the corps. I recall saying, 'Father Donovan, I'm sorry, I'm gonna have to quit the Drum and Bugle Corps: I got my rock band.' And he said he was sorry to see me go."

Mickey Hart became one of the two drummers known as "the Rhythm Devils" in the Grateful Dead. In his absorbing book *Drumming at the Edge of Magic*, Hart revealed his close connection to the world of marching bands and rudimental drumming: "My father, Lenny Hart, was a national and world champion rudimental drummer. My mother, Leah, took up drumming to get close to him; he was her drum teacher at the Coney Island American Legion drum and bugle corps, and together they won the mixed doubles competition at the 1939 World's Fair in New York. Two years later they married and settled in Brooklyn. I was born two years after that, but by then the marriage was over, and my father had vanished, leaving a hole in our lives."

Hart, who grew up on Long Island, gave a wonderful description of how marching bands affected him as a boy: "If there was a parade when I was a kid, I'd always be as close to the drums as I could get, running alongside for block after block. The hairs on the back of my neck quivered with excitement as the snare drums, in perfect synch, roared out their rhythmic tattoos. The bass drum was like a blow to the stomach, leaving me breathless."

The British drummer Steve White recalled a similar moment from his youth in south London. "My 'flash moment' with drumming was being eight years old, outside on a Sunday morning with my dad in Lewisham," he said, "and we watched a Boys' Brigade band walk towards us. And it was like the trumpets and drums of heaven, as far as I was concerned: it sounded so amazing. From that moment on, I was obsessed. It just spoke to me, and I wanted to play the drums like that."

Further inspiration came when White, now a teenager, saw his idol Buddy Rich play at Ronnie Scott's jazz club in London in the early 1980s. "I just thought he was doing everything you could possibly want from a drum solo. He played with such emotion, and it just blew me away. And then I got to meet him afterwards. He was sweating and he was wrapped in tinfoil, like a tinfoil cape, and he looked really small. He was using an office there a makeshift dressing room, and I walked into the office and said, 'Mr. Rich, I just want to say that was absolutely amazing . . . and can I have a pair of your sticks?' And he went, 'Kid, this is my dressing room, not my drum room.' I said, 'I'm sorry, Mr. Rich: that was very rude.' And he said to this guy, 'Get the kid a pair of sticks,' and the guy went off and took the actual sticks that were on his kit and gave them to me, which I still have."

Other modern drummers have been inspired by jazz greats such as Rich. "I remember seeing the film *Jazz on a Summer's Day* [1960]," said Nick Mason, "and there's a lovely sequence where Chico Hamilton plays a drum solo, but he plays it with mallets, and I thought, 'That's interesting.' That influenced my playing on 'Set the Controls for the Heart of the Sun.'" Mason was already in the nascent Pink Floyd Sound in 1966 when he saw Cream play Regent Street Polytechnic college in London, but Ginger Baker's performance made him think differently about drumming. "When I saw him playing his champagne sparkle kit, I just thought, 'Yes!' Ginger Baker is the reason I'm here, really."

When Blondie played the Roundhouse in London in July 2013, Clem Burke honored his usual practice of decorating his dressing room with pictures of his heroes Ringo Starr and Keith Moon. But he revealed that he also had a strong admiration for Earl Palmer, who started performing in the 1940s. "When I was a kid, Moon was my hero—he still is—but he taught me more about what not to do than what to do. John Bonham as well. They were both brilliant drummers, but there's a life lesson to be learned from their pitfalls. I knew Earl Palmer in the last ten years of his life, and he was always a gentleman. He worked with everybody, from Fats Domino to Frank Sinatra. He carried himself well and was dignified, and he was a real role model for me. He played right into his eighties: he saw it all and did it all, and he was still here to talk about it—he wasn't destroyed by it."

Multitudes of American drummers, famous and lesser-known, can put a date on the moment they decided to become a drummer. On February 9, 1964, the Beatles appeared on *The Ed Sullivan Show*, and millions of viewers saw twenty-three-year-old

Ringo Starr bashing a beautiful drum kit, perched on a tall drum riser above his three mop-topped bandmates. Starr was unlike the jazz and rock 'n' roll drummers who had previously appeared on TV: he was instantaneously charismatic, he was holding his sticks using the modern "matched grip" (unlike the "traditional grip" derived from military drumming, with the left stick held almost as if it were a chopstick), and he was bashing the drums in a solid rock-pop style.

A record seventy-three million people across the USA were watching the show that night—approaching one third of the entire nation—and inevitably some of those people had latent drumming skills. One was a thirteen-year-old boy in California called Terry Bozzio who had already been fooling around for several years on improvised drum kits made from bits and bobs. He later remembered the impression that Starr's TV appearance had on him:

"That was it. I told my dad I had to have drum lessons. Ringo had a small kit and he sat high, so you could see him play. So I sat in front of a mirror we had in the living room and I emulated his movements. By the time I took my first drum lessons I was ready to go, because I had practiced it in my mind and mimed it so much. My teachers told me I was four or five weeks ahead, as far as coordination and that stuff."

Watching the same show over on the East Coast, in New Jersey, was a twelve-year-old boy called Max Weinberg, destined to become the drummer in Bruce Springsteen's E Street Band. Weinberg later wrote: "More than any other drummer, Ringo Starr changed my life. The impact and memory of that band on *The Ed Sullivan Show* in 1964 will never leave me. I can still see Ringo in the back moving that beat with his whole body, his right hand swinging off his sock cymbal while his left hand pounds the snare. He was fantastic, but I think what got to me the most was his smile. I knew he was having the time of his life."

A little farther north, Joey Kramer and his family were watching that show in Yonkers, New York. As the future Aerosmith drummer sat on the floor in front of the family's shabby old orange couch, he found himself transfixed. "My eyes were glued to Ringo up there on the riser in the center with a smile on his face, occasionally giving his head that signature shake," he later wrote. "It was like he was sitting on top of the world, the coolest guy on the planet. His partners were spread out in front of him, and he was the man in the middle. I was mesmerized; I felt it. I imagined it was me at that moment on stage in front of all those screaming fans."

In some ways, by inspiring so many Americans, Starr was doing the equivalent of selling snow to Alaska. Not only was his style of playing derived from the rock 'n' roll and R&B drummers of the USA, but he was playing an American drum kit as well. His Oyster Black Pearl kit was made by Ludwig, the same business that, half a century before, had marketed the first bass-drum pedal. At its headquarters in Chicago, Ludwig was soon overwhelmed with orders for drum kits like the one Starr had played. The company quickly increased its production, running its factory 24/7 to keep up with this unprecedented demand for its products. For three years after that TV show, the factory closed only for Thanksgiving, Christmas, and New Year's Day. In 1964 its sales totaled $6.1 million, but that had more than doubled two years later to $13.1 million.

And just as a young drummer risks the wrath of his neighbors by practicing late into the night, Ludwig was now annoying the locals with the noise of its factory. The company's then president, William F. Ludwig Jr., went into public-relations/damage-limitation mode, visiting neighbors, inviting them on factory tours, and buttering them up in a local bar. "Over beers, we worked out compromises," he later explained. "I agreed to shut down certain machines after 10 o'clock, like the stick lathes and the scarfing machines, and the neighborhood allowed us to expand."

Frequently, it becomes apparent that a young person is going to be a drummer when he or she starts attacking household objects in a percussive manner. The infant Nicko McBrain would bash on the objects he found in his parents' kitchen, including the cooker. As a child, Charlie Watts of the Rolling Stones became frustrated at his inability to play a cheap banjo, so he took the instrument apart and started playing it like a drum. Paul Thompson, the man who gave British art rockers Roxy Music their solid rhythmic foundation, told me that he put together his earliest kit as a child in the 1950s using biscuit tins, cardboard boxes, and metal parts from his Meccano toy engineering set before graduating to a snare drum bought in installments from a mail-order catalog.

The young Dave Grohl improvised a drum kit using ordinary furniture and bedding. "The house that I grew up in was pretty small," he once explained, "so we didn't have room to put a drum set anywhere, and I didn't have enough money to get a drum set for myself. But I knew the configuration of a drum set, so I'd set up a pillow between my legs as a snare drum and I'd use my bed as a tom and a chair as a hi-hat, and I'd just play along with the records all day long, till there was sweat dripping from my windows! I was so into it. And I wasn't playing along with Beatles albums or AC/DC records: I'd play along with these really fast hardcore punk-rock albums like Bad Brains and Minor Threat."

"When I was six years old I started beating on things," remembered Ndugu Chancler. "I made me some drums out of oatmeal boxes and coffee cans. I didn't have any formal training till I was thirteen, but before then I just beat on things and kept a rhythm going."

Chad Smith was another early starter, drumming in earnest from the age of seven at his home in Michigan. The future Red Hot Chili Pepper's first drum kit comprised a series of cardboard ice-cream tubs, which had been rescued from the back of a Baskin-Robbins store when his parents noticed early percussive tendencies. "I would hit these tubs with Lincoln Logs," he revealed, "wooden sticks from a kids' building toy." There were no cymbals on this makeshift kit, let alone a hi-hat or a cowbell. "It was a very tribal sound," he laughed. "I ended up putting holes in those ice-cream tubs, and then I got a little crappy drum set from a department store. I think my parents just wanted to see if I was going to stick with it, before they would be nice enough to help me get a decent, real drum set. In the Midwest, where I grew up, a lot of the homes had basements, and that's where I played my drums, playing along to all this music. Even though I was down in the basement, it was still loud—so I'd play when I came home from school. And my mom would say, 'Okay, I'm going shopping now. Now would be a good time for you to play your drums.' My parents were very supportive, because they saw that it was something that I was really passionate about."

"I was always tapping and fiddling," said Rich Jupp of Elbow, "and I still do." Jupp recalled putting together a "monstrous kit" as a boy in his bedroom in Greater Manchester, begging and borrowing bits and pieces from different places. "It was whatever I could get my hands on—bits that I found at school, and bits that I could afford to buy from shops." The bass drum was broken, so he repaired it with a large quantity of gaffer tape, and he didn't have proper stands for his cymbals: he used test-tube clamps from his school's chemistry department instead. "I nicked those from Tottington High School. Sorry, guys!"

Phil Collins said he remembered being given a toy drum for Christmas when he was a three-year-old boy in Hounslow, west London, in the 1950s. He had two resourceful uncles who noticed how much he enjoyed playing it and decided to make him something better. "They made me a drum kit that consisted of two pieces of wood in the shape of a cross, and at each of the four ends there was a hole. There were metal rods in all four holes, and at the ends of the rods there was attached a tambourine, a snare drum, a cymbal, and a triangle, I think. I would sit down and play this kit in the living room—probably concentrating less on the triangle. I played it from the age of five until I was ten. You could dismantle the kit and put it in a suitcase. I often wonder what happened to that, because I never threw it away: it just disappeared. It's something I'd love to have now."

Collins progressed to a real bass drum and snare drum, bought from a boy across the road, and then asked for a complete drum kit for his twelfth birthday in January 1963. "My mum insisted that I make some kind of sacrifice, because the drum kit was fifty-five pounds, which was a little bit above her budget, so I sold my train set and put the money towards the kit. It was actually my brother's train set!"

Novice drummers have often benefited from lessons with experienced players. The young Keith Moon took lessons from

Carlo Little, a drummer he admired greatly, who played with Screaming Lord Sutch and had drummed in an early incarnation of the Rolling Stones. Moon later gave lessons to Zak Starkey, son of Ringo Starr. The story goes that when Starkey asked Moon how he could execute a fantastic Moon-style roll when he only had a couple of toms, the older drummer's response was to buy his pupil a drum kit.

Other teachers could be more demanding, and even downright peculiar. "My first drum teacher was an old gentleman, in his eighties," said David Lovering. "My dad would take me to him every Wednesday night. I just sat at a table learning how to read and write sheet music and doing rudimentary things, and I did that for two years. I knew that he had a drum set down in the basement, but I wasn't allowed to play it yet. When he felt you'd learned everything, you graduated to downstairs—you got on the drum set. And I remember going for years, learning to read and write and doing all the rudiments, and then finally it was, 'Okay, come on into the basement.' And I was like, 'Oh yeah!' So we went down, and there was this drum set from the 1920s, with a big calfskin kick drum, and I started learning how to play all this stuff from old 78 records, all big-band and bebop stuff. The newest thing he gave me to learn was a song called 'Put Your Hand in the Hand,' by a Canadian band called Ocean, and even that was pretty dated by then.

"I learned as much as I could with that teacher, and after that, when I was still in high school, I had another instructor, a Berklee graduate who came to my house to teach me. That was interesting, because he taught me some really complicated jazz stuff, and he taught me how to transcribe Neal Peart's drum parts on my Rush albums. And we'd talk about weed!"

"I'd tried studying the drums and taking lessons, and it never really resonated," said Joey Waronker. "But then I hooked up with Freddie Gruber, who was this great old jazz musician and a fantastic educator. He was like a weird version of Mr. Miyagi from *The Karate Kid*: he had this very abstract and spiritual system of teaching you to develop great technique, and it involved a whole year of not even playing. You would sit and hold the drumsticks, and he would study how you were sitting and how you were holding the sticks. Gradually we moved on to letting the sticks fall on a drum pad, and that went on for months! And then at the end of it all, suddenly I had this very natural technique, and I could do things that I could never do before and not hurt myself. I would spend hours with him, and I would show up and watch other students have lessons with him. We all knew he was nuts! But he was helping all of us become the best possible players we could be. I definitely wouldn't have got to where I am today without that experience."

Another novice drummer who had to show considerable patience was John Densmore of the Doors, who had private lessons at a west LA shop run by a drum teacher called Mr. Muir. But for a long time, Densmore was only allowed to play on a practice pad. "It was terribly frustrating having to be taught the nine essential drum rudiments on a silly piece of rubber while being surrounded by sparkling drums of every color," he has since recalled. "But Mr. Muir insisted that I wasn't quite ready for the big, loud drum set—or his ears weren't ready to hear my earnest pounding . . . I suspected my parents of paying Mr. Muir off to keep me away from those cacophonous drums until the last possible moment. It was for the best. Those damned nine essential rudiments gave me my touch. It made the difference later on between a tree-trunk-slamming, heavy-metal technique and a subtler jazz-rock style."

When the student is ready, the saying goes, the teacher will come. Omar Hakim was definitely ready from an early age, but he wasn't thinking of drum teachers when he started flirting with a pretty girl at his elementary school in Jamaica, Queens, New York, in the 1960s. "I was one of those kids who walked around with drumsticks in my back pocket all day," Hakim told me. "And I remember there was a little girl in the school that I was very fond of, whose name was Rochelle Perkins. One day we were in the schoolyard and she saw the drumsticks in my back pocket and she said, 'My daddy plays the drums.' And I was like, 'Wow. Really? Cool! Who's your daddy?' And she said, 'I live right across the street.' And I said, 'Well, can I meet him?' And so I'm hanging out with this girl that I thought was super-cute, I can't believe I'm going to her house, and when we got to her house and opened up the door, there was this Slingerland drum set in the living room. I flipped out—and at that point I ended the relationship with Rochelle and began the relationship with her dad, Walter Perkins, who was a fantastic jazz drummer. His pro name was Baby Sweets. Rochelle introduced me to her dad, and he offered to give me drum lessons for free. But he said I had to ask my parents first.

"So I went to my dad, who was also a jazz musician, and told him Mr. Perkins said he would give me drum lessons, and he said, 'Oh . . . Walter!' It turned out they were friends. So my dad and I walked over to Walter's house, and they gave each other a giant hug and started talking. Walter said, 'I didn't know this was your son.' So Walter started teaching me the rudiments, and he got me started in the right direction, in terms of getting my technique together. But then a couple of years later when I was about eleven, I met another teacher, Clyde Lucas, who had the biggest impact on my technical development. This was a drummer of tremendous finesse, who was playing with the Count Basie big band when I met him. Clyde said something very interesting to me. He said, 'You play very well, but you're working too hard. I'm going to teach you how to make the sticks work for *you*.' And that's what he did. One of the first lessons he gave me was 'the Anatomy of the Drumstick.' He told me how you should understand this instrument that you're holding in your hand, and how it interacts with your body, and by doing that you will be able to play much better."

Drumming can be highly technical, very clever, and extremely complex. But it is also a noisy business, so drummers are often people who have a special relationship with noise. In his book, Mickey Hart said that loud sounds had attracted him for the whole of his life. "Twenty feet from Grandfather's house a trolley kept up an insistent, clattering rhythm," he wrote. "It was the timekeeper, pulsing every twenty to forty minutes, never diminishing or increasing, rain or shine, summer or winter, dawn or dusk. At the other extreme, humming and atonally melodic, was the constant surge of traffic up and down Nostrand Avenue, flowing into the big artery of Quentin Road. And layered in on top was the drone of TVs and radios, exuberant sometimes angry yelling, and the slap-slap-slap of gangs of kids running the territory. Loud, percussive, industrial, urban sound.

"I've always been temperamentally on the side of untamed sound. If it was charged with the unexpected, then I loved it. It didn't have to be aggressive; it could be soft like a raindrop or sharp and harsh like a barking dog. The point is, it tugged at me with an almost painful excitement."

That primal desire for noise, and the urge to express rhythms, gives these special people a dedication to their art and a determination to create, invent, and continually fiddle with their equipment in the cause of music. Drummers are endlessly resourceful and go to great lengths to improve and perfect their instruments. The spirit of drumming, with all its restlessness and cleverness, has given the world such inventions as the African talking drum, the snare drum, the bass drum, the cymbal, the hi-hat, and the whole set of "traps"—plus thousands of unique, customized drum kits, tailored to the needs of specific drummers.

You don't find this drum dedication in a great number of people, and it doesn't arrive suddenly in the middle of your life: it's highly unusual to switch one day from being a Wall Street trader or an international arms dealer to being a passionately committed, full-time drummer. Hart's friend Remo Belli, who founded the famous Remo drum company in 1957, told him that around 1 percent of the world's population are drummers, and Hart has suggested that drummers have an innate talent: "There is a need to drum. I believe that. No drummer really knows why, you're just born with it, it's what makes you part of Remo Belli's one percent. You can acquire technique but not this need, it's a birthright. There have been times when I wished I'd been born without it. When I was younger, if I didn't play well, I'd feel like killing myself. I used to slip on stage before a show and pray—pray that I didn't screw up, that my energy and talent and will would be strong enough to carry me to the Edge one more time."

If people are truly born to drum, drumming must have an overwhelming genetic component. And there may well be, because a significant number of children of drummers become drummers themselves. Ginger Baker's son, Kofi, is a brilliant drummer in his own right and has played in the new-generation tribute band Sons of Cream. Jason Bonham is also a fine drummer, and just happens to be the son of the late John Bonham. Steve Gadd's son Duke has played in a band called Boneyard—on drums. Woody Woodmansey, formerly of David Bowie's Spiders from Mars, formed the band 3-D with his sons Nick and Danny, who are drummers like their father. Max Weinberg's son Jay also plays a mean kit, as does Bill Bruford's son Alex. At the end of the show "An Evening with Nicko," I watched Nicko McBrain perform a drum duet with his son Nicholas McBrain.

Other drummers spoke proudly of the percussive proficiency of their offspring. "My son Rufus Tiger Taylor is a fabulous drummer," said Roger Taylor. "He's a natural. He's been touring with the musical *We Will Rock You* all over Europe, and he's also done a bit of work with Jeff Beck, which is really impressive—you've got to be pretty good to work with Jeff."

"My younger son, Cary, has got a kit and plays quite well now," said Nick Mason. "My daughter Holly's got a kit too, but she hasn't played in years."

Phil Collins seems to have produced at least two drummers as well. His eldest son, Simon, plays drums in a prog-rock band called Sound of Contact (and sings incredibly like his father). "Simon is a fantastic player," said Phil. "And Nicholas, who's twelve and the elder of my two youngest sons, has been playing since he was a toddler. Matthew, my youngest, who's nine, had a drum kit but he went off it a little bit, and maybe that's because Nicholas was proving to be so good that Matthew got a little shy of doing it."

Some famous drummers are the progeny of other skin bashers. As we have seen, Mickey Hart's father was a champion drummer, and Zak Starkey is the son of a drumming Beatle. "My dad was a drummer," revealed Clem Burke. "He had a society dance band with his brothers and his dad, and they played at weddings and funerals and things like that. He wasn't pro, but my first drum kit was inherited from him."

Bev Bevan of ELO became the drummer in his first rock 'n' roll band by default, because the other members of Rocking Ronnie and the Renegades owned guitars. And it was only after he started playing drums that his mother revealed that his father, Charles "Bev" Bevan, had been a drummer too—keeping the beat in the Bev Bevan Danceband and playing ballrooms and workingmen's clubs in the Midlands of England.

There are plenty of siblings who share drumming abilities, too. Steve White's brother is Alan White, who used to play in Oasis (and is not to be confused with Alan White of Yes). Carl Palmer has a younger brother named Steve who plays the drum kit extremely well. Carmine Appice and Vinnie Appice are both fine rock drummers who happen to be brothers. Tommy Lee's younger sister, Athena, used to bang on her brother's drums in the family garage when he wasn't at home, and she became a rock drummer too—winning an award for Best Female Drummer in the 1997 LA Music Awards. She hasn't played a flying drum kit—not yet.

But there is a whole class of drummers we have yet to meet. These are people who play the drums—or have played the drums at some point in their lives—but are not necessarily famous for being drummers. It's time to lift the veil off the secret drummers, the part-time drummers, and the multitasking drummers of this world.

8

SECRET DRUMMERS

Life doesn't always pan out the way we want it to. We may set our hearts on becoming a sporting legend, a software billionaire, or a globally adored supermodel, but we end up flipping burgers, driving buses, or balancing the books for small-time fire-hydrant manufacturers. So it goes. And this happens to drummers as well. Many young, percussively able people dream of spending their lives sitting behind a gleaming drum kit, bashing out multiplatinum hits for an audience of insanely devoted fans; and while a few will realize that ambition, many others end up among the buses, the burgers, and the fire-hydrant ledgers, wondering where it all went wrong.

What you need, if you're going to be a successful drummer, is not necessarily insanity or flashiness or tattoos, but an unfailing determination to work hard in order to achieve your dream. On top of that, of course, you need luck. Without luck, all the hard work in the world won't give you the opportunities you need to show your skills and get yourself noticed.

However, there are a good many drummers whose luck took them in a different direction—not to a disappointingly dull job, but into the limelight. These are the people who may have initially thought they were going to spend their professional lives drumming, but instead found great success in a different occupation. And it is astonishing how many famous singers played the drums before they found the vocal vocation that would change their lives. Vocals and percussion are the earliest musical instruments used by the human race, and these artists hit the big time after merely switching from one primitive means of making noise to another.

Several important makers of soul music started out with sticks in their hands. Before he began belting out impassioned soul songs like "If You Don't Know Me by Now" as part of Harold Melvin and the Blue Notes, Teddy Pendergrass was belting a drum kit in the Cadillacs, a 1960s doo-wop group from Harlem, New York. The songwriter Lamont Dozier would go on to co-write many No. 1 Motown records as part of the Holland-Dozier-Holland songwriting and production team, but as a teenager he played drums in a band in Detroit, and in the early 1960s became a session drummer for the pre-Motown label Anna Records. One of his colleagues at Anna was the future soul legend Marvin Gaye, who was also playing drums there. Gaye was also a session drummer for another Detroit label, Tri-Phi Records, and he progressed to playing drums for Motown, backing acts such as the Miracles and the Marvelettes. But in 1962 he had his first solo hit, "Stubborn Kind of Fellow," and Gaye was on the way to stardom as a singer.

Years before James Brown told us to "Get Up Offa That Thing" and declared that he wanted to be a "Sex Machine," this African-American bundle of energy from Barnwell, South

Carolina, spent time in a juvenile detention center for robbery. After his release, he tried a series of different jobs and activities, including boxing, baseball, shining shoes, and singing in a gospel group before becoming a drummer and singer in a band called the Famous Flames in the 1950s. He soon left the drum kit behind when his vocal talent and showmanship became evident, and he was crowned the Godfather of Soul. But what he learned behind the kit didn't go to waste: Brown's most successful records display an extraordinary understanding of rhythm, and as a bandleader he employed some exceptionally skillful drummers, such as Jabo Starks and Clyde Stubblefield.

Though he is miles apart stylistically from the Godfather of Soul, the Godfather of Punk also had an early passion for the drum kit. Jimmy Osterberg, born in the US in 1947, was a lively boy who was raised in a shabby trailer park in Michigan. While at high school in the town of Ann Arbor, little Jimmy pursued his enthusiasm for the drums, keeping the beat in a series of bands, including one called the Iguanas. He kept up the drumming after moving to Chicago, where he played behind the drum set in blues clubs. But that wasn't how Osterberg eventually made his name. The world had to wait until he left the drums behind, formed a group in 1967 called the Psychedelic Stooges, and launched himself as their highly energetic lead vocalist. The band eventually dropped the "Psychedelic" and Osterberg changed his name too. At school he had been nicknamed Iggy, because of the Iguanas, and a local newspaper journalist resurrected the name in a review of one of the band's gigs. Osterberg changed his second name to Pop, and Iggy Pop, the wild man of rock, was born.

One of the world's most unlikely ex-drummers is Donovan Leitch, known simply as Donovan. Born in Glasgow, Scotland, in 1946, he became a prolific Dylanesque folk singer and scored a string of hits in the 1960s including the US-chart-topping "Sunshine Superman." Donovan joined the Beatles during their Transcendental Meditation adventure in India in 1968, and even passed on some of his guitar-picking skills to members of the Fab Four. But in his teens, Donovan had worshipped jazz drummers such as Gene Krupa and Art Blakey, and he looked set to become a professional drummer himself. As a young man he was seized by wanderlust and was desperate to run away from home, to hit the road and become a traveling musician. But that was only possible when he changed his instrument to the much more portable acoustic guitar. As he later explained, "You can't carry drums on your back."

Donovan has revealed that his experience as a young drummer gave him a rhythmic sense that strongly affected the way he plays guitar: "I can cook up rhythms, and I had to cook them up myself, because I only had one guitar. So I'd be doing bass parts, I'd be doing Latin rhythms out of the middle of the guitar, and I'd be picking melodies out of the top of the guitar. I was a one-man band . . . And drummers would say, 'I don't have to find a pattern, because you're playing the pattern inside the guitar anyway.'"

The gravelly, bluesy voice of Joe Cocker has graced many hit songs, from his storming version of the Beatles' "With a Little Help from My Friends" (played to great effect at Woodstock in 1969) to his duet with Jennifer Warnes, "Up Where We Belong," which boosts the tear-jerking ending of the 1982 film *An Officer and a Gentleman*. But in his first band in the late 1950s, the Sheffield-born singer was behind the drums. As the 1960s dawned, he came out from behind the kit and fronted the band Vance Arnold and the Avengers, which toured the pubs of

Britain playing standards such as "Sixteen Tons" and "Georgia on My Mind." Cocker has a peculiar habit of moving his arms around while singing, which he has connected to his former job as a drummer, saying that when he started singing without drums in front of him, he wasn't sure what to do with his hands.

David Essex and Suzi Quatro were both singers who found fame and UK chart success in the early 1970s. Born as David Cook in 1947, Essex became the drummer in a semiprofessional band called the Everons after leaving school, bashing his kit in east London pubs for a while in the 1960s. After switching to vocals and releasing a series of flop singles, Essex received his big break in 1971 when he was cast as Jesus Christ in the religious rock musical *Godspell*. His self-composed 1973 single, "Rock On," featuring a sparse percussive backing track, launched the former drummer's face onto the bedroom walls of thousands of British girls and kicked off a long chart career.

Born as Suzi Quatrocchio in Detroit in 1950, Suzi Quatro was taught to play drums and piano by her father, and played basic hand drums as a small child in his jazz band, the Art Quatro Trio. As a diminutive student at high school, she was encouraged to play the big bass drum. "I'm sure the music teacher was a sadist," she joked years later. "Little, tiny kid like me with a mammoth bass drum!" She took off in the 1970s as a leather-clad singer, dwarfed this time by a big bass guitar, scoring glam-rock hits such as "Can the Can" and "Devil Gate Drive."

Another bass player and sometime singer who flirted with the drum kit was John Ritchie, who came into the world in 1957 not far from Ginger Baker's birthplace in Lewisham, southeast London. Ritchie was given the sobriquet "Sid Vicious" by his friend and future bandmate John Lydon, and the two of them would busk in the streets, with Vicious bashing a cheap tambourine. Caught up in the burgeoning British punk-rock scene, nineteen-year-old Vicious was behind the drum kit when Siouxsie and the Banshees played their debut gig on September 20, 1976, at the 100 Club Punk Festival, organized by punk svengali Malcolm McLaren. Vicious, of course, would join Lydon in the Sex Pistols, attempting to play bass guitar. The punk icon died in 1979, just twenty-one years old, his death certificate blaming "acute intravenous narcotism."

Before she co-founded the Go-Go's in the 1980s, Belinda Carlisle enjoyed a brief spell as a punk-rock drummer. In 1977 she joined the Los Angeles band the Germs on drums, calling herself Dottie Danger. But Carlisle never had the chance to show what a dangerous drummer she was in public, because she never played with the band live, owing to an extended bout of glandular fever.

Dana Gillespie played Mary Magdalene in the first London production of the musical *Jesus Christ Superstar*, and has since had a long career as a singer and movie actress. But as a teenager, her passion was drumming. While attending theater school, she worked in the mornings and evenings to raise money for a drum kit and drum lessons. Around that time, she became the drummer in a band, but when the singer pulled out, she stepped to the microphone and began her career as a vocalist.

Soon after the little-known Madonna Ciccone began dating the musician Dan Gilroy in New York in the late 1970s, they formed a rock band called the Breakfast Club, in which the charismatic Ciccone was frequently seen wielding a pair of sticks behind the drum kit. But the band was just one of a series of stepping stones to Madonna's ultimate destiny as a sing-ing, dancing, acting, self-reinventing, children's-book-writing, African-child-adopting megastar.

Steven Tallarico, better known as Steven Tyler of Aerosmith, was a back-of-the stage man before he was a front man. By the age of sixteen, the Yonkers-born Mick Jagger lookalike was playing the drums in his first band, the Strangeurs (apparently an attempt to Frenchify and exoticize "Strangers"). Peter Gabriel played drums in bands while he studied at Charterhouse, the English public school in Surrey, but when the band Genesis emerged from that institution, he became the lead singer. Onstage, he wasn't completely divorced from his previous role: he often had his own bass drum to play at the front of the stage. After leaving Genesis in 1975, he became a successful solo singer with a taste for powerful and distinctive drum sounds.

Shortly before becoming a 1990s grunge god as the lead singer and guitarist in Nirvana, Kurt Cobain played the drums in short-lived mid-1980s bands with his bass-playing and guitar-playing buddy Krist Novoselic, including the Sellouts—a covers band playing, improbably, the songs of the West Coast band Creedence Clearwater Revival—and the Stiff Woodies, which had various guitarists and vocalists, and which changed its rather adolescent name to Skid Row and then to Nirvana.

Cobain went from playing the drums to smashing them up. In 2011, I found a sad remnant of a smashed Tama bass drum on display in the showroom of Christie's South Kensington auction house in London. It had been played twenty years before by both Dave Grohl and Cobain during a Nirvana gig at the Cabaret Metro in Chicago on October 12, 1991. Grohl had switched to guitar and Cobain had moved behind the drum kit for the last two numbers of the evening, "Four Enclosed Walls" (the PiL song) and "Endless, Nameless." Cobain had deliberately destroyed the drums at the end of the gig, and this piece at Christie's had been thrown into the crowd and claimed as a trophy by a member of the audience. After the auctioneer's hammer fell, the drum remnant—plus a set list from the same gig, scrawled on a paper plate—went to an anonymous buyer for more than $13,000.

Becoming a charismatic lead singer is certainly not the only road to success for failed drummers. Why not try photography, acting, modeling, movie directing, politics, or the food industry? David M. Overton founded the American restaurant chain the Cheesecake Factory, but he is also a music lover who played drums in a band from the early 1960s, when he was a teenager. He later moved to San Francisco to try to make his fortune as a drummer, but eventually gave up and joined his parents in their small wholesale cheesecake business in Los Angeles in the mid-1970s.

Jamie Oliver started playing in the British band Scarlet Division in the late 1980s, when he was just thirteen, and played many gigs across the UK in the 1990s. But Oliver had also started working as a restaurant chef, for which he seemed to have a special talent. In 1996 he was spotted by a television producer who was making a documentary—he was cooking in an Italian restaurant in London at the time, rather than playing the drums—and he was given his own TV show, *The Naked Chef*. Although his band was signed by Sony and released a single, "Sundial," Jamie Oliver's culinary career quickly overshadowed his percussive life. He became a household name in the world of cookery, selling millions of cookbooks and his own brand of culinary equipment, and promoting high-profile campaigns to improve the nutritional value of Britain's school meals and to encourage Americans to eat more healthily. Since then, he has occasionally been seen out of the kitchen and behind the drums, as when he appeared onstage with Blur bassist Alex James at the Big Feastival [*sic*] in the Cotswolds in the summer of 2013. He is sometimes confused with another drummer called Jamie Oliver, who is a longtime member of the British punk band UK Subs but may not be quite as handy with pots and pans in the kitchen as his namesake.

Long before LA Reid was a Grammy-award-winning American record executive and a judge on *The X Factor*, he was captivated by the drums. As a young man growing up in Cincinnati, Ohio, he worked in a barbershop and saved up a few dollars from tips to buy a pair of drumsticks, which he used to bang on his floor as he listened to records by James Brown. His real name was Antonio Reid, but one day, when he was drumming in a band, he happened to be wearing a Los Angeles Dodgers T-shirt, and one of his bandmates called him "LA" because of it.

In the early 1980s, Reid became the drummer in the local band the Deele, who had R&B hits with "Body Talk" in 1983 and "Two Occasions" five years later. He then moved into songwriting and production, forming the record label LaFace with his business partner, Kenneth "Babyface" Edmonds. In 2000, LA Reid succeeded Clive Davis as president of Arista Records, and he later became CEO of the Island Def Jam Music Group and subsequently CEO of Epic Records. If Reid had stayed put behind the drum kit rather than becoming a music-business hotshot, several big-selling artists would probably have been a good deal less successful: he was the man who signed Avril Lavigne and Pink to Arista, and he has assisted the careers of artists as diverse as Mariah Carey and Justin Bieber.

As one of Britain's most prolific and stylish photographers, Terry O'Neill has photographed a long list of famous and beautiful people since the 1960s, from Frank Sinatra to Brigitte Bardot, and from David Bowie to Amy Winehouse. He even married into celebrity in 1983, tying the knot with the Hollywood icon Faye Dunaway. But O'Neill may have never lifted a professional camera if he hadn't picked up a pair of drumsticks first. As a teenager in London in the 1950s, his ambition was to travel to the USA to study with the country's greatest jazz drummers, and he decided he could cross the Atlantic Ocean frequently and inexpensively if he became an air steward. He applied to the airline BOAC (British Overseas Airways Corporation, which would later merge with another airline to create British Airways), which had no steward vacancies but did have a vacancy in its technical photographic unit, which sounded intriguing. O'Neill took the job and began learning about photography, and went on to take pictures at airports for the British press. In the early 1960s he was swept up in the excitement of Swinging London, with its feast of highly photogenic actors, models, and pop stars, and his drumming ambitions were left far behind.

There are American politicians who might have become famous drummers if life had taken a different turn. Mary "Tipper" Aitcheson married the Democratic politician Al Gore in 1970, having dated him since an encounter at his senior prom five years before. Tipper Gore became the woman who protected young people from overtly sexual lyrics on records in 1985, when she helped to create the Parents Music Resource Center (PMRC), which pressured the recording industry to put warning labels on albums with "explicit lyrics." This followed her purchase of Prince's *Purple Rain* album for her daughter, and her outrage at some of the naughty words in the song "Darling Nikki." Opponents complained she was anti-music in general, but that was far from the truth: as a teenager, Tipper had been the drummer in a 1960s all-girl band, the Wildcats. She had received a drum kit at the age of fourteen and played along to records at home in Washington, DC, including Sandy Nelson's classic "Let There Be Drums." The band—named after her mother's car, a Buick Wildcat—were allowed to practice at the Aitcheson home, and played covers of Beatles and Bob Dylan songs. You can be sure that there were no offensive words in anything they performed.

Another famous Democrat, the former secretary of state Madeleine Albright, recently discovered the drums in her seventies. Albright made a surprise appearance onstage at the Kennedy Center in 2011, accompanying the jazz trumpeter Chris Botti, and the following year was back on the kit at the same venue, hitting cymbals and toms with a pair of mallets as Botti played Puccini's "Nessun Dorma."

Great dancers need an excellent sense of rhythm, and many dancers have shown an aptitude for the drum kit. Sammy Davis Jr. was a true all-around entertainer who could not only dance but could sing, act, tell jokes, and play the piano and the vibraphone. He was also a competent jazz drummer, and showed off his skin bashing on various television shows, including *The Ed Sullivan Show* in 1963.

The young British supermodel and *Vogue* cover star Cara Delevingne, known for her luxuriant eyebrows, enjoys posing for fashion shoots, but she also loves playing drums when she gets a chance. In 2013 she made a public appearance at the launch of a makeup collection at the Selfridges store in London, drawing an appreciative crowd as she played a Pearl drum kit with a Zildjian Custom Dark Crash cymbal. And in true drummer style, Delevingne has had her lucrative body decorated with tattoos, including the words MADE IN ENGLAND on her left foot, the head of a lion on her right forefinger, and her lucky number, 12, in Roman numerals (XII) near her right breast.

Given the fact that so many drummers have a penchant for comedy, it is not all that surprising that other professional comedians, besides Sammy Davis Jr., have had a bash on the drums from time to time. Rosie O'Donnell has whacked the skins behind Cyndi Lauper, and on a 1998 edition of her TV show, *Rosie*, she performed in a drum battle with the singer (and drummer) Chaka Khan. As a boy growing up in Philadelphia, Bill Cosby was obsessed with jazz and yearned to be a cool, swinging drummer in a band. The comedian has said that he would shine people's shoes until he had a few dollars, and then go to a local musical-instrument store called Wurlitzer's, where a man charged $1.25 for half an hour's worth of drum lessons. Cosby's mother eventually bought young Bill a kit for seventy-five dollars from a pawn shop, and he would play along to jazz records in his bedroom. Cultivating his image as a cool young drummer, he painted the tips of his drumsticks blue and would walk around town with them poking out of his back pocket.

After the drum legend Max Roach died in 2007, Cosby paid tribute to his hero with a comical speech about how, as a "boy from the projects," he desperately tried and failed to imitate his favorite jazz drummers, including Roach and Art Blakey, on that seventy-five-dollar kit. When he finally met Max Roach, he claimed, Cosby told him: "Let me tell you something. You owe me seventy-five dollars."

Mel Brooks, the Brooklyn-born director responsible for laugh-a-minute movies such as *The Producers*, *High Anxiety*, and *Robin Hood: Men in Tights*, had aspirations as a young man to be a jazz drummer in a big band, and he had a fantastic start: he was taught to play in the early 1940s by none other than Buddy Rich. Brooks once told *Billboard* magazine that Rich had become emotional in 1974 after the filmmaker found success with his famous comedy western, *Blazing Saddles*: "When I made *Blazing Saddles*, which was the first big hit I ever had, Buddy Rich hugged me and he was weeping. I said, 'Buddy, why are you crying?' And he said, 'It's such a great movie, Mel. You're going to be a movie director.' I said, 'So? So?' He said, 'You coulda been a good drummer.' Brooks found the master's choice of adjective amusing: "He didn't even say '*great* drummer.' He said, 'You coulda been a *good* drummer.'"

Chevy Chase, who found fame on *Saturday Night Live* and starred in many comedy movies, including National Lampoon's *Vacation* series, could have been a reasonably good drummer too. He was lucky enough to go to Bard College, in New York State, at the same time as two even more promising musicians, Walter Becker and Donald Fagen. The three students played together in an ensemble called the Leather Canary, which Chase later remembered as "a bad jazz band." In his twenties, Chase played drums in the short-lived late-1960s rock band Chamaeleon Church (he clearly had a fondness for the "Ch" digraph), also contributing keyboards to their one and only album, now something of a cult psychedelia favorite. Meanwhile, Becker and Fagen went off and formed Steely Dan, recorded several classic albums, and sold tens of millions of copies.

Peter Sellers, the London-born comedian who would achieve global fame playing characters such as Inspector Clouseau on the big screen, played the drums for local dance bands when he was a teenager in the early 1940s. Other British comedians with drum chops include John Thomson, whose TV appearances include many episodes of *The Fast Show* (the catchphrase-based sketch comedy adored by Johnny Depp), and Al Murray, famous for playing his character "the Pub Landlord" on stage and TV. "When I was sixteen, all I wanted to do was play the drums," Rowland Rivron told me. Rivron, a familiar face in British television comedy since the 1980s, had his drum epiphany as a boy at Abbotsford secondary school in Middlesex, which had its own jazz band. "The guy running the band was a French teacher called, bizarrely, Mr. Bean," Rivron recalled, "and he would actively recruit kids and encourage them to take up various instruments. Of course, when people left the school, they had to leave the band as well, and the drummer was due to leave in two years, so I was asked if I wanted to take up the drums. I gave it a go and I became very interested in it. And the drummer I took over from was Ian Mosley, who went on to become the drummer in the band Marillion."

Rivron would stay behind for an hour after school, sitting behind the kit and playing along to big-band music on a reel-to-reel tape recorder. "I was about sixteen when I played my first professional gig," he said. "My mother drove me to a hotel near Heathrow Airport, where I played in a band, and she came back after midnight and picked me up. And from there I got onto the jazz circuit in west London. I ditched school, and when I was eighteen and nineteen I was gigging almost every night."

In Rivron's case, playing the drums became an accidental route to a career in comedy. But first he was in on the birth of the New Romantic movement, which spawned bands such as Culture Club and Duran Duran, when he became the resident drummer for a cabaret act at London's famous Blitz club. Then he became the drummer for the Comic Strip, a group of alternative comedians who performed above Raymond's Revue Bar, the city's most famous strip club. The rising stars he accompanied included Dawn French, Jennifer Saunders, Rik Mayall, Ade Edmonson, and Alexei Sayle. While performing as a warm-up man for the American comedienne Ruby Wax, Rivron was spotted by a TV producer, which led to him fronting *The Bunker Show*, a late-night showcase for pop videos, and then becoming the comic foil to a young Jonathan Ross on *The Last Resort*.

Rivron has been on and off the kit for most of his life. He has toured with bands including Jools Holland and His Rhythm & Blues Orchestra, stepping in when their regular player Gilson Lavis fell ill, and he has played in an ensemble of musically talented British comedians known as the Idiot Bastard Band, comprising Rivron, Ade Edmonson, Neil Innes, and Phill Jupitus. Rivron told me he had his own idea about why so many drummers are comedians, and vice versa. This relates to the kind of personality that is drawn to the drums—or, perhaps, the kind of personality you develop by playing them. "I think there's something about the drum kit that makes drummers a lot more slapdash in their approach to playing," he said. "As a drummer, what you have to do in a band isn't nearly as introverted as someone playing a melodic instrument."

However, some of those players of melodic instruments are versatile musicians, and it's not uncommon for guitarists, bass players, and keyboardists to play a little percussion on the side. Paul McCartney enjoyed having an occasional bash on the kit when the Beatles were in the studio. In Ringo Starr's own words, "Every time I went for a cup of tea, he was on the drums!" And when Starr briefly left the band during the sessions for *The White Album* in 1968, following an argument with McCartney about the drum part on "Back in the USSR," it was McCartney who filled in, contributing drums to that song as well as "Dear Prudence." The following year, when Starr was away again, acting on the set of the movie *The Magic Christian*, Macca was back on the drums for "The Ballad of John and Yoko."

Drums were one of the instruments played by McCartney

on his 1970 debut solo album, *McCartney*. And he was obliged to pick up the sticks again three years later when the drummer Denny Seiwell abruptly left Wings before they flew out to record the album *Band on the Run* in Lagos, Nigeria.

In addition to being a skilled songwriter, singer, and harmonica player, Stevie Wonder is also an accomplished drummer who has laid down cool grooves on many of his own compositions, such as "Superstition." He is particularly admired for his distinctive hi-hat work. Listen to his inspired, funky drum pattern on "I Wish" from *Songs in the Key of Life*; the drums were credited to a session player on the album, but Wonder has since revealed that he was behind the kit on that song. And who was the musician named the "greatest drummer of our time" by Eric Clapton in 1974? Stevie Wonder.

Prince has played drums on many of his own records. He once said that he started drumming at the age of thirteen, when he would turn on the radio and drum along on cardboard boxes to whatever song was playing. One of his biggest influences as a drummer was another multi-instrumentalist: Morris Day of the Time.

Graham Coxon is best known as the guitarist in Blur, but he too has hidden talents. "Graham's a very good drummer," said the producer Ben Hillier, who has worked with him on some of Coxon's solo albums. "It's not his first instrument, but his feel and his musicianship are so good that it totally works."

Lenny Kravitz isn't averse to playing the drums, in addition to other instruments, on his own records. A few years ago, a choir of high school students from Lewisville, Texas, began performing in a park during a visit to New Orleans. They happened to be singing Kravitz's hit song "Fly Away" and, to their amazement,

Kravitz himself suddenly appeared in person, sat behind their drum kit, and started playing along. Kravitz, who had a residence in New Orleans at the time, just happened to be nearby and had pricked up his ears when he heard the familiar music.

Steven Drozd told me he had been "playing keyboards and guitar and all kinds of stuff for years" before he joined the Flaming Lips. In fact, back when he was about twelve years old, it looked as if Drozd might devote his life to keyboards. "We had this old Yamaha organ in the den of our house that was just gathering dust, and I'd try to pick out things from the radio, and I learned a couple of Beatles songs. And after a couple of years, my dad bought a junky old upright piano and we put that in the living room, and that's when I really started teaching myself piano and music theory."

But multi-instrumentalism can bring its own complications. When he joined the Lips in 1991, he "just wanted to be a crazy, intense rock drummer." But as he settled into the band, it seemed natural for Drozd to start playing keyboards and guitar on their albums, as well as drums. That created a problem when the band played live, since even Drozd couldn't play drums and guitar, or drums and keyboards, simultaneously. The drummer Kliph Scurlock told me how they solved the problem. In 2002, when Scurlock was roadying for them, the band was due to go on tour with Beck, playing as his backing band for the main set. The Lips' lead singer, Wayne Coyne, was discussing the arrangements for the tour with Beck. "As it was getting nearer the time to go to LA for rehearsals," said Scurlock, "Wayne said at one point, 'Y'know, I'm not entirely sure that he knows we don't have a drummer per se, that our drummer plays all this other stuff when we play live.' And he said to me, 'You're going to LA with us anyway. Maybe bring your drums just in case, because we need some drums.' We got there and, sure enough, there was nobody else to play drums. So I started practicing with them, and they said maybe I should play with the Lips properly some-time. I started playing that night, and they haven't been able to get rid of me since," he laughed. (Scurlock may have been tempt-ing fate with that joke: he left the band in 2014.)

Roger Taylor of Queen has earned considerable praise as a percussionist since the 1970s. In 1975 his bandmate Brian May called him a "great drummer," explaining: "He's got his own special style. I don't know what it is, but when he plays, I know immediately that it is him. It's so distinctive." I was surprised, therefore, when Taylor told me recently that he didn't specif-ically identify himself a drummer. "I think of myself as a mu-sician, really, more than just a drummer," he said. "I just think of it as all one thing—just being musical." In 2013 he released his fifth solo album, *Fun on Earth*, on which he sang lead vocals and played keyboards, guitar, bass guitar, and a Stylophone toy electronic keyboard as well as drums and percussion.

Omar Hakim enjoys playing so many instruments that he has been criticized by fans for not playing enough drums on his solo albums. He corrected that on his 2014 release, *We Are One*, by the Omar Hakim Experience: in addition to writing his own compositions and playing guitar, keyboards, bass, and vocals, he contributes exciting drumming of the kind he has performed in the past for Weather Report, Miles Davis, and Daft Punk. Hakim's multi-instrumentalism started early, when he made a deal with his music teacher at elementary school in New York. "I was falling in love with the drums," he said, "but I was in third grade and too young to join the school concert band—you had to be in fourth grade. But my teacher said that if I played violin that year, he'd make sure I was in the band playing drums the following year. I guess the school needed a violinist. I ended up learning violin and liking it, and I won an award for it."

When you look back at the story of Foo Fighters now, it might seem like Dave Grohl's master plan to reinvent himself, effecting an extraordinary transformation from drummer to singing guitarist, but it didn't happen that way at all. Grohl simply decided to record some songs he had been writing in the Nirvana and pre-Nirvana days. He played most of the instruments on the songs, used "Foo Fighters" as a pseudonym, and released them in 1995 as a limited-edition album on cassette for some friends. It was only after the music attracted serious attention within the industry that Grohl signed to a major label, formed a proper band, and stepped into the spotlight. Although Foo Fighters became a phenomenal success, there was considerable whinging from some die-hard fans who wished that Grohl would get back behind the drum kit for keeps, instead of fannying about with a guitar and a microphone at the front of the stage like some grunge dilettante.

The miracle for Grohl is that he is still highly regarded as a drummer. When other drummers diversify, they don't always receive the praise and fame they deserve as percussionists. Ndugu Chancler is a case in point: his drumming is all over Michael Jackson's *Thriller*, the best-selling album of all time. Chancler played on "Billie Jean," "Baby Be Mine," "P.Y.T. (Pretty Young Thing)," "Human Nature," and the title track, and yet somehow has not achieved household-name status, perhaps because he has also been a composer and producer and played a lot of vibraphone during his career. "I was having this discussion with someone recently," Chancler told me. "Myself and the other drummers that have also been songwriters and producers, like Narada Michael Walden, who produced soul singers including Whitney Houston—we never got as much acclaim as drummers. We were always doing more than playing drums, so we got overlooked on that level a lot."

I remember meeting Phil Collins briefly in January 1974 outside the Theatre Royal, Drury Lane, London, after a particularly enjoyable Genesis gig. I was a fifteen-year-old fan waiting by the stage door, happy to meet any members of the band—such as Peter Gabriel, keyboardist Tony Banks, or Collins, whose drumming I considered exciting and technically brilliant. Two men eventually emerged into the frosty London night: the very tall guitarist and bassist Mike Rutherford, and a much shorter man in a tatty sheepskin jacket, his small face almost hidden by his longish hair and his beard. It took a few seconds for me to realize that this unprepossessing, stoop-shouldered man in his early twenties was the mighty Phil Collins. I blurted something witty like "Great gig, Phil!" and he grunted something back.

Little more than a decade later, this man was a singing superstar, selling millions of records, with a single at No. 1 on the Billboard Hot 100, and his face—now beardless and with considerably less hair—plastered across thousands of billboards. It was hard enough to believe when it happened, and it would have been impossible to predict back in 1974, when his only featured vocal on the latest Genesis album was on a drumless ballad called "More Fool Me" (cowritten with Rutherford), a track I usually skipped when I played the record. Considering the trajectory of his career, the title of his first American No. 1 hit seems very appropriate now: "Against All Odds (Take a Look at Me Now)."

By the mid-1970s Collins had become the lead singer in Genesis, but fortunately he hadn't abandoned the drums completely. He continued to play them on Genesis records; he drummed on the first Band Aid charity single, "Do They Know It's Christmas?"; and he famously played on both sides of the Atlantic for Live Aid, using the supersonic aircraft Concorde to carry him swiftly across the ocean. He also played brilliantly on a series of albums by Brand X, the British jazz fusion band.

Because he was now mostly front-of-stage when he toured with Genesis or a solo artist, Collins had to hire another drummer, but he still managed to do some drumming himself during the shows. Nevertheless, owing to the success of his solo records, there are whole generations of fans who regard him as a singer rather than a drummer, and many people don't even know he plays the drums. "Yes, that's true," said Collins when we spoke again, thirty-nine years after that first encounter outside the Theatre Royal. "There have been people who have come to a gig and seen two drum kits onstage, and they've wondered why. Then they realize, 'Oh! He plays a bit of drums as well.' I find it quite humorous that they think, 'He can knock about a bit on the drums,' because they don't know my history. It all depends on what period of my career you come in on."

Skill, and the mysterious workings of chance, may determine whether someone has a successful career as a drummer. Some exceptional drummers are highly successful part-timers who sing or play other instruments, like McCartney, Collins,

Grohl, Wonder, Hakim, Taylor, Coxon, Drozd, and Kravitz. And there are many other potential drummers who go off and find success elsewhere and end up being would-be drummers, former drummers, or occasional drummers.

But we still haven't discovered exactly why anybody becomes a drummer. It's time now to enter murkier territory, and to investigate a possibility that has been bothering me for some time. Do people begin playing this instrument because they have something a little bit naughty on their minds?

9

DO YOU THINK I'M SEXY?

While drummers go on and on about how they were inspired by the sound of Buddy Rich or John Bonham, and about how playing great music with other musicians is the best thing in the world, and about how they love to hear the applause of their fans, perhaps there's something they're deliberately not mentioning. It's not unknown for attractive young women to throw themselves at rock musicians, and it has certainly been known for the phenomenon of "groupies" to be an incentive to the occasional budding musician. What if people become drummers simply to improve their sex lives? What if they are only expending all that energy, learning their instrument, practicing and playing all those songs and drum solos and percussive tricks, just so they can enjoy some necking and fornication between the gigs and the recording sessions?

Some people, including a reasonably large number of guitarists and lead singers, will laugh at that idea. How can drummers possibly arouse anyone sexually? They sit at the back, out of the spotlight and covered in sweat; they're either crazy or dumb or both; and they have to spend so much time setting up their equipment and taking it all down again, they don't have time to do anything else—even if they do have a shred of energy left after bashing things all night.

Drummers' chances are severely limited when their band's lead singer is a wildly charismatic groupie magnet like Jim Morrison. John Densmore noticed this after the Doors were given a residency at the famous Whisky A Go Go club in LA in 1966. The drummer later confessed: "I must say it bothered me a bit at first when one particular blonde and her girlfriends stood at the front of the Whisky stage and stared at Jim and not me. They could almost reach out and touch him. They seemed to be completely hypnotized. Jim was now wearing tight velvet pants and no underwear. The blonde stared right at his crotch without embarrassment and kept giggling excitedly to her friends. For a twenty-two-year-old with a perpetual hard-on like me, her brazenness was tantalizing to the point of pain."

But the occasional confessions of other famous drummers tell a different story. "I remember I was in this band in the 1970s when I was fourteen years old," said Omar Hakim, "and after we played a show in Connecticut we were loading the van, and this girl—who was absolutely gorgeous—walked up to me and just grabbed me and started kissing me. The other guys in the band were like, 'Woo-hoo!' She didn't pick anybody else in the band: she came right up to me. Drumming is such a primal thing, and when it hits the body in the way it does, it can be interpreted as a sexual energy. Dancing is a human mating ritual, isn't it? So, drums being the instrument that kick-starts that whole party, it would make sense that females would respond to a male that they see that's moving them in that way."

Never the most handsome of drummers, Ginger Baker nonetheless admits to a series of raunchy extramarital encounters in his autobiography, *Hellraiser*. They include the time he "chatted up" a "gorgeous-looking Norwegian head stewardess" on a Pan Am flight to New York in 1968. She subsequently visited Baker at his hotel "all made up and dressed in a suit and high heels, and we jumped into bed together." Then there was Baker's secret apartment in Fulham, southwest London, where, in the words of his daughter Ginette, "he used to install certain women." And then there was the "crazy threesome" that the drummer enjoyed one night in the early 1970s with a female singer and the girlfriend of one of his bandmates in Ginger Baker's Air Force.

Phil Varone has not only drummed with the bands Skid Row and Saigon Kick, but has also been a *Playgirl* centerfold. In his recent book, *Unphiltered: Real Life On and Off the Rock 'n' Roll Tour Bus*, Varone discusses the intimate moments he has had with some of the three-thousand-plus women he claims to have slept with. And Tommy Lee's autobiography, *Tommyland*, begins with an imaginary conversation between the Mötley Crüe drummer and his penis, and features touching reminiscences such as this: "I have been with two chicks many, many times and it isn't all it's cracked up to be. Something drastic happens when you've got one person left out in the cold. There are only so many things you can all do together and there are a few lovely things you can do to both of them at the same time and them to you. But when it comes time for fucking, unless there's something out there that I don't know about, you've only got one dick." The solution, writes Lee, is simple: "The thing to do is have foursomes: three chicks and just you."

Go on the Internet, that international hothouse of spilled secrets and raunchy confessions, and you will discover how certain drummers are regarded by their female admirers. Judging by Twitter tweets, personal blogs, and the occasional piece of erotic fiction, there seem to be plenty of women who desire drummers, both generally and specifically. Here's a tweet from 2011, from someone with a feminine handle: "Still daydreaming about the sexy drummer last night." Here's another: "I think Neil Peart had the cutest smile back when Rush first started." Here's one from 2013: "Some girls wanna marry doctors and athletes. I wanna marry a tattoo artist or a drummer."

"I was never kissed by a drummer before," tweets another young woman. "Thanks for the great experience!" And somebody else tweets that they have noticed a pattern here: "I'd be a millionaire if I had a dollar for every time I heard a girl say 'Ooohh, who's the drummer? He's cute.'"

Here are some extracts from a blog, also by a woman, that first appeared online in 2008:

> So, I am now secretly infatuated with drummers. *Blush*
> Well, all right, it's only secret to people who don't read
> my blog. But I don't think any drummers read my blog,
> so my secret is safe. Yes, I'm infatuated with all of them!
> Um, okay, maybe particularly the good-looking ones. A
> girl has to be discerning where she directs her infatua-
> tions. It all started eons ago when I watched a Metallica
> tour video and noticed Lars Ulrich, who is not really
> good-looking but his drumming more than makes up

for it—he's like the god of drummers. Even now, after so many years of listening to Metallica, my heart still skips beats listening to him play.

Another woman recently posted an excruciating story online about "the time I was at a concert when I was 17. I had a really bad crush on the drummer at the time, and sneaked into the front row. I peeled off my shirt, and wrote his name across my boobs. The band came on stage, and there I was jumping around . . . I looked toward the drummer, and just as he smiled at me, I saw my UNCLE, horrified, just 15 feet away. It was awful, I just wanted to fall into a hole and die."

Here is part of another revealing post by a woman:

I have a definite "thing" for drummers, but I think I am somewhat unique. I was raised by musicians and had my first crush on the drummer in my parents' band, who ended up being only one of many—my first love was also a drummer. For me it's the way they move and that they are the backbone to the music; you watch a drummer move and it's hard to keep from being inspired to move, dance, whatever. Also depending on the skill or temperament of the drummer, just the style can give you insight into their intellect, the choice when to "fill" or not . . . the spaces too, how they use the instrument . . .

Drummers certainly can use the love. In 2013, a little-known Australian drummer named Glen Fredericks spontaneously decided that one day of every year should be Hug a Drummer Day. He chose October 10—partly because 10/10 is catchy, the 1s look like drumsticks, and the 0s could be drums or cymbals. "Drummers are often heard but not seen, so it's nice to share some of the limelight that is usually taken by the guitarist or lead singer," he explained. Thousands of people shared the idea on Facebook, and some drummers may have received real physical squeezes from people as well. Hug a Drummer Day also prompted an articulate young Texan blogger named the Good Groupie to discuss her passion for drummers. She is brave enough to confess that the first drummer who caught her eye was Zac Hanson of the Oklahoma teenybop band Hanson.

"Since age 13 when I developed my first drummer crush on Mr. Zac Hanson, I have been a drummer boy devotee," she writes. "Their instruments sparkle and gleam on stage in a way that's always caught my eye before guitars, bass or keys. Drummers sit in the back, quietly keeping everything going in their own little world—they're always the most interesting person on stage to me . . . Plus, as Rob Sheffield so smartly notes in his book *Talking to Girls about Duran Duran*, drumming is girl code. Go to a show, and you will find nearly every girl in the place tapping her foot along to the beat. There's something about rhythm—we can't help but be overcome by it."

The Good Groupie goes on to list the drummers she loves, including Jon Shiffman of Steel Train, Jason Schwartzman of Phantom Planet, the late Dennis Wilson of the Beach Boys, and Ned Brower of Rooney. "When I'd see Rooney live," she explains, "I'd quite literally stand there with my eyes glued on Ned, watching his every move. Up until then, I'd never seen someone play like him. The way he'd get completely into the song, swinging his hands and head back and forth to the exact beat he was keeping—flawless . . . I lived for those moments during Rooney shows. Plus he sings. Is there anything better than a singing drummer?"

If you care to search, you will find some extremely raunchy stories online about women and male drummers. Some are pure fiction—stock tales of fans having sex backstage with drummers, dreamed up by writers to titillate specialist audiences—while some have the ring of true confessions about them. In 2014, the Illicit Encounters site, which calls itself "the UK's largest dating website for married people," put a question to more than a thousand of its female members who had admitted to having an affair with a musician. What instrument, it asked, did their best-ever musically talented lover play? Forty-two percent of them said lead guitar, but the drummers knocked the guitarists into second place with a score of 67 percent. "Ladies stereotypically fancy the front man," said an Illicit Encounters spokesman, "but they often give a short-lived performance in the bedroom, as they are more interested in themselves; whereas drummers are used to being pushed aside and are therefore way more interested in you without a need to boost their ego."

I asked Joey Kramer if he had ever seen evidence that certain women were turned on by the drums. "Of course!" he fired back. "I left a trail of them in the seventies! But I don't know what that's about, because I'm not the woman."

Confronted directly with questions about their sex lives, most drummers are understandably coy. Even Ginger Baker was irritated when, before he published his book, a potential biographer "wanted to go into graphic detail about sexual relationships." And when I asked many of my interviewees if they had seen any evidence that drumming made them sexually attractive, a few said that they would be unsettled or even offended if they found that their girlfriends or wives had been drawn to them purely because they played the drums. While they were happy to be regarded as professional percussionists, there was so much more to them than that—personality, intellect, the whole enchilada. Nick Mason, with typical jocularity, quipped: "Oh no, I've always put it down to my eyes." If I asked his wife why she went for a drummer, suggested Mason, "she'd probably say it was because the guitar player was already taken."

But why wouldn't a drummer be a great catch? There have been plenty of surveys exploring the qualities that women find attractive in men generally, and many conclude that a good sense of humor is somewhere near the top of the list—hence all the requests for "GSOH" in lonely-hearts ads. A recent survey found that "playfulness" was the most important quality, and most surveys highlight confidence and physical fitness as well. A typical drummer—being the well-toned, assertive musician who is often the funniest member of the band—would tick so many boxes there, whereas a politician or insurance broker, or even a guitarist, might not.

"I've got to say," said Roger Taylor of Queen, "that a great by-product of being a drummer is that it gives you tremendous physical stamina, and it gives you a kind of fitness. It's a generalization, but drummers are usually in physically better condition than the other members of the band."

The ever-comical Nicko McBrain had a lot of fun with the subject of sexually attractive drummers. "There's a lot of prejudice against drummers," he said, "and when the drummer pulls all the decent-looking birds, then it really gets bad! I always say that the drummer is the best-looking bloke in the band. They may not be physically the best-looking bloke, but I think from a girl's point of view, the stamina of a drummer is appealing. And this is why I've got a big drum set: the rest of the band won't let me have a little one, because then all the girls could watch me, and then the rest of them wouldn't get the attention that they feel they deserve!"

Stamina, fitness, and those "drummer arms" score highly for many women. Another online comment observes that "Drummers are incredibly attractive . . . not only are they musically talented, but they are going to have strong arms. I love the way their arm veins pop out after playing. So hot."

Sweaty drummers will also have an irresistible appeal for a large number of women. A recent scientific study found that around 70 percent of women are genetically equipped to detect a powerful pheromone in male sweat known as androstenone, and that a proportion of these women find androstenone sexually arousing.

But sometimes physique and pheromones are irrelevant. One of the reasons that drummers are fun to watch is that so many of them are clearly enjoying themselves when they play. One female drummer fan recently observed online: "I have found that people who look as if they are having a great time appear to be more attractive; even if they aren't in fact better-looking. And really, drummers just seem to always be having such a good time. Mostly I don't even notice their actual looks, but their expression of pure joy just seems to radiate outward and bathe us all in their glow. Their body language tells you they are totally into what they are doing. Yeah!"

The Danish fine artist Rose Eken has a keen interest in musicians. Her artwork, she explains, "revolves around the paraphernalia and detritus of rock 'n' roll culture." She has studied the drum kits of many famous drummers, from Lars Ulrich to Ginger Baker and Phil Collins, and has meticulously created her own enchanting miniature versions, which have been displayed in galleries. "It's about the beauty of the instrument," she told me, "and each one becomes a kind of portrait of the drummer who plays it." When I spoke to her, she was also working on an embroidery project involving drummers, in which she took well-used drum heads and used stitching to recreate the marks left on them by repeated playing. In this way, she is transforming the unique pattern left by each drummer into art. "The patterns are all so individual," she told me. "It's like the handwriting of each drummer. The drum heads of jazz drummers look different from those of rock drummers."

Eken revealed that her boyfriend was an artist and drummer and that she had dated "a lot of drummers," and we discussed the qualities that she saw in them. "You could generalize and say that drummers are the shyer ones," she said, "which is more appealing to some people. They're not so extroverted as guitar players. But that's not necessarily true: I've met a lot of drummers, and their temperaments are all different." Reflecting more on the subject, she said: "They have so much rhythm; they never sit still and they always want to tap on something. It's sort of an excess of energy. And maybe it doesn't bother me that someone is drumming on everything all the time." Does she actively like all the tapping? "Yes, I think so." Perhaps she finds it comforting, somehow? "Yeah. It's something about rhythm. I haven't really thought that much about it."

Let us not forget female drummers, too, who inevitably receive a certain kind of attention when they play. Sheila E. is well-known for playing the drums in sexy high heels. But when she answered fans' questions live online in an AMA (Ask Me Anything) "interview" in 2014 to celebrate forty years in music and to promote her latest album, *Icon*, this devout Christian may have received more than she bargained for. The nicer comments included "I wish I had aged as well as you have. You're still beautiful," "how you play in stilettos I don't know," and "Sheila I think you're one of the sexiest drummers I've ever seen, just a Babe!" There were a few moderately cheeky questions, including "Who do you think had sexier legs, you or John Bonham?," "Want to go out for a pizza?," and "Will you marry me?" And then there were some downright naughty questions and remarks, like "Is it true that Prince has a very small package?," "Can I smell your ass?," "Favorite sex position?," and "I just want to state that I masturbated to you numerous times as a teenager in the 80s." The ruder comments elicited a stony silence.

When a YouTube clip showed the drummer Samantha Maloney behind a new "drum rack" fitted with cooling fans, it elicited various "rack" jokes, and this response from one man: "I would love to be one of those fans mounted on your rack. What is it about female drummers that brings out the pervert in me?"

"When you're drumming as a woman, you're immediately sexualized," said Mindy Abovitz, editor of *Tom Tom* magazine. "As soon as you get on the kit, men think you're hot and they want to get with you. There are always comments about women being sexy if they're drummers. One reason may be that when you're behind a kit, with your right foot on the bass-drum pedal and your left foot on the hi-hat pedal, you have to spread your legs—and women are not supposed to do that."

"That's true. Men can sit like this," said Julie Edwards of Deap Vally, spreading her legs in her dressing room at London's Electric Ballroom, "but women aren't meant to. People used to compare me to Tori Amos, because I've got long red hair and because she would spread her legs over her piano stool. And I think also there must be something about watching a woman who is completely engrossed in something. It's like watching a dancer. For me there is a link between playing drums and sex, but I think it's more tenuous than people think. I don't personally get aroused by playing drums, but in terms of being completely engrossed and in the moment, I think that drums are akin to sex."

Edwards pointed out something else about drummers, both male and female, that was thought-provoking. "One thing I've noticed is that drummers tend to be married," she said. "I'm married, and when we're touring and I meet drummers, they'll tell me they're married too. They're often the only married ones in the band."

Here was an aperçu that deserved further investigation. Of course, a great many musicians of all kinds are married, or have been married. But it is certainly true that the majority of the thirty-eight drummers I interviewed for this book were married. And I was already aware of that wonderfully romantic story about the Santana concert at Tinley Park, Illinois, in 2010. Shortly after a typically brilliant solo by the drummer Cindy Blackman, the bandleader and guitarist Carlos Santana proposed marriage to her onstage, and she accepted. "Cindy and I are blessed to have found each other," Santana said later. "Being in love is a gift from the universe, and the spirit and vibrations that come with it are infinitely powerful. I look forward to expressing that incredible energy through my music, and in helping to tip the balance toward more love in the world with what Cindy and I share." The happy couple tied the knot the following year on the Hawaiian island of Maui. The bride wore a custom-made Zoro silk dress.

When you probe a little deeper, you discover that many drummers have been married an alarming number of times.

Kit bashers who have been hitched twice include Ringo Starr, Chad Smith, Dave Grohl, Joey Kramer, Nick Mason, and Roger Taylor of Queen. Phil Collins has been married three times, as have Mick Fleetwood, Omar Hakim, Terry Bozzio, and Tommy Lee. Ginger Baker is on his fourth wife, and two late giants of jazz drumming, Earl Palmer and Art Blakey, both had four successive wives. Hal Blaine has been up the aisle no fewer than five times. But blowing all of these off the stage, equaling the score of King Henry VIII with six marriages, is that late, fast-living Beach Boy Dennis Wilson.

This may be an astonishing coincidence, but it may also be explained by the gregarious nature of drummers generally—so often, during the research for this book, I heard people (not only drummers themselves) remark on the advanced social skills of people who play the drums. Or it could be a result of the impetuous nature of many drummers, who have a way of rushing headlong into their lives—hence all the injuries and car crashes. Another explanation could be that collector's mentality with which countless male drummers are blessed: if they're not collecting drums, cymbals, cars, or souvenirs from the Alamo, they're collecting women. It's also difficult to ignore the fact that wedding bells are a percussion instrument.

Do these anomalous marriage statistics prove our hypothesis: that people only play the drums to get laid? I really don't think so. Firstly, it doesn't explain why, when these drummers have fallen in love and/or become happily married, they continue to play the drums. If sex is the prime motivation, what's the point of carrying on when you can have all the hanky-panky you need without lifting another drumstick? They could get a proper job instead—one that doesn't carry such a high risk of exhaustion, injury, and tattoos. Okay, there may be some drummers who are out-and-out lotharios who have affairs in every city they visit. But I think this is a ridiculously tiny minority, and not even the hell-raisers John Bonham and Keith Moon fitted that description. Bonham desperately missed his wife, Pat, when Led Zeppelin toured overseas. Moon was similarly besotted with his own wife, Kim. In 1973, fiercely jealous when she took off with the keyboard player Ian McLagan, lovable old Moonie is said to have paid an unpleasant character £250 to break McLagan's fingers. (The story goes that Pete Townshend, learning of the plot, paid the gorilla another £250 not to go ahead with it.) When Phil Collins was married to his second wife, Jill, he told an interviewer: "I am a very loyal person. I have never taken advantage of stuff on the road. Some guys can't wait to get out of the house so they can go and sleep around. It's never really interested me, because I've always felt, 'Well, if I'm doing that, maybe she's doing that.' So I'm very loyal."

Secondly, becoming a drummer is certainly no guarantee of easy sex. For all the online comments about women fancying skin beaters, there are plenty of comments from women who don't, and from drummers who are unsuccessful in that department. Here's a very forlorn post from an unknown male drummer: "I have tried dating lately and it seems like every time I get on a steady even pace, I tell her I'm a drummer and they all seem to dislike me. I even asked the latest one, if I was a guitarist or singer would you like me more? And she said yes, definitely."

And thirdly, the drummers I spoke to, to a man or woman, were obviously passionate about music and about playing the drums. If they weren't just pretending, they wouldn't have become such brilliant musicians. They hadn't spent years mastering this complex instrument for the sole purpose of rumpy-pumpy with the fans.

I really do believe, after my extensive research for this book, that drummers are seriously misunderstood. It's time to take a hard look at what they really go through, how they really suffer for their art, and to detail the many extracurricular duties that are expected of them. You're about to discover that the word *drummer* carries an awful lot more baggage than you may realize.

10

THE FINAL
COUNTDOWN

Drummers are everywhere. It's very likely that you walked past one today without knowing it, spoke to one without realizing it, stood in line behind one, or sat very close to one in a restaurant or bar. They don't always wear giveaway T-shirts with pictures of drum kits or portraits of Keith Moon on them. There are certainly thousands and possibly millions of these people, which means that you're never far away from a drummer.

The magic of statistics means that even if you're not a drummer yourself, you're very likely to know somebody who is. And whenever you meet somebody else, there is quite a strong likelihood that they know a drummer too. Mentioning my book at a couple of social events recently, I was quickly introduced to several drummers. And I was sitting on a London Tube train recently when a fellow passenger, an American woman called Michelle who lived in California, attracted my attention and asked me something about the destination of the train. I happened to mention that I was en route to the London Drum

Show, explaining that it was a big showcase for the drum industry and for famous drummers, and that I was going to watch a
performance by the incredible Terry Bozzio and interview the
fantastic Russ Miller. "Oh!" said Michelle. "My neighbor Mike
is a very good drummer."

For some people, the sheer ubiquity of drummers may have
apparently unpleasant consequences. Perhaps somebody on
your street or in your apartment block has been playing a set of
acoustic drums recently, interrupting your thoughts and conversations or distracting you from the television. Your reaction
might have been to cuss, fly off the handle, and complain to the
person concerned or to a higher authority. You might choose
to come over all high and mighty, like Dame Helen Mirren
dressed as the queen, striding into a London street—"Shut the
fuck up!" But before you do that, you might consider an alternative reaction.

Do the drummers sound as if they are having fun? Are they
laying down a nice groove? Perhaps they're rehearsing for an
important gig, making sure they get their drum chops into
great shape for their big moment, playing for an audience at a
dive bar in Cleveland, at a cool café in Amsterdam, at the Royal
Albert Hall, or at Madison Square Garden. You never know.
They're doing something they love, trying to make music,
being creative and artistic, trying to make something out of
their lives, and getting some exercise into the bargain. Would
you rather they were unemployed and bored, robbing banks, or
mugging people in the street? When you think about it, give
them a larger context, cut them some slack, I would argue that
there is surely more to admire than to complain about.

Other drummers are cool about this sort of thing, as they
should be. "There's a kid who lives in one of the houses beyond

the bottom of our garden in London," said the comedian Rowland Rivron, "who I hear every now and again drumming on a kit, thrashing away. And it's quite nice—I quite like it, because I'm a drummer."

Drummers don't just have hypersensitive neighbors to worry about: they suffer in so many other ways. Did you hear the one about the drummer who went into a recording studio and spent days laying down drum tracks for an important record, which turned out to be a total waste of time and effort because the powers-that-be then decided that they weren't going to use any of his drum parts? It's actually not funny at all, and it happens over and over again.

The very capable Ash Soan was booked to play some studio sessions for Dido, recording tracks for the album that became *The Girl Who Got Away*. He knew the singer well: he had previously worked with her when they had performed with the band Faithless. "I did four tracks for the album," he said, "and then I got a message from Dido saying she really loved what I'd played, it was absolutely beautiful. But then a bit of time went by, and she had a child, and they ended up redoing it all, and none of my drums made it. They used synthetic drums instead. That's what's really annoying about the business: a bit of paranoia sets in somewhere, and somebody says, 'It's not modern enough—let's change it.' It's a real shame, because I really enjoyed playing on those tracks, and I enjoyed seeing her again after all those years."

It has happened to the best of them. September 11, 1962, saw the Beatles arrive at EMI Studios in London's Abbey Road for their third recording session, with the aim of nailing their first single, "Love Me Do." It wasn't a great day for Ringo Starr: although he had played the song seven days before, he wasn't considered good enough for the job by the producer George Martin, who hired the session drummer Andy White for the new recording. Starr was permitted to play a pair of maracas on the B-side, the drippy "P.S. I Love You."

Fourteen years later, Starr met the singer Cat Stevens by chance when they were both staying in Copenhagen, and Stevens invited the drummer to play in a recording session for his next album, *Izitso*. They played several songs and had fun jamming on some old numbers they both knew, but none of Starr's beats made the album. The drummer later reflected that this happened during a bad period for him, when he was drinking a lot, and said he had no animosity toward Stevens: "I mean, I can't blame him because around those years, I was losing control! It's funny because you cop such a resentment at the time: 'What! He wiped me off!' God knows what I played for him."

Patty Schemel's nightmare came in 1998, when Hole were recording the album *Celebrity Skin* with the producer Michael Beinhorn. "He had a reputation for replacing drummers with his own session players," said Schemel. "He kept making me play my drum parts over and over again. I didn't understand what was going on, and I just carried on. I wasn't giving up until he said, 'Okay, that's it!' He had to call it, because I wasn't going to stop. Usually, I guess, when he does that kind of stuff, the drummer will just be like, 'Okay, forget it, I give up.'" Eventually a session drummer called Deen Castronovo appeared in the studio to take over.

Schemel said she was deeply scarred by the experience, which is documented in the riveting 2012 film about her life in Hole, *Hit So Hard*. "It's still tough to talk about," she told me. "I felt that I had to do something with the feeling, and making the film was my way of expressing that and letting it out."

Something downright peculiar happened to the drumming on Ozzy Osbourne's second solo studio album, *Diary of a Madman*. When it was released in 1981, it had drum parts recorded by Lee Kerslake. But when it was reissued in 2002, fans noticed that something had happened to the rhythm section. Kerslake's drum tracks, as well as the original bass playing, had been removed in favor of new parts recorded by the drummer and bass player who were then in Osbourne's band, Mike Bordin and Robert Trujillo. The bizarre decision was reversed in 2011 when a thirtieth-anniversary edition restored the original drums and bass.

Even when drummers are allowed to leave their beats on a successful record, they might not receive an adequate credit for their efforts. Joey Waronker played all the solid and tasteful drum parts on R.E.M.'s 2001 album, *Reveal*, but his name only appears near the bottom of a list of "Additional Musicians" on the CD sleeve, and there is no indication that he played drums. The casual reader might guess that he contributed a snatch of trombone or Appalachian dulcimer to one or two of the tracks. Worse, at the point when I spoke to Waronker, the Wikipedia page for *Reveal* didn't mention him at all, and listed the drummer on that album as Barrett Martin. "Oh . . . That's not correct," Waronker said when I pointed out the anomaly. "When I came into the R.E.M. world, they were just finishing the previous album, *Up*; Bill Berry had left and they didn't have a drummer. They had Barrett helping out, and we both play on that album. But *Reveal* is all me." This fact having been confirmed by other descriptions of the making of that album, I amended the Wikipedia page to give Waronker an overdue credit.

Many drummers have lost out in the financial department as well. This is because drumbeats, no matter how creative or catchy they may be, are not recognized for the purpose of songwriting royalties. These go to the people who write the tunes and the lyrics of the songs. "It's so weird, and it's always astounded me," said Ash Soan. "One of the most important things in pop music is the beat. But in the eyes of the law, it's melody, harmony, and lyrics. I'm not bitter or angry about it personally, because I've had a great career, but you can see why some people would be." However, Soan explained that many drummers receive "performance royalties" when recordings they have drummed on are broadcast or played in public.

When I met Ginger Baker, he was still annoyed that he hadn't been credited for his work on two specific Cream songs in the late 1960s. "When Jack Bruce played the riff of 'Sunshine of Your Love' the first time, it sounded way too fast, and I said so," Baker told me. "I suggested he slow it down, which transformed the whole rhythm of the song. Then there was 'White Room,' where I suggested that introduction, which is a bolero in 5/4 time. It totally makes the song. But I didn't get any credit for either of them."

Of course, drummers can earn songwriting royalties if it is accepted that they have written part of the music and/or lyrics. A more satisfying solution is for bands to draw up their own special royalty-sharing arrangements for their music—as Shirley Manson, Duke Erikson, Steve Marker, and Butch Vig of Garbage have done. "We decided right away," said Vig, "that if we were going to stay together as a band, we'd have to split everything equally, so the money never becomes an issue." This can now be seen as an important step for a band that has sold upward of seventeen million albums. "Even if I write a song on my own and bring it in, or Shirley writes one, it ends up being credited to all four of us. That's how U2 does it, that's how R.E.M. did it, and those bands have had long careers."

"Yeah, a lot of bands today split everything," said Nicko McBrain. "That works really well until there's a big hit, and the girlfriend of the bloke who wrote it goes, ''Ere, do you know you could've had one hundred percent? That's your bloody song—you 'ave the lot!'"

Most drummers are simply like other honest, hardworking people: they want to do a job they can be proud of, they want to be allowed to do it properly, and they appreciate a little recognition every now and again for their efforts. When I spoke to Steven Drozd of the Flaming Lips, he was recovering from the shock of being omitted from an important list. "*Spin* magazine just did a list of the one hundred greatest alternative drummers, and I didn't even make the list," he said. "At first, I was kind of pissed off and my ego was, like, really bummed out. But then I saw that they'd left all these other people off as well. They didn't have Steven Morris of Joy Division, who to me pretty much invented alternative drumming. Larry Mullen of U2, Bill Berry of R.E.M., and Grant Hart of Hüsker Dü— they're not on the list either. And they had, like, ten drummers from these bands that came out four years ago that no one gives a shit about. It's crazy!"

Michèle Drees has had a long career in drumming, during which she has played in an impressive variety of styles, from jazz, funk, and R&B to pop and heavy metal. She has backed the British singers Kirsty MacColl and Marc Almond, and was once the house drummer for Jonathan Ross's popular UK television chat show. "I do feel I deserve a little bit of acknowledgment now," she said. "It would be great if people said, 'You know what? Michèle swings! My God, she's such a fine player.'"

It's particularly unfair when hardworking drummers are insulted by their bandmates. Asked the unlikely question of whether Ringo Starr was the best drummer in the world, John Lennon is supposed to have quipped: "He wasn't even the best drummer in the Beatles." The line has been quoted over and over again in books, magazines, newspapers, on the Internet, and in countless conversations, and has developed its own mini-mythology. People often add that Lennon was referring to the fact that Paul McCartney also played drums, and had to get behind the kit for some songs on *The White Album* when Starr briefly left the band in 1968. It does sound like the kind of remark that Lennon might have made in one of his more caustic moods. The trouble is, I've tried for years to find the reporter or broadcaster who obtained that famous quotation from Lennon, but I've always drawn a blank. He never said it. The indefatigable Beatles expert Mark Lewisohn recently traced the remark to a joke told by the British television comedian Jasper Carrott in 1983, three years after Lennon was killed. Somehow, through a process resembling Chinese whispers, the line was reattributed to Lennon as it was spread from person to person, with nobody bothering to do any fact-checking as they passed it on.

During the early days of Aerosmith in the 1970s, Joey Kramer overheard a conversation between a manager and other members of the band that made it plain that he was considered just a sideman, an accessory to the band rather than one of the stars of the show. He was just the drummer—a phrase to raise the hackles of drummers everywhere. "I have a completely different outlook now," Kramer told me in 2014. "I don't feel as though I'm 'just the drummer.' I feel as though I'm an integral part of what makes Aerosmith Aerosmith. I think it takes a lot of intestinal fortitude to be a drummer, because you have to deal with a lot of shit and you've got to love what you do. And I love what I do more than anything else in the world, but at the same time I'm not going to be a doormat for anybody, and I'm not going to take any shit from anybody. And I did for a long time, but those days are long gone and are over forever."

Kramer has faced a particular disadvantage because Aerosmith's lead singer, Steven Tyler, is also a drummer, and has had some strong ideas in the past about Kramer's drumming. "Let's just say that he had a lot to say about what I was playing," said Kramer. "And that's magnified when the drummer, being me in this situation, also has a strong personality and also has a strong idea about how he wants to play and what he wants it to sound like. I was able to decipher the kind of direction that Steven was giving me in the beginning of the band, because I had a lot of respect for him as a musician and as a drummer, so my attitude has always been: if there's somebody that's doing what I'm doing and it's plain to me that they're doing it better, then I can learn from it, obviously. The only thing that's going to prevent me from doing that is my own ego—and I've tried to not get in my own way for quite some time now. So I learned a lot of things from him. But then you get to a point where, okay, the teacher lets the student go. But Steven, being the way that he is, never lets go. So I just deal with it."

Drummers suffer in so many other ways. A player who doesn't have a band to play with might consider becoming a session drummer, imagining what a wonderful life he could have formulating brilliant drum parts and hearing himself on hit records, like Ash Soan or Ndugu Chancler. But it's a tough world out there, with hundreds of drummers competing for a limited amount of work, and many talented players struggle, fail, and eventually give up. The American player Russ Miller endured a period of grinding poverty while he tried to get a foothold in the business. After growing up in Ohio and moving to Florida to go to college, Miller came to Los Angeles in 1996. "And I lived in a ten-foot-by-eight-foot storage closet at a rehearsal facility for a year," he recalled. "I had a little burner you could plug in, and I had the phone company come and install a phone in there. I joined a gym so I could go for a shower. And I crawled up on top of the closet and put an air conditioner there with a garbage bag on it, so it would blow cold air into the closet." When he wasn't living in his tiny closet, Miller was haunting casual entertainment offices, asking if they would book him as a drummer for weddings or other events. "I would play events and meet other musicians, and I figured that the more guys I played with, the better chance I had of them knowing other people and recommending me." Although there were days when he did more valet parking than session drumming, Miller said he always had the right mind-set. "I was a professional drummer who this week was valet parking: I was never a valet parker who wanted to be a professional drummer."

"If you talk to ten different session drummers about how they made it," said Omar Hakim, "you would probably hear ten very different stories. When I was trying to get more work in the sessions scene in New York in the 1970s, it was a challenge, because the drummers who were already there were the likes of Steve Gadd and Bernard Purdie. So why are they going to hire me? But one of the things on my business card at the time was 'percussionist': one of my drum teachers was a conga player, and I learned djembe drums and timbales and all of this other stuff as well. So when I didn't get gigs on the drum set,

I could market myself as a percussionist. I thought, Okay, if they're not going to hire me as a drummer, I could slip in and play percussion. And I remember when everything shifted. I was on an advertising-jingle session, playing percussion opposite the drummer Allan Schwartzberg, who was one of the top drummers in New York. This session was going overtime, and Allan had another session afterward with a pretty big pop star that he didn't want to be late for, and at a certain point he just stood up and said, 'I gotta go!' So the producer looked at me and said, 'Omar! You're up.' It was the first time that that group of people in the room had heard me on a drum set, and that really helped: after that, I started getting a lot more calls for drumming work."

Drummers who join bands have to struggle as well sometimes. A drummer who plays for a long time in the same band is usually at a severe disadvantage when the group breaks up, explained Nick Mason. "You have to bear in mind that the drummer is the one person who can't operate without the others," he said. "All the others can go off and do something on their own—go off and sing on their own or play guitar on their own, for example. But no one's that interested in listening to two and a half hours of drumming. Well, apart from other drummers!" he laughed. "The public at large are not going to buy lots of tickets to hear solo drummers."

This echoes a point that Robert Wyatt has made: that a drummer needs a band; that drumming is a "social act." With a few exceptions, drummers are not celebrities on their own. Proof of this particular injustice comes from the websites that help journalists to find contact details for famous people. When I logged in to one such useful website and typed the names "Ringo Starr," "Phil Collins," and "Sheila E.," the site showed their publicists' contact details. However, the names of many brilliant virtuoso drummers such as Omar Hakim, Vinnie Colaiuta, and Cindy Blackman Santana were not recognized at all. When I started typing the name "Terry Bozzio," the site suggested I might be looking for the wrestler Hulk Hogan (evidently because his real name is Terry Bollea, which is vaguely similar).

It has been said that Keith Moon, despite his independent notoriety and evident insanity, was fiercely loyal to the Who and secretly terrified that they would split up. He did try his hand at some studio session work, but found he wasn't adaptable enough: his frenetic style worked well in the Who, but not in most other musical settings. As he once explained, "I'm not used to being told to play a certain way. I'm a lousy session musician." Ultimately he became the only member of the Who to die before he got old, passing away while his beloved group was still together.

Ringo Starr was bereft when the Beatles broke up in 1970. As he recalled years later, "I went back to my luxury home in Weybridge and just sat in the garden for months, wondering what on earth I was going to do with myself. Playing with the Beatles had been my whole life for ten years, and now it was over and I didn't feel qualified to do anything else. The initial breakup was so emotional, mainly for me but not so much for the others. We had been together for so long, and then suddenly I had nothing to do. I sat in my garden thinking, 'My God, where do I go from here?' I felt so absolutely lost." Starr soon began hitting the cognac and suffering blackouts, and ended up in rehab for a while.

David Lovering shuddered as he recalled how the Pixies had split suddenly in 1992. "I loved the Pixies; it was something that I had done for years, and I enjoyed it. It was a blow when I heard about the breakup. I was upset about it and I didn't know what to do. Before the band I'd worked in electronics, but after all those years I couldn't just go back and get an electronics job: I'd have to learn a lot of new things, and also I'd become disenchanted with it. So I started doing session work. I had a lot of friends who wrote music, and they helped me out. But I found out after a while that I can't do it: I'm not that good at going into a studio and immediately coming up with something good. So that was very hard, and I stopped doing that."

Adding to the pain of the Pixies' dissolution, said Lovering, was the fact that he had just acquired a shiny new red Gretsch drum kit when the band called it a day. "I joined a band called Cracker for a couple of years, and we did some touring, but after that I gave up the drums. I put the drums away, in storage. Luckily, I had some money from the Pixies, so I had the freedom to have a little vacation. But the vacation kept stretching."

Lovering was lucky to find another showbiz role in the mid-1990s, though adapting to it was initially a struggle. "I decided I wanted to be a magician, and then I had to figure out how to take on that career," he said. "I did thirteen-year-old girls' birthday parties. Don't do thirteen-year-old girls' birthday parties! If you think being a musician is hard, being a magician is a billion times harder. But I love magic and I wanted to do it, so I had to come up with something. You need a big stage show to make money." A lightbulb suddenly appeared above his head, and he transformed himself into the Scientific Phenomenalist, presenting science-based tricks onstage, dressed in a white lab coat. He became one of the world's strangest support acts, opening for shows by Pixies-related acts such as the Breeders and Frank Black. "People love smoke and fire, so if I had fire and smoke in my show, I could do no wrong. I used my kick drum in my act: I filled it with smoke and shot smoke rings out of it."

Despite his success in the world of conjuring, Lovering eagerly put his kit together again when he heard that the Pixies were regrouping in 2004. "That was great news, because I was at a very low point, and I had a terrible girlfriend at the time."

It was Nick Mason who revealed one of the most profound facts about drummers. Because it's such a struggle for the drummer when a band splits up, he explained, it is very much in the drummer's interest to keep the band together. This is why he or she is very often the band's diplomat and peacemaker, breaking up fights and pacifying feuding band members. "I've had people say to me that I was the one holding it all together," said Mason. "Bands are very interesting in the way that they group together and show solidarity when there's adversity, and when they fragment it's at the point when they're loved by all and sundry and they don't need each other anymore."

Debbi Peterson explained that she and the rest of the Bangles have made great strides with band harmony and diplomacy after suffering from infighting in the 1980s. "We all used to keep things to ourselves and not discuss things. Probably one of the reasons we broke up in 1989 was because everybody was keeping their own angst and frustrations to themselves. There were mean, catty looks at each other—all this bitchy girl stuff. It would have been better if we'd actually tried to punch each other out or yell at each other: we might've lasted longer. It's different now that we're back together: we've learned over the years that hey, come on, if there's a problem, let's talk about it. We are a lot more open with each other now. And I'm definitely the one who will say, 'Okay, you guys, let's stop, let's sort this out.' I'm like lukewarm water. I'm pretty much the diplomat, I think."

Carl Palmer recently said that his role in the prog super-group Emerson, Lake & Palmer was "kind of referee-cum-juggler," despite the fact that he was several years younger than his two bandmates. And in 1970, when Phil Collins became the drummer in Genesis, joining Peter Gabriel, Tony Banks, and Mike Rutherford, he also found himself taking on the role of mediator. The guitarist Anthony Phillips had just left the band, and his replacement, Steve Hackett, would climb aboard later that year. "When I joined the band," said Collins, "my social background was very different from that of Tony, Mike, and Peter. They were very tightly wound public schoolboys, and there was a lot of stress and bickering around the time when Anthony left. Peter and Tony had a love-hate relationship. Whether you played an F-sharp-major chord or an F-sharp-diminished was really important in those days, and nobody wanted to appear to be wrong. Steve Hackett hit the nail on the head a while ago when he said that there'd still be arguments about who had stolen whose protractor at school! But I found myself coming in from a stage-school background, where anything goes, and being a lot looser as a person. And I would be watching these arguments, looking from one side to the other like I was watching a tennis match, and it would sometimes be down to me to deflate the atmosphere, which I might do with a joke. If you make a joke, people tend to relax a bit."

Collins's point suggests that the drummer's diplomatic tendencies are inextricably tied up with the role of "the comedian in the band." "Comedy is a great icebreaker," said Ross McFarlane, "and I've been told that I've been a great tonic on tours with my sense of humor. And there are a lot of other drummers I know who are funny. There is a lot of ego in singers and guitar players, and I always take the approach of 'Let's all work this out.'"

"Drummers are basically the friendly ones in the band," said Steve White. "I remember when I was in the Style Council in the 1980s, we did a TV show with a lot of other acts on the Polydor label. And all the singers were shut in their dressing rooms, or looking around to make sure that everyone was looking at them. But the drummers were hanging around the coffee machine, chatting to each other. I think as drummers we're in touch with something that goes back a long, long way. Not being too hippie-dippy about it, but in Africa, people get together to play the drums if somebody dies, if somebody marries, if somebody's born, or if they're going into battle: drumming is a communal thing. And drummers never have a problem with hanging out together, and taking ideas from other drummers and incorporating them."

"There's quite a lot of sharing among drummers," concurred Nick Mason. "Drummers play a lot of master classes for other drummers, and they're very social. My impression of guitarists is that they're a bit more separated, whereas drummers really like to get together and talk. Even wildly tattooed, television-out-the-window-brigade drummers are still absolutely charming and love to talk about drumming. Tommy Lee, for instance, is delightful."

"Drummers sit at the back and see everything that's going on in the band," said Butch Vig. "A good drummer is able to work within the context of a band and deal with some of the more ego-centered issues that might occur between, say, a lead guitarist and a lead singer. A lot of drummers are more grounded and can be more objective about the music. Look at Larry Mullen in U2—he's sort of their bullshit detector. Bono and the Edge will often experiment, going off in tangents, and Larry is the one who will say, 'That doesn't sound like U2 . . .'"

For me, it was the producer and drummer Ben Hillier who put his finger on the main reason why drummers are often more socially skilled than other musicians. "You can quite easily learn to play guitar or keyboards on your own, just sitting in a room and practicing for a long time," he told me. "But with drums, you really can't learn how to play them all on your own. You can practice to a certain extent, but you're not going to get a huge grasp of dynamics and tone unless you're playing in a live situation, with other people. So most drummers have grown up playing with other musicians, whereas a lot of guitarists and keyboard players and other musicians have grown up playing on their own."

"Drums are really hard," said Julie Edwards. "They're exhausting and it's a relentless job. I just think that the drummer's job is so different from anyone else's in the band—so drummers can bond with other drummers in a way that they can't necessarily with other musicians. Drummers understand each other."

There was a notable bonding session for drummers at the Greek Theatre, Los Angeles, in the summer of 2011, when Steely Dan arrived to play their *Aja* album in its entirety with Keith Carlock behind the kit. "Steely Dan are my favorite band," said David Lovering, "and every one of their drummers has been great. I went to see them play *Aja*, and there was a little meeting area in the theater where people were having drinks before the show. I looked around, and I couldn't tell you how many drummers I saw there. There was everyone from Josh Freese to Danny Carey, and it went on and on; Pat Wilson from Weezer was there too. I was like, 'Are you kidding me?'"

Drummers aren't just beat keepers, explained Ben Hillier: they also make an enormous contribution to the sonic distinctiveness of a band. As well as producing acts including Blur and Elbow, Hillier has worked as a sound engineer with U2 and believes that there is a unique chemistry between the band's drummer, Larry Mullen Jr., and their bassist, Adam Clayton. "Larry and Adam are amazing," said Hillier. "Larry usually plays the same distance ahead of the beat. If there's a perceived beat that drives through the song, he will push it to the front of the beat as far as he can. So even when U2 play a slow song, it sounds fast and exciting. But Adam is the opposite: he's behind the beat. And the two of them create this unique combination; you could get them to play almost anything, and it would still sound like U2."

According to Hillier, Blur had an equally intriguing chemistry, thanks to the interplay between drummer Dave Rowntree and bassist Alex James. "Dave is metronomic; few drummers are more in the center of the beat than Dave. He's absolutely square in his feel. And then, on the other hand, as a bass player, Alex is quite laconic."

The list of skills and qualities that people require from drummers just gets longer and longer. Not only are they expected to keep the beat and provide sonic distinctiveness, but they are also supposed to be highly sociable people who can be very funny and can defuse disagreements. As if that weren't enough, there is another role that many of them take on: that of the chronicler and historian of the band they play in. Nick Mason has penned *Inside Out: A Personal History of Pink Floyd*. Mickey Hart has written about his experiences as a member of the Grateful Dead, while John Densmore has written not one but two books about the Doors, including the recent volume *The Doors Unhinged: Jim Morrison's Legacy Goes on Trial*. The late Mitch Mitchell documented his time in Jimi Hendrix's band in *The Hendrix Experience*. Tony McCarroll put out *Oasis: The Truth: My Life as Oasis's Drummer*, Peter Criss wrote *Makeup to Breakup: My Life In and Out of Kiss*, and other drummers including Joey Kramer, Bill Bruford, and Ginger Baker have pitched in with their own autobiographies, describing what it was like to play the drums in bands such as Aerosmith, Yes, King Crimson, and Cream. One of the most charming and original pop-music memoirs ever published is Ringo Starr's *Postcards from the Boys*, which reproduces many of the postcards he was sent through the mail by the other three Beatles.

I was at the ICA in London when Clem Burke gave a public reading of extracts from a book he was writing about Blondie. "I'm telling the story from my perspective," he told me afterward. "I think I have a pretty good recollection of what went on. The beauty of keeping a diary is that you can go back and relive the experience, which is what I'm trying to do. I'm not trying to make any great statement about my life being so wonderful and everybody needs to know the story of my life, but I think the anecdotal stories I tell give some insight into being there. It's like descriptive narrative: what color the wallpaper was and what kind of cigarette I was smoking; all that kinda stuff."

Although Dale "Buffin" Griffin didn't write a book about Mott the Hoople, he became an enthusiastic archivist of their music. "A while after Mott split up, most of us lost interest in the band," said Mott's bass player, Overend Watts. "I wasn't interested because I was doing other things, and the rest of the band were doing their own things. But all through the lean years, Buffin was raiding recording archives in London, finding old things we'd never finished off, and then getting me or someone else to play a bit on them to finish them off. He took the best of the stuff—and he found some amazing stuff—and mixed it and got it all sounding good, and got it released. And he did all the research on the tracks and wrote the sleeve notes.

"A lot of that work, like the sleeve notes, has fallen to me now, because Buff has Alzheimer's and can't do it anymore. I curse him: I think, 'You bugger, you've left me to do all this!' It's not my sort of thing at all, whereas it was his. I think if there had been a proper book about Mott the Hoople, it would have come from Buffin. He was a good writer. He was very articulate, and was a stickler for good English grammar."

The role of historian may seem an unlikely one for a drummer. But there are certain key qualities, possessed by a wide range of skin beaters, that would be extremely useful in this field. One of these qualities is an outstanding memory. Reflecting on the qualities of the late Keith Moon, Pete Townshend once said: "The most interesting aspect about Keith was the excellence of his mind, the rapidity of his memory. You often find this with drummers, that they have the most extraordinary memories. It's an extension of their work. Maybe their memories are centered in a different part of their brain, because they have to remember long musical phrases as pure data. It's almost binary. They must know exactly where they are in a song at any given time."

When Mike Portnoy played drums in Dream Theater, he boasted that he had "an elephant's memory" and went on to explain: "The guys in my band, they joke about it, because when we did our twentieth-anniversary tour a couple of years ago, one of the things we were doing on that tour was playing the first song we ever wrote together from back in '85, a song called 'Another One.' And basically, when it came time for tour rehearsals, I never even listened to it. I just sat down with a kit, and it was still stored in there from twenty years earlier."

Nick Mason identified another quality, also common in drummers, that helps them write the histories of their bands. "The reason I'm the historian is that I kept more stuff relating to the band than the others did," he told me. Mason—a prodigious collector, like so many other drummers—has preserved "ephemera" including concert programs, T-shirts, and ticket stubs from various Floyd tours, and clippings of press articles about the band, which he started methodically sticking into scrapbooks in the 1960s.

Mason is one of those drummers who have transcended the role of simply playing the drums in a band. He has been a record producer whose production work includes the classic album *Rock Bottom* by Robert Wyatt and the album *Music for Pleasure* by the British punk band the Damned. "I like producing," he told me. "I like being on the other side of the glass and trying to make it sound right." Other drummers who have worn the producer's hat include Phil Collins, Omar Hakim, Butch Vig, Questlove, and Ben Hillier.

Drummers are sometimes inventors as well. When I saw Russ Miller play, I noticed he had something attached to the front of his bass drum that looked like a baby bass drum. This, he told me afterward, was one of his own inventions, the Subkick, a "low-frequency capture device" that amplifies some of the deepest sounds of the drum. "I was doing these hip-hop records," recalled Miller, "working with these guys who were programming stuff on drum machines. The beats they made sounded huge, but they didn't feel good, so they had me playing beats over the top. But the natural drum sound was a little small-sounding in relation to the machine beats, and I thought, 'We need to get some more bottom end here.' So I got a seven-inch speaker, wired it so it became a microphone—which is an old trick—and put it in a little drum shell. It only picks up the low end of the drum sound, and adds so much more to it." Other drummers now use Miller's Subkick to give more oomph to their bass drums—and his invention can even be seen on the drum-kit tattoo adorning Miller's left arm.

A few drummers have ventured into the rarefied world of fine art. Bill Ward, formerly of Black Sabbath, has worked in the medium of "rhythm on canvas," making abstract light paintings based on the movements of his drumsticks. Carl Palmer and Rick Allen have produced work in the same medium.

Mickey Hart has also created dazzling displays with his drumming, after collaborating with California neuroscientist Adam Gazzaley. In 2012, Hart and Gazzaley presented a show in which Hart drummed in front of a live audience while his brain activity was captured by electrodes and converted into a light show. This isn't just trivial entertainment, as Hart has explained. "This is about breaking the rhythm code, our genome project," he said. "Once we know what rhythm truly does, then we'll be able to control it and use it medicinally for diagnostics, for health reasons. To be able to reconnect the synapses, the connections that are broken in Parkinson's, Alzheimer's— that's where we are heading."

Another American neuroscientist who has explored the world of drumming is David Eagleman. The scientist was intrigued by a story that the British musician and producer Brian Eno had told him about U2's drummer, Larry Mullen Jr. As a 2011 feature by Burkhard Bilger in the *New Yorker* explained, Eno was working with Mullen in the studio, and the drummer was playing to a recording of the band that had a click track on it. But Mullen complained that he couldn't play to the click track, because it was ever so slightly out of time—a tiny fraction too slow. Eno disagreed, but discovered later that Mullen had been correct: the click was several milliseconds out. It was clear that the drummer had an extraordinary perception of timing.

Was Mullen a freak of nature, or was there something special about drummers' brains? Eagleman decided to conduct an experiment. Drummers were invited to Eno's studio, and each one played while wearing an EEG monitor on his head. They discovered that the drummers did have something happening in their brains that wasn't going on in the brains of other randomly selected subjects—people who were not drummers who were used as controls in the experiment. Their sense of timing really was exceptional. Not any old Tom, Dick, or Harry can become a drummer.

However, drumming is an equal-opportunities gig: drummers can be male or female, from any race, straight or gay, intellectual or moronic, dyslexic or highly literate, perfectly sane or certifiably crazy. They can be carnivores or herbivores— Omar Hakim, for example, has been a vegetarian for over thirty-five years. "When I was on tour as a young kid in the 1970s," he said, "I ate a lot of junk food that started taking a toll on my digestive system. So by the time I was nineteen years old I was not feeling so great, and I went to a doctor who suggested that I try a vegetarian diet for six months. I immediately started feeling better, and I feel my drumming got better too: it helped my endurance and my focus and concentration."

Even sinistrality—left-handedness—is no impediment to drumming success. Just as some musicians manage to play guitar and bass despite being left-handed, there are plenty of brilliant southpaw drummers. But this is where life gets a little confusing. When you start classifying drummers as right-handed or left-handed, you discover that there are actually three classes of drummer, not two. The majority of the world's drummers are right-handed people who play standard, right-handed kits. Then there are left-handers who play left-handed kits—drum sets that resemble a mirror image of an ordinary kit, with the snare drum and hi-hat to the right instead of the left. Phil Collins and Joey Waronker are two drummers in that category. But then there are other left-handers who play right-handed kits, such as Ringo Starr and Clem Burke.

"I took formal lessons when I began drumming," Burke told me, "and the drums were set up the traditional right-handed way, and I just took to it and was taught to play that way—although I do lead with my left hand quite a bit, which makes my style somewhat unusual, which also makes Ringo Starr's style somewhat unusual. I feel I'm somewhat ambidextrous, but Ringo has said he has a hard time going around the whole kit, because he's starting with his left hand and going the wrong way round."

"Ringo basically plays the kit backwards," explained Joey Waronker, "which is why his approach to drum fills is so unusual—going from the low toms to the high toms, when we're all used to hearing drummers go from high to low." Waronker made a surprising discovery when he was in the studio with Paul McCartney, contributing to the ex-Beatle's 2005 album *Chaos and Creation in the Backyard*. "I set up my kit left-handed, as usual. And Paul plays guitar and bass left-handed, but when he tried to play my kit he found it really difficult. He couldn't do it." Like Clem Burke and his old bandmate Ringo (whose kit he often played when Ringo was out of the room), it seems that the sinistral McCartney learned to play the drums on ordinary, dextral kits.

So many drummers are so different from each other in so many ways. But is it still possible to ascertain a type—a particular sort of person who becomes a drummer? What's obvious is that it's usually an energetic, resourceful person who loves music and doesn't mind sitting at the back of the stage and being the butt of endless jokes. And the evidence of all my research suggests a bit more. Just as a professional drum kit is really a collection of instruments, the best professional drummers need a collection of qualities—including physical endurance, a good memory, excellent timing, loyalty, a healthy sense of humor, diplomatic inclinations, and perhaps even the ability to write books about the bands they've kept the beat in.

But my ideas about the type of person who makes a great drummer were shaken up severely as I finished this book. There was a short documentary film circulating on the Internet, popping up on social-media networks, and steadily gathering an audience of hundreds of thousands of people. Created in 2012 by the filmmakers Ross Harris and Stanley Gonzales, it's called *Drummer Wanted*. The star of the film is Dean Zimmer, a rock drummer in his early fifties with a fantastic feel for rhythm, who lives in Southern California. There's nothing too unusual about that, of course, but Zimmer has a rare congenital condition called arthrogryposis, which stiffens the joints and severely restricts the movement of the limbs. He has used a wheelchair since he was very young, and accomplishing most tasks is hard work for him, and yet here he was in this film, laying down a fantastic groove on a drum kit. Zimmer has played many gigs behind the kit and has opened for big acts such as Styx, Kansas, and Thin Lizzy; he has even managed to play demanding prog rock and speed metal. But he recounted how, one day, he had responded to a "drummer wanted" ad, arriving in person in his wheelchair. The musicians who had placed the ad "looked at me like I had three heads," he said.

"What we didn't realize when we came to make the film,"

said Ross Harris, "is how long it would take Dean to set up his drum kit. It took hours. We helped him, because it was taking forever, but he insisted on doing most of it himself, because he was very particular about everything. I think many other people would've been exhausted at the end of it, but Dean is so patient. I think he has the greatest attitude of anybody I've ever known."

Zimmer's disability has forced him to find a unique way of playing the drums. He holds the sticks the other way round, so that the fatter ends hit the drums and cymbals, and he has to strap the sticks to his hands so that he doesn't let go of them. "And in order to hit the drums on time," said Harris, "Dean has to throw his arms well in advance, way ahead of the beat. And he uses his back and his shoulders to propel his arms. I'm sure it took him years even to reach a basic level of playing. But here's the thing: he loves really technical drumming. His favorite drummers are people like Terry Bozzio."

Many drummers around the world have been wowed by the film, and by its star. "We had a really nice note from a guy in Brazil who has the same rare condition as Dean," said Harris, "and he said that Dean was such a huge inspiration." Zimmer recently received an endorsement from the DW company, whose drums are played by the likes of Dave Grohl, Clem Burke, Sheila E., and Terry Bozzio. "And DW gave him a brand-new, personalized drum kit," said Harris. "That was beyond what we'd ever imagined when we made the film."

Never mind drummers—Dean Zimmer should be an inspiration to people in general. Born with all those odds stacked against him, he has nevertheless pursued his passion with almost superhuman persistence, battled through the pain, disregarded the skepticism of others, mastered his instrument, and become an Internet celebrity. Next time you find yourself complaining about a teensy-weensy problem or setback in your life, it would be salutary to consider Dean Zimmer and what he has accomplished despite the overwhelming problems that he has faced.

That's what drummers are like. They're not loonies and nut jobs—not many of them, anyway. They're not sex-mad, masochistic show-offs—not all of them. They simply play the drums because they have an overwhelming urge to do so. It's a vocation—just as much as medicine, philosophy, painting, or politics are vocations—and it calls out to all kinds of people around the world, regardless of race, sex, class, or physical ability. I asked an old friend of mine, an extremely talented and versatile drummer named Glenn Harris, why he chose to play the drums. He sipped his beer and pondered for a while.

"I didn't choose the drums," he said, in all seriousness. "They chose me."

ACKNOWLEDGMENTS

Thanks are due to the many drummers who patiently answered my questions, including some true wizards and gentlemen of the drum kit—Ginger Baker, Jack Bevan, Clem Burke, Ndugu Chancler, Phil Collins, Steven Drozd, Tom Grosset, Omar Hakim, Col Hatchman, Ben Hillier, Ralph Johnson, Richard Jupp, Joey Kramer, David Lovering, Boo McAfee, Nicko McBrain, Ross McFarlane, Nick Mason, Russ Miller, Rowland Rivron, Kliph Scurlock, Chad Smith, Ash Soan, Roger Taylor, Paul Thompson, Butch Vig, Joey Waronker, and Steve White—and some phenomenal female drummers—Jess Bowen, Julie Edwards, Cherisse Osei, Debbi Peterson, Anna Prior, and Patty Schemel. Belated thanks are also due to Sheila E. for giving me an interview back in 1984.

Special thanks go to Dr. Marcus Smith at the University of Chichester for his assistance and scientific expertise; to drummer and *Tom Tom* editor Mindy Abovitz for her brilliance and enthusiasm; to my friend Mel Bradman for permission to use two amazing interviews; to Ginette Baker, Rose Eken, Ross Harris, Jean Smith, and Overend Watts for their exceptional insights and stories; and to my drummer friend Michael Burgess for some inspirational conversations.

I'm also very grateful to Denise Oswald, editor and drummer, for her meticulousness. And none of it would have happened without Robin Morgan and Carrie Kania, who helped me start the beat in the first place.

The rest of you know who you are.

BIBLIOGRAPHY

PRIMARY BOOK SOURCES

Baker, Ginger: *Hellraiser: The Autobiography of the World's Greatest Drummer*, John Blake Publishing, London, 2009.

Bruford, Bill: *The Autobiography*, Jawbone, London, 2009.

Cohan, Jon: *Star Sets: Drum Kits of the Great Drummers*, Hal Leonard Corporation, Milwaukee, 1995.

Coleman, Ray: *Phil Collins: The Definitive Biography*, Simon and Schuster, London, 1997.

Copeland, Stewart: *Strange Things Happen: A Life with the Police, Polo and Pygmies*, The Friday Project, London, 2009.

Criss, Peter, and Larry "Ratso" Sloman: *Makeup to Breakup: My Life In and Out of Kiss*, Scribner, New York, 2012.

Densmore, John: *Riders on the Storm: My Life with Jim Morrison and the Doors*, Arrow Books, London, 1991.

Doole, Kerry, and Chris Twomey: *Crowded House: Private Universe*, Omnibus Press, London, 1996.

Fletcher, Tony: *Dear Boy: The Life of Keith Moon*, Omnibus Press, London, 1998.

Forrester, George, Martyn Hanson, and Frank Askew: *Emerson, Lake & Palmer: The Show That Never Ends*, Helter Skelter Publishing, London, 2001.

Hart, Mickey, and Jay Stevens: *Drumming at the Edge of Magic: A Journey into the Spirit of Percussion*, HarperSanFrancisco, 1990.

Kramer, Joey: *Hit Hard: A Story of Hitting Rock Bottom at the Top*, HarperOne, New York, 2009.

Lee, Tommy, and Anthony Bozza: *Tommyland*, Simon & Schuster, London, 2004.

Starr, Ringo: *Postcards from the Boys*, Genesis Publications, Guildford, 2003.

Thompson, Ahmir, and Ben Greenman: *Mo' Meta Blues: The World According to Questlove*, Grand Central Publishing, New York, 2013.

Welch, Chris, and Geoff Nicholls: *John Bonham: A Thunder of Drums*, Backbeat Books, San Francisco, 2001.

PRIMARY FILM SOURCES

Hit So Hard: The Life and Near-Death Story of Patty Schemel, directed by P. David Ebersole (Ebersole Hughes Company, 2012).

Neil Peart: Anatomy of a Drum Solo, directed by Matthew Wachsman (Hudson Music, 2005).

ABOUT THE AUTHOR

Tony Barrell is a British journalist who has written frequently about pop music and popular culture for the *Sunday Times* (UK), among other publications. He lives in London.